Studying the Sikhs

SUNY Series in Religious Studies
Harold Coward, Editor

STUDYING THE SIKHS

ISSUES FOR NORTH AMERICA

Edited by
John Stratton Hawley
and
Gurinder Singh Mann

STATE UNIVERSITY OF NEW YORK PRESS

Published by
State University of New York Press, Albany

© 1993 State University of New York

Printed in the United States of America

For information, address State University of New York
Press, State University Plaza, Albany, N.Y. 12246

Production by Diane Ganeles
Marketing by Dana E. Yanulavich

Library of Congress Cataloging-in-Publication Data

Studying the Sikhs : issues for North America / edited by John
    Stratton Hawley and Gurinder Singh Mann.
        p.   cm. — (SUNY series in religious studies)
    Includes bibliographical references and index.
    ISBN 0-7914-1425-6 (CH : acid-free). — ISBN 0-7914-1426-4 (PB :
acid-free)
    1. Sikhism—Study and teaching (Higher)—North America.
I. Hawley, John Stratton, 1941–   . II. Mann, Gurinder Singh.
III. Series.
BL2017.35.S88   1993
294.6'07'073—dc20   92-16469
                                                         CIP

10 9 8 7 6 5 4 3 2 1

*Prepared under the auspices of
the Southern Asian Institute,
Columbia University*

Contents

Introduction

*

John Stratton Hawley and Gurinder Singh Mann

In the course of the past decade, remarkable changes have taken place in the way the world views the Sikhs and in the way Sikhs view the world. Many of these changes have been generated by the swirl of violent events that have so fundamentally changed life in the Punjab, the prosperous northwestern state of India that is home territory to Sikhs. These include the rise of a newly militant Sikh religion; demands for an independent or semiautonomous Sikh state; the invasion of the Golden Temple, Sikhism's central shrine, by troops of the Indian government; the assassination of Indira Gandhi in response; the massacre of thousands of Sikhs in Delhi in counterresponse; and a continuing cycle of killings in the Punjab itself. These events make the papers and create a context within which the many Sikhs who have emigrated overseas must explain themselves to their non-Sikh neighbors—and themselves. Not only that, they reflect the activities of some of those same overseas Sikhs. The idea of an autonomous Sikh state, a "homeland" that came to be called Khalistan, received persistent support abroad; and when Khalistan was publicly proposed at a major Sikh educational conference held in the Punjab in 1981, it was a Sikh citizen of United States who did the speaking.

Such matters highlight the fact that not all Sikhs around the globe still think that their home community, the Sikhs of the Punjab, belong within the borders of India. Whether this is the majority or the minority opinion, it is founded on a perception of Sikh religion and culture that is very widely shared—the conviction that Sikhism is an independent religious tradition. Ten years ago it was common for introductory textbooks in world religion to dispense

1

with Sikhism by means of a paragraph inserted in the section on Hinduism. No longer. Political events of the last decade have made it plain that such an approach is seriously askew. And if that is true when the Sikhs are studied from the point of view of their religion, it is no less true when they are studied for their history, their literature, or their identity as an ethnic community abroad.

The aim of this book is to open up the major issues involved in pursuing Sikh studies in the context of higher education in North America. The first four chapters take a field-by-field approach to the problem. The next three address issues of overall educational structure and specific pedagogical needs. The final chapter is bibliographic in nature; it presents a review of literature in the field.

Mark Juergensmeyer begins by describing difficulties and opportunities that face students and teachers of Sikhism in the context of the field of religious studies. He distinguishes four aspects of Sikh studies—studies of the historical origins of the tradition, its major texts, its beliefs and practices, and the sense of communal identity it has spawned, especially abroad—and suggests how these interact with major currents shaping the academic study of religion in Western universities. He goes on to separate out the major ways Sikhism has been treated in textbooks on world religion, and he explains why there are such disparities and outright omissions.

N. Gerald Barrier continues by addressing significant issues posed by the study of Sikh history. He describes two major approaches, one emanating primarily from academic institutions in the Punjab and the other more at home in Western universities. The one stresses the organic integrity of the Sikh historical experience; the other is more interested in its intersection with forces and events that were not intrinsically Sikh. Barrier goes on to isolate several themes that recur persistently at various points in Sikh history and show how, in addition, each historical period demands the consideration of a set of issues uniquely appropriate to itself.

W. H. McLeod takes as his subject the study of Sikh literature. He highlights the issue of canonicity by describing the spectrum of texts that extends from the clearly scriptural *Adi Granth* all the way across to such influential but extracanonical documents as the hagiographical *janam-sakhi* and *gurbilas* literature. Questions relating to the textual status of these various documents figure prominently in McLeod's discussion, and he shows how, in the current political environment, the attitude one takes to such questions is apt to put one in serious conflict with scholars and/or believers who take a different approach.

In the fourth and final chapter dealing with a field of study as it relates to the Sikhs, Arthur W. Helweg discusses Sikhs under the rubric of ethnic or migration studies—the study of Sikhs living elsewhere than in the Indian subcontinent. Like Barrier, he devotes considerable attention to the major historical phases that need to be distinguished by anyone approaching his subject, but the time span he considers is only one century, as compared with Barrier's five, and the geographical spread is much larger. In relating the study of the Sikh diaspora to studies of other replanted communities, Helweg stresses the point that a bilateral approach will not do. One cannot merely understand a migrating community in relation to the society in the midst of which it settles. One must also take into account the sending community—in this case, Sikhs living in the Punjab—and understand the importance of ever more intense interactions between the Punjabi Sikhs and those who have settled elsewhere.

With the fifth chapter, written by Gurinder Singh Mann, the book comes to a major turning point. In the first four chapters, all written by scholars outside the Sikh tradition, much attention is given to demands placed upon the study of the Sikhs by the Western academic tradition. Mann takes up the other side of things: the educational heritage that has been built up over the centuries within the Sikh tradition itself. Yet in the course of doing so, he shows that this is a tradition which has been in lively dialogue with Western modes of study for a full century, ever since the British succeeded in making a colony of the Punjab. In fact, Mann uses the experience of the so-called Singh Sabha period in Sikh history (1873–1920), when Sikhs first systematically confronted Western notions of education, as a base from which to think about the prospects for Sikh studies in North American universities today. He brings directly to the fore the often thorny question of what should be the relation between North American universities teaching about Sikhism and the Sikh communities that exist in the populace at large.

This question also plays a great role in the chapter that follows, where Joseph T. O'Connell charts the historical course of programs in Sikh studies at Canadian and American universities. O'Connell repeatedly draws attention to the financial and ideological force that has been exerted upon these programs by Sikh foundations and local Sikh communities, and he concludes by describing a current movement among some Sikhs who would shield the Sikh tradition from the critical scrutiny it is apt to receive in North American universities. O'Connell suggests ways in which such concerns can appropriately be met. For him, as for Juergensmeyer, McLeod, and Mann, the tension between scholarship and religious experience is not just one that confronts Sikhs; every religious tradition must deal with this problem. Moreover, one feels this element of strain not just in relations between Sikhs and outside observers, but within the Sikh community itself. This is undeniably rough terrain, both for the critical student and for the staunch believer, but Sikhs are not alone in having to confront it.

The marked tensions between academics and believers that have affected the field of Sikh studies in recent years—and sometimes made it difficult for one side of a single person to live with the other—create a concern that surfaces in almost every chapter of the book. Although the field of Sikh studies is very much intact, and in India well established, such tensions have on occasion made the last decade a troubled period for Sikh studies in North America. At the same time, however, they have undoubtedly helped make it a formative period, too.

How these tensions will play themselves out in the 1990s remains to be seen, but a second theme that unites the chapters in this book is an exploration of one important context where such conflicts are sure to arise: the college classroom. Contributors to the first half of the book explain issues that will face teachers approaching the Sikh tradition from each of four vantage points—religion, history, sacred literature, and ethnic or migration studies. In several cases these authors also suggest how their own aspect of Sikh studies might fit into courses covering a wider range than the Sikhs, and they explain what resources are available to teachers of such courses.

In the seventh chapter, Gurinder Singh Mann goes a step farther by describing an actual course on Sikhism that he has taught for three years in the combined religion departments at Barnard College and Columbia University. He explains what decisions he faced in structuring his course and points out issues that emerged as central. As a way of guiding our perception of the logic of the course, he draws out the themes and tensions that he believes have given a coherent, overall shape to the development of Sikh history and religion. Mann's course on Sikhism is not the only course on Sikhism that has been offered at universities in North America, but it is one of only a handful, and it provides readers with at least one paradigm against which to react. Gerald Barrier's detailed description of issues he faced in a course that also had a chronological format provides some counterpoint.

The book concludes with a bank of materials that we hope will be of use as reference tools for teachers who wish to approach Sikh subjects but do not consider themselves experts in the field. There is a glossary of Punjabi terms used at various points throughout the book, and a select bibliography of works in English about the Sikhs. The bibliography is organized by topic—many corresponding to those suggested in Mark Juergensmeyer's essay—so that readers can review the literature according to its major divisions. Additional help in understanding major contours in Sikh studies as expressed in published books is provided by J. S. Grewal, who is widely acknowledged to be one of the preeminent figures in the field. His historical review of major works published in English since the middle of the nineteenth century is the final chapter in this book.

Studying the Sikhs began as a conference held at Columbia University in the spring of 1989. The event was cosponsored by Columbia's Southern Asian Institute and by the Sikh Cultural Society of Richmond Hill, Queens, and represented the sort of happy cooperation for which several contributors to this book so fervently hope. The editors are grateful to both sponsoring organizations for their confidence and, we hope, foresight and to Kristie Contardi, who has so meticulously helped us in typing the text of the manuscript. We also acknowledge the kindness of the University Seminars program at Columbia for assistance in preparing the manuscript for publication. The ideas presented here have benefitted from discussions in the University Seminar on Tradition and Change in South and Southeast Asia. Finally, we wish to express our thanks to one another for a mutually enlightening, if sometimes dogged, experience in bringing these essays to the light of print.

Note on Transliteration and Pronunciation

No diacritical marks are used in the text, but the pronunciation of the Punjabi words is recorded in parentheses in the glossary. The vowels /a/ /i/ /u/ /e/ and /o/ are fairly close to the corresponding sounds that appear in the English words *but, bit, book, bet,* and *boat.* A macron (ˉ) is used to indicate an increase in the length of /a/ /i/ and /u/, and these sounds correspond to vowel sounds in the English words *balm, beat,* and *boot.*

The Punjabi stops /kh/ and /ph/ correspond closely to the aspirated /k/ and /p/ in English as used in the initial syllabic position in words such as *cat* and *pat.* The other Punjabi stops, /ch/ and /sh/, correspond to English affricates used in words like *chair* and *share.* As will be noticed, our system of transliteration prefers /ch/ to the /c/ that would be standard for transliterating the unaspirated palatal stop in Sanskrit. The corresponding aspirated stop is given as /chh/, not /ch/. The Punjabi /th/ matches the dental fricative in the English words *thick* and *myth.* In English, there are no corresponding sounds for the Punjabi retroflexes /t/ /th/ /d/ /dh/ and /n/, nor for /r/, which is a flap. These sounds are marked in the glossary with a subscript dot.

1

Sikhism and Religious Studies

*

Mark Juergensmeyer

In some ways the field of Sikh studies has never been in a better position for expansion in North American and European universities. There is now such a sizeable population of Sikhs living outside India that they can no longer be ignored by the scholarly community; there is a critical mass of excellent scholarship in the field, and this encourages other scholarly work in response; and the recent political events in the Punjab, tragic as they have been, have increased the awareness of the importance of the Sikh community throughout the world.

But there are important questions to be answered before this expansion can occur smoothly. Are academic disciplines in Western universities ready to accept Sikh studies, and on what terms? And are Sikhs ready to have their tradition scrutinized by Western scholarship?

Part of the problem of absorbing the study of the Sikhs into Western scholarship is that it will inevitably have to be a part of some existing academic field, such as anthropology, comparative sociology, world history, South Asian studies, or religious studies. It might be nice if American and European universities could create entire departments of Sikh studies and adopt wholesale the standards and concepts related to the field that have been developed in India. Realistically, however, this will not soon be the case. There is only one permanently allocated position in Sikh studies in the whole of North America, and it will be a long time before the field has the numbers and the intellectual respect to be accorded its own department. Until then, if it is to be taught at all, Sikh studies will always have to be a part of another field.

Religious Studies: The Shape of the Field

When Sikh studies is located in another field, it inevitably becomes subject to that field's limitations, interests, and academic fads. We can see this clearly in the case of religious studies, which is the department in which Sikh studies will most likely be located in Western universities. Religious studies is an expanding discipline, and one that is relatively hospitable to new areas of growth, but even so it offers a series of particular conditions to which the study of the Sikhs will have to be adapted.

To indicate how Sikh studies would currently be viewed from the perspective of religious studies and to explain the problems that proponents of Sikh studies might encounter if they were to enter the field, I will have to digress a bit and describe some aspects of the recent history of religious studies as a field of concentration in North American universities. All academic fields change over time, but in the last thirty years the field of religion has changed and expanded more than most. Up until the 1960s, religious studies was concerned almost solely with the Christian and Jewish traditions. Indeed, the field of religious studies began as the secular university's nod toward the theological disciplines it had so rudely discarded in the previous century. By the turn of the twentieth century, Christian theology and the training of clergy had been dispatched to seminaries, which were financially supported by churches and usually institutionally separate from universities, though often located adjacent to them. Even before the sixties, certain university faculties became aware that something had been lost from the curriculum of general education by this excision of religion, and they allowed some courses related to religion back in, often under the rubric of comparative literature or philosophy. These included especially courses on the Bible and, to a lesser degree, the history and theology of Christianity and Judaism. In some cases there was a sufficient number of such courses that they could be grouped under the heading "religion" or "religious studies," and departments or programs bearing that name were founded. Inevitably, however, it was Christian and Jewish religion that was meant, although a course in world religion or comparative religion was often thrown in to cover the rest of the world. Sikhism, if it was taught at all, typically came as an addendum to the lecture on Hinduism in the world religions survey. It was, as I called it a dozen years ago, a "forgotten tradition."[1]

In the 1960s all this began to change. Several things happened at about the same time. For one thing, young Americans began to-take a personal interest in cultures dominant in other parts of the world, especially Asia. More important, changes in immigration laws allowed a far greater number of persons to emigrate to the United States from Asian countries than ever before. Because of the increasing pluralism of American society one could no longer teach a course in religion at a major university and assume a certain Judaeo-Christian homogeneity of faith and religious identity. At Berkeley, where I taught for fifteen years, I saw a steady increase in the percentage of Asian students, until in 1988 30 percent of the entering students were of Asian ancestry. At the University of Hawaii, where I am now affiliated, Asian students are in the majority. Some of these are Christian, of course, but most are not: they are Buddhist, Confucian, Hindu, Muslim, or Sikh, or like many students of European ancestry they are indifferent to religion altogether. The point is that when one teaches courses on religion, one can no longer assume that the students taking such courses will be united by a single biblical heritage.

In the 1960s and 1970s, the subject matter of religious studies changed dramatically, as if to recognize the new religious pluralism in American society. Another factor, of course, was the nation's attempt to provide a cultural component that would reflect its changed image of itself as a world power. Religious studies provided an obvious arena for making it clear to students that America represented but one in a multiplicity of cultures rather than being the singular leader of what used to be called "the free world." The changes that occurred in this period were increasingly registered in the meetings of the American Academy of Religion, which for similar reasons superseded the Society for Biblical Literature as the field's major professional association. Presentations on "comparative religion," which once were rare, became central to the program, and working groups were established on what a generation ago would have been regarded as "exotic" religions. In recent years scholars from Berkeley, Chicago, and Harvard have held a series of training institutes for college teachers of religious studies sponsored by the National Endowment for the Humanities intended to facilitate this new "global approach" to the teaching of religion in the liberal arts. The NEH was sufficiently impressed with the importance of the topic to award the project the largest grant it had ever given in that category of funding.[2]

Needless to say, these developments in the field of religious studies are good news for proponents of Sikh studies, as they are for anyone who cares about the study of non-Western cultures. There is now more receptivity to courses on religious traditions other than

Christianity and Judaism than there has ever been in the history of Western academic institutions.

The departure from Christianity and Judaism as the norm of religious studies has also been the occasion for another development within the field, however, and this development may create a problem for some scholars of Sikhism. It is the attempt to make the field of religious studies less pious, less "religious" in its orientation—more objective and "intellectually respectable." Many scholars in religious studies seem to bend over backward to show that they have shed their allegiances to Christianity or any other religion and that they are ready to take up the cause of rational, objective scholarship. The rallying cry for this new trend is "methodology": the adoption of theoretical frameworks, usually borrowed from literary analysis and the social sciences, that serve to surround texts, rituals, and other aspects of religion with an aura of objectivity. Scholars of religious studies want to show that they can examine the various traditions of religion that constitute their subject in a spirit as value-free as that of a botanist scrutinizing the phyla into which plants are classified.

This attempt by scholars of religious studies to align their field with the rational, Enlightenment ethos of the secular university has had a series of important effects. First, it has encouraged scholars to apply methods that have been successfully employed in one tradition (such as certain kinds of textual scholarship) to similar phenomena in other traditions. Second, it has led scholars to look for aspects of religious experience that appear to be universal: those that cut across religious traditions—myths, for example—and are not peculiar to any one. Third, it has moved scholars to examine the cultural contexts in which the histories of particular traditions occur rather than seeing them as self-contained entities. Hence when I taught the introductory course in world religions at Berkeley, I presented Christianity not as a timeless set of revealed doctrines but as something that began as a Jewish cult, merged into the culture of Mediterranean mystery religions, then by a fluke of history became the state religion of the Roman Empire, and developed further in relation to various times and cultures. I treated the other religious traditions of the world in much the same evolutionary way, often emphasizing the point that these traditions have frequently intersected. Such concerns about the historical connections among traditions are not mine alone. Recently the Berkeley search committee for a new faculty position in the field of early Christianity was adamant that the position not go to a conventional historian of Christianity. What they wanted—and eventually got—was a scholar who could treat the early development of Christianity as an aspect of ancient Mediterranean history and culture.

These developments in the field of religious studies have serious implications for the way in which the study of Sikhism will be received by scholars of religious studies. From what I have said, it should be clear that while the scope of the field has enlarged sufficiently to embrace traditions originating in far-flung quarters of the globe, such as Sikhism, the guardians of standards within the field will look for Sikh scholarship that is objective, methodologically *au courant*, cross-cultural in its significance, and contextual in its historical analysis.

Unfortunately, these expectations are somewhat out of kilter with recent trends in Sikh scholarship. This is especially so in the area where the largest number of scholars of the tradition reside and the greatest enthusiasm for Sikh studies exists: the Punjab. In India, one of the main thrusts of recent Sikh scholarship has been to show the distinctiveness of the faith rather than its connections and similarities to other traditions. Another main emphasis has been to demonstrate the relevance of scholarship to the community of believers, and this has often meant projecting the Sikh heritage as one in which the heterogeneity of belief has been bound into an integral, unified, and autonomous culture. Not just for social reasons, therefore, but for intellectual ones, the proponents of Sikh studies are proud to be identified with the Sikh community and determined to be understood on its terms. They do not want the salient features of their faith to be coldly dissected by the methods of social science or to have their textual truths reduced to a level that comparative literary analysis can easily understand.

It seems, then, that the stage is set for an unhappy confrontation between these two views of scholarship, a conflict that has in some parts already begun. But perhaps the prognosis is not so dismal as I may seem to have implied. For one thing, I have described these positions as starker and more inflexible than they actually are. There are many scholars within the mainstream of religious studies who care about subjective views of faith and struggle to accommodate them in intellectually respectable ways; and there are many Sikh scholars who are knowledgeable about, and appreciative of, the methodological developments on American and European campuses that relate to the study of religion. So in many cases the gap is not as severe as, for purposes of discussion, I have portrayed it.

Four Areas of Sikh Studies

Moreover, there are some areas of study within the Sikh tradition in which the gap between the two points of view is not so wide as in others. And even in the more difficult areas there is a potential, not just for tension between Western and Sikh scholars, but for accommodation and collaboration. Let me isolate four such fields within Sikh studies and show how this potential for fruitful scholarship exists in each. The four fields are: historical origins of the tradition, textual studies, beliefs and practices, and Sikh identity. A reader wishing to locate English-language works published in each of these fields should consult the select bibliography at the end of this book. The category "beliefs and practices" appears there; the category "textual sources" contains books I have called "textual studies." Works relating to the historical origins of the tradition are listed under "early Sikh history and religion." Those relating to what I call Sikh identity will be found under "Sikhs in independent India" and "the Sikh diaspora."

The first area of Sikh studies, the *historical origins of the tradition,* is one in which a great number of controversies have arisen between traditional Sikh scholars and scholars trained in the Western mode. From what I have said about the trend in Western scholarship toward looking at historical contexts and interconnections among traditions, it is clear that this point of view contrasts sharply with one that insists that a religious tradition can begin *sui generis,* as a revelation unique in history. The issue in Sikhism is the degree to which one places the early years of the tradition within the context of fifteenth- and sixteenth-century India, especially the milieu of the medieval *sants,* and the degree to which one regards Guru Nanak as the bearer and exemplar of a unique revelation. There are also other controversial matters in the study of Sikh history, such as those regarding the role of the Singh Sabha in the nineteenth century: whether it manufactured the notion of an orthodox Sikh religion or simply standardized preexisting canons of idea and practice. But the greatest controversy centers on Guru Nanak.

The focus for this controversy in recent years has been the scholarship of W. H. McLeod. McLeod is a historian from the University of Otago, New Zealand, who is now also associated with the University of Toronto; he lived and taught in the Punjab for many years and has a master's grasp of Punjabi language. McLeod has written a series of books on Sikh history and literature, many of which were published by Clarendon Press at Oxford. The first book, *Guru Nanak and the Sikh Religion,* which appeared in 1968, remains among the most controversial. The approach adopted by McLeod in this book seems to most Western scholars to be commonplace, even conservative: he attempts a doctrinal catalogue of Guru Nanak's writings and examines the information relevant to Guru Nanak's life with the purpose of separating hagiography from historical fact and placing the historical figure in his contemporary cultural and political context. McLeod's work is not so different from, say, Albert Schweitzer's *The Quest for the Historical Jesus,* written almost a hundred years ago. Like McLeod's book, Schweitzer's thesis—that the life story of Jesus could be examined for its accuracy just as the biography of any other historical figure could be—was intimidating to many conservative religious thinkers of his day. What makes the McLeod issue even more sensitive, however, is that whereas Schweitzer was a Christian examining a problem in the Christian understanding of Christian history, McLeod is a non-Sikh examining a problem in Sikh history for an audience consisting primarily of outsiders: Western academics.

The fact that McLeod's audience is largely the Western academic community, and that his scholarly standards are so rigorous and impressive from that community's point of view, has in one way been a great boon for Sikh studies. Without question, McLeod is regarded in North America and England as the premier scholar of Sikhism, and his work has given studies of the Sikh tradition an intellectual respectability that they otherwise might have taken some years to attain. When in 1986 he was chosen from an international pool of scholars to give the nationwide lectures on the history of religions sponsored by the American Council of Learned Societies, it was a distinction that no other scholar of Sikhism, and few other scholars of South Asian studies, had achieved. This was not only an honor for McLeod; it was an indication that the study of Sikhism had finally been given its due by the Western scholarly establishment.

It is poignant to consider how much respectability McLeod has given to Sikh studies in American and European universities, for in Sikh communities in India and elsewhere he is often caricatured as being hostile to the faith. Sometimes the attacks on him are personal, but the issue ultimately is not one of personality but of approach to scholarship: is a tradition's own understanding of its history to be explicated and affirmed or are the historical data of a tradition available for cross-cultural analysis? The question for those within the Sikh tradition—or any other religious tradition—is whether its uniqueness is challenged when scholars treat it in the same way they might approach any other religion. There is a certain school of Christian scholars who feel about historical scholarship on their tradition the same way the Sikhs hostile to McLeod feel about theirs, and they often feel uncomfortable in the modern university. Such fundamentalists often teach at church-related colleges or seminaries and often find it hard to locate a place for themselves within the field of religious studies, especially in secular universities. Similarly, it is possible that some scholars of Sikhism will always experience the modern university as forbidding. Let us hope, however, that their numbers will not be large and that most Sikhs who study their tradition in a scholarly way will, like their Christian counterparts, find modern modes of analysis congenial to faith and not alien to it.

In a second area, *textual studies,* we may expect to find less friction between scholars within and outside the faith. This is true of textual scholarship in general, whether it be carried out by Christian, Jewish, and secular scholars studying the Bible or by Sikh and non-Sikh scholars examining the *Guru Granth Sahib* (the central Sikh scripture, also called the *Adi Granth)* and other Sikh texts. One can debate the accuracy of the translations of such scholars as Gurbachan Singh Talib, G. S. Mansukhani, Khushwant Singh, or W. H. McLeod without having to discuss their interpretations of Sikh belief or their perspective on the faith. Here techniques of textual reconstruction, translation, and analysis are often more important than one's interpretation of the meaning of the texts themselves, and it is possible for scholars to agree about matters relating to their scholarly tasks even when they disagree over matters of faith.

One of the few areas of scholarship in which fundamentalist Christians have made a widely respected contribution has been in biblical archeology, and conservative Sikh scholars have made similar contributions to the recovery and analysis of manuscripts related to the Sikh tradition. At the other end of the intellectual spectrum is the nineteenth-century German linguist, Ernest Trumpp, who prefaced his English translation of the *Adi Granth* (the *Guru Granth Sahib)* with the nasty remark that it would hardly attract many readers since "Sikhism is a waning religion, that will soon belong to history."[3] Yet his translations and his field notes of discussions about the translations with *granthis* (the keepers of the *Guru Granth Sahib)* at the Golden Temple in the late nineteenth century continue to be valuable reference works for scholars of all religious persuasions.

A third area, the study of the *beliefs and practices* of a religious tradition, is one in which disagreement need not arise if the scholarship in question is largely a matter of description and not interpretation. Of course, to some extent any descriptive study is interpretative in that it selects some things for emphasis more than others. But in general it is possible for an outsider to state the basic beliefs of a faith and to describe its practices in such a way as not to bring radical dissent from the believer. The writings on guruship by Owen Cole and Clarence McMullen, for instance, have been fairly well received within the faith, and for many years the summary of the teachings of Guru Nanak that W. H. McLeod gave in his otherwise controversial *Guru Nanak and the Sikh Religion* were published in a little pamphlet that was distributed by pious Sikhs at the Golden Temple in Amritsar as an accurate description of central tenets of their faith. The introductory textbook on Sikhism that was jointly authored by Owen Cole and Piara Singh Sambhi is another indication that this is an area of scholarship in which insiders and outsiders to the faith can happily collaborate.

Since descriptive analyses of beliefs and practices in Sikhism are a relatively uncontroversial area of scholarship, it is something of a pity that they are not pursued more actively. Scholars living in India apparently consider these matters to be the domain of religious functionaries, while outside of India scholars who are interested in the comparative study of ideas and religious practices often overlook Sikhism for other reasons.[4] These have to do with the still-dominant Western perception that Sikhism is only a syncretic blend of Hinduism and Islam. It follows that most ideas and practices of the Sikh faith can be subsumed under one of these other great traditions. This perception is wrong, of course, and the familiarity with Sikhism that many Western scholars have gained in recent years may help to change it. Because of the political situation in the Punjab, however, it may be some time before foreign scholars will be allowed to undertake anthropological studies of Sikh beliefs and practices in India.

Studies of Sikhism outside the Punjab are another story, and in places like England, Canada, and America, there has been quite a bit of scholarly interest in studying aspects of Sikhism. The main concern there has been with a fourth area of scholarship, which I would describe as the study of *Sikh identity*. Or perhaps it might more accurately be termed "the maintenance of the Sikh community abroad." Some of the most interesting recent scholarship on the Sikhs has focused on the shaping of the Sikh community in the last century and early in this one—Richard Fox's and Rajiv Kapur's work are excellent examples—and on the maintenance of the Sikh community in diaspora in this century. The Barrier and Dusenbery book called *The Sikh Diaspora* is a useful example of the range of work that has appeared.

This is an area of scholarship in which there is virtually no area of disagreement between scholars within and outside the faith, for at least until now the primary interest of those who pursue this area of scholarship has been the survival of the community, its sustained identity. Most Western scholars who write on this topic are sympathetic toward the attempts of the Sikh community to maintain its dignity and integrity. After all, they have those attempts to thank for the coherency of their own subject. Furthermore, the conditions of modernity that fragment community relationships and alienate individuals from their own cultural pasts are of concern not only to Sikhs but to all other sensitive inhabitants of modern urban societies.

As we can see, then, some aspects of Sikh studies lend themselves easily to being taken up by Sikh and non-Sikh scholars alike, without any major risk of controversy. Alas, this is not possible in all areas of scholarship, and we are liable to see many difficult moments before scholars, both Sikh and non-Sikh, feel comfortable with the way Sikh studies is handled within the field of religious studies.

Sikhism within a Course on World Religion

In the meantime, teachers responsible for shaping courses on the religious traditions of the world need to know what to do when faced with the task of integrating the Sikh tradition into their more general subject. With that in mind, it might bear repeating one aspect of my earlier article on "The Forgotten Tradition," namely, that most courses on world religion treat Sikhism shabbily. In part this is because the issue of where to locate the Sikh tradition within a syllabus for such a course and how to describe it puts the teacher face to face with matters that are culturally sensitive to many Sikhs and are still being debated among scholars who specialize in the field. But there is a broader problem, for issues that are critical in the case of the Sikh tradition arise when teaching any religion:

what makes a tradition, when does a tradition become a tradition, and how is it related to other traditions from which it emerges and with which it historically interacts? For courses in world religion that have a basically historical orientation, in particular, these questions must be answered.

In surveying a number of textbooks on world religion, I have looked at the ways the authors have tacitly dealt with these questions in approaching Sikhism. Unfortunately, the results are not always encouraging. One way is to ignore Sikhism altogether. Sikhism is not a religious tradition, as far as Huston Smith is concerned in *The Religions of Man*.[5] In the English translation of Hans-Joachim Schoeps's *The Religions of Mankind*,[6] the existence of Sikhism is acknowledged, but barely, in only five lines, and most of these are inaccurate. According to Schoeps, the founder of the faith "built this combined Hindu-Moslem religion around the god Rama."[7] (In fact, of course, Sikhism rejects all names and anthropomorphic forms of God, including Rama, and as I have mentioned earlier, it is not a combination of Hinduism and Islam at all.) The main problem with ignoring Sikhism, aside from insulting the Sikhs, is that it gives a false impression of Indian religious culture: that it is composed solely of a monolithic Hinduism and that minor and schismatic movements do not exist.

A second way of dealing with the problem is to present Sikhism as a tradition but to present it as if it had no relationship to any other tradition whatsoever. This is essentially the approach that John Noss takes in *Man's Religions,* which is typical of his way of dealing with each of the world's religious traditions: as discrete and relatively uniform entities.[8] While this approach has the practical value of making the material easy to summarize and present, it gives a misleading view of the way in which history actually works. Traditions evolve and change over time, and the changing character of traditions is an important fact to present in an introductory course.

Often textbooks will opt for a third approach to the presentation of religion, which will be revealed in the way they organize the chapters: the section on Sikhism will be sandwiched in between those on Hinduism and Islam, giving the appearance of what many will actually (but falsely) state to be fact: that Sikhism is a syncretic amalgam of the two faiths. Ninian Smart, whose two pages on Sikhism in *The Religious Experience of Mankind* are otherwise fairly accurate, describes it as "a faith designed to bring men of good will in Islam and Hinduism together."[9] The Jesuit scholar, John A.

Hardon, in *Religions of the World,* starts out well by admitting that Sikhism is "sometimes lightly dismissed as a hybrid of two old religions, Islam and Hinduism, made into one," but then he unaccountably decides to label Sikhism as "conscious syncretism, one of the few that has ever been successful."[10] Noss, taking a different tack, claims that Sikhism is a spontaneous rather than a calculated fusion: "the religion of the Sikhs is not to be confused with the rationalistic syncretisms whose adherents have been engaged in a reworking of philosophy rather than in a revival of religion, properly conceived."[11]

The syncretist notion is not wholly based on fiction, for Muslims certainly have had some influence on Sikhs. The reverence that Sikhs accord the *Adi Granth* and the emphasis they place on congregational worship may have resulted, in part, from early Sikh interactions with Islam. Guru Nanak mentioned Muslim teachers among the *yogis,* Brahmans, and other religious people with whom he was in contact. Yet these contacts and influences do not constitute syncretism, and the credit for the promotion of that idea must go to a Sikh, Khushwant Singh, who for years was the major source of information on Sikhism for Western scholars, and who was quite fond of the Hindu-Muslim syncretic view—a position that, unfortunately for him, no other major scholar of the tradition has held before or since.[12]

A more creditable view, the one most clearly articulated by W. H. McLeod, is that the Sikh tradition emerged from medieval Hinduism. McLeod derives its origins from the *sants,* the poet-saints among whom Guru Nanak himself is to be numbered and whose verses contribute to the *Adi Granth.* Many textbooks that are devoted solely to Hinduism will quite properly mention the rise of Sikhism in the context of their discussions of the medieval *sant* movement. But although they avoid the error of classifying Sikhism as a synthesis, these textbooks are not altogether satisfying in their presentations of Sikh tradition. They are, after all, determined to present Hinduism as a distinct and separate tradition of its own; and the Hindu aberrations and offshoots, such as Sikhism, tend to receive short shrift.

Several examples will illustrate the problem. In an otherwise thoughtful and lengthy section on the medieval *sants,* A. L. Basham, in his chapter on Hinduism in *The Concise Encyclopedia of Living Faiths,* edited by R. C. Zaehner, dismisses Nanak and the Sikhs in seven sentences.[13] K. M. Sen's *Hinduism,* which in its Penguin paperback version is perhaps the most familiar of the introductory textbooks on that tradition, is subtitled "The World's Oldest Faith," and the text appears determined to keep it that way since all but twenty pages are premedieval. The two sentences on Nanak and Sikhism in Sen's book are buried in a paragraph on another *sant* figure, Kabir.[14] The first edition of the two-volume *Sources of Indian Tradition,* compiled by a team of scholars under the general editorship of William Theodore deBary, excluded Nanak and the Sikhs altogether. This glaring omission has been corrected in the revised edition prepared by Ainslie Embree, but again the concentration is on Nanak and the early Sikh tradition rather than on a full exposition of the history of the faith and its theological evolution.[15]

For a truly accurate portrayal of the Sikh tradition, then, one must turn to the scholarship devoted solely to the Sikhs and their historical interactions with other traditions. Quite a bit of work has been done on Sikhism since 1948, owing largely to the Punjab government's support of Sikh educational institutions and research projects. Notable among works by Indian scholars are J. S. Grewal's *Guru Nanak in History* and Harbans Singh's *The Heritage of the Sikhs.*[16] Other research has been conducted by scholars from abroad, the most prominent of whom is W. H. McLeod. In addition to his *Guru Nanak and the Sikh Religion,* his *Early Sikh Tradition* should be required reading. He also has a brief and readable introduction to Sikhism in *The Penguin Dictionary of Religions,* and the title essay in his collected essays, *The Evolution of the Sikh Community,* is a classic. Recently McLeod has also compiled a useful series of primary materials for classroom use entitled *Textual Sources for the Study of Sikhism.*[17] A British scholar, Owen Cole, has produced important works as well, including *The Guru in Sikhism* and *Sikhism and its Indian Context, 1469–1708.*[18] An overview and assessment of the state of scholarship on Sikhism as it was twelve years ago may be found in Mark Juergensmeyer and N. G. Barrier, eds., *Sikh Studies: Comparative Perspectives on a Changing Tradition.*[19] For more current estimations of the field, insofar as it concerns prospective teachers, the reader is referred to the chapter by N. Gerald Barrier in the present book and to Gurinder Singh Mann's review of issues he faced in structuring a full course on the Sikh tradition.

Before closing, let me add that local communities of Sikhs are a rich resource for classes in world religion. Sikhs enjoy talking about their beliefs and customs, and a classroom visit from a Sikh, or a field trip to a local Sikh temple (*gurdwara,* "the Guru's place,") will enliven a presentation of the Sikh tradition. Americans who have

joined a Sikh Dharma (3-HO, i.e., Healthy, Happy, Holy Organization) ashram are usually quite knowledgeable about Sikh history
and customs as well, but their perspective on the tradition is somewhat different from that of the Punjabis who have grown up with
the faith, and many of the American Sikhs' practices (such as wearing only white garb and undertaking yogic meditation) are not followed by the rest of the Sikh community. If local Sikhs are not
available or one wants to supplement their perspectives, films and
slides are also a resource.

The best introductory book on Sikhism currently available for
classroom use is Owen Cole and P. S. Sambhi's *The Sikhs*. It incorporates the best recent scholarship on the origins of Sikhism into a
readable account that devotes much attention to actual Sikh religious practices—more, in fact, than any other book now in circula-
tion.[20] If one has the luxury of creating an entire course on the Sikh
tradition, however, one will want to rely on the original sources,
many of which are now available in readable English translations.

Notes

1. "The Forgotten Tradition: Sikhism in the Study of World Religions,"
in Mark Juergensmeyer and N. G. Barrier, eds., *Sikh Studies: Comparative
Perspectives on a Changing Tradition* (Berkeley: Berkeley Religious Studies
Series, 1979), pp. 13–23.

2. Three volumes of essays produced by this project have recently been
published by Scholars Press. The first, of which I am the editor, is entitled
Teaching the Introductory Course in Religious Studies: A Source Book.

3. Ernest Trumpp, trans., *The Adi Granth, or The Holy Scriptures of the
Sikhs* (1877; reprint, New Delhi: Munshiram Manoharlal, 1970), p. viii.

4. See my "The Forgotten Tradition," especially pp. 13–17.

5. Huston Smith, *The Religions of Man* (New York: Harper, 1958). The
book continues to be reissued in this form despite the existence of a revised
edition, entitled *The World's Religions* (San Francisco: Harper, 1991), which
does a bit better by appending an "appendix on Sikhism" to the chapter
on Hinduism.

6. Hans-Joachim Schoeps, *The Religions of Mankind* (Garden City: An-
chor Books, 1966 [in German, 1961]).

7. Schoeps, *The Religions of Mankind*, p. 167.

8. John B. Noss, *Man's Religions* (1949; rev. ed., New York: Macmillan,
1974).

9. Ninian Smart, *The Religious Experience of Mankind* (1969; rev. ed., New York: Scribner's, 1976, p. 152.

10. John A. Hardon, S. J., *Religions of the World,* 2 vols. (1963; rev. ed., Garden City: Doubleday, 1968), vol. 1, p. 224.

11. Noss, *Man's Religions,* p. 226.

12. Khushwant Singh, *A History of the Sikhs,* 2 vols. (1963; rev. ed., Delhi: Oxford University Press, 1991), vol. 1, pp. 17–48.

13. A. L. Basham, "Hinduism," in R. C. Zaehner, ed., *The Concise Encyclopedia of Living Faiths* (1959; reprint, Boston: Beacon Press, 1967), p. 240.

14. K. M. Sen, *Hinduism* (1961; reprint, Harmondsworth: Penguin Books, 1965), pp. 99–100.

15. William Theodore deBary, gen. ed., *Sources of Indian Tradition,* 2 vols. (New York: Columbia University Press, 1958); Ainslie T. Embree, ed., *Sources of Indian Tradition,* vol. 1 (New York: Columbia University Press, 1988), pp. 491–510.

16. J. S. Grewal, *Guru Nanak in History* (Chandigarh: Panjab University, 1969). Harbans Singh, *The Heritage of the Sikhs* (New Delhi: Manohar, 1983).

17. W. H. McLeod, *Guru Nanak and the Sikh Religion* (Oxford: Clarendon Press, 1968); *Early Sikh Tradition: A Study of the Janam-sakhis* (Oxford: Clarendon Press, 1980); *The Evolution of the Sikh Community* (Oxford: Clarendon Press, 1976); W. H. McLeod, ed. and trans., *Textual Sources for the Study of Sikhism* (Totowa, N.J.: Barnes and Noble, 1984).

18. W. Owen Cole, *The Guru in Sikhism* (London: Darton, Longman & Todd, 1982); *Sikhism and its Indian Context 1469–1708* (New Delhi: D. K. Agencies, 1984).

19. Mark Juergensmeyer and N. G. Barrier, eds., *Sikh Studies: Comparative Perspectives on a Changing Tradition* (Berkeley: Berkeley Religious Studies Series, 1979).

20. W. Owen Cole and Piara Singh Sambhi, *The Sikhs: Their Religious Beliefs and Practices* (London: Routledge and Kegan Paul, 1978).

2

Sikh Studies and the Study of History

*

N. Gerald Barrier

The Sikhs and their homeland, the Punjab, have received increasing scholarly and public attention during the last decade. At present there are several centers in India, England, and North America that focus on one or more aspects of the religious and political life in the region. Nevertheless, the study of Sikh history tends to be downplayed except in India, and particularly within educational institutions in the Punjab itself.[1]

This is unfortunate for two reasons. First, historians and the public in general can learn much from trends and controversies that appear in current discussions of how Sikh politics, society, and religion have evolved over the last five hundred years. Perhaps more importantly, the Sikh community has had a persistent need to define itself, and to communicate an understanding of what it means to be a Sikh to other Sikhs as well as to a broader audience. This process of defining boundaries and highlighting basic tenets was prominent in the Singh Sabha era, circa 1880–1920, and has assumed a new importance today. Efforts to formalize the study of Sikh history in a Western setting may help resolve some conflicts among contemporary Sikhs or serve to widen ideological and institutional differences. Whatever the consequence, the discussions among Sikhs and with those outside the religion will be lively and necessary. Sikhs are now a world community, and in the long run, such intellectual activity can only strengthen the rich legacy that gives Sikhism its vitality.

This chapter introduces some patterns and problems inherent in discussing Sikh history. The first section highlights a tension between two approaches to Sikh historiography, the one more familiar inside the Punjab and the other more at home in Western universities. I will attempt to place this debate in a broader context. In the second section, I will raise the question of how the study of Sikh history fits into academic programs in North America: Why and where should the subject be taught, by whom, and with what resources? What issues should be conveyed in the classroom? Finally the chapter concludes with a survey of themes and issues that arise naturally from the study of Sikh history. I will discuss these with an eye to showing how they relate to matters that have stimulated the interest of historians generally.

Two Schools of Sikh History

The institutional base for Sikh studies has tended to center on a network of institutes and university departments within the Punjab. The funding and intellectual milieu within that state affect the focus of research and the understanding of how Sikhism has evolved. Whether lay or professional, most Sikh commentators on Sikh history share certain preconceptions and commitments. They are concerned to reinforce a respect for the Gurus, a sense of historical continuity, a clear differentiation between Sikhism and Hinduism from the time of the first Guru, and to provide an almost hagiographic treatment of historical figures seen as political or religious heroes, whether Maharaja Ranjit Singh or various leaders of reformist sects and revolutionary bands. Most recently, they have shared an insistence that nonviolence has never been a cardinal element within Sikh ideology. They wish to show that the defense of Sikhism through the use of force is a traditional Sikh value.[2] There are striking parallels between such contemporary concerns and the ideology and writings of a network of reformist leaders and organizations in the period stretching from 1880 to 1920, the period loosely associated with the "Singh Sabha movement" dedicated to religions and educational reform among Sikhs.[3]

Much of the historical writing and research that emerges from such Sikhs reflects a common method and a uniform treatment of sources. One underlying assumption is that quotations from the *Adi Granth* are self-validating. If they can be made to support a given interpretation of history, contrary historical evidence counts for nothing. In addition, the paucity of historical documents from the eighteenth and early nineteenth centuries, a critical time in the evolution of Sikh thought and institutions, has led to an uncritical acceptance of other texts such as a number of the *janam-sakhis* (hagiographic biographies of the first Guru) and scattered political accounts. Indigenous sources are not the only ones used to buttress accepted interpretations. In particular, the work of Macauliffe (c. 1900) is generally seen as validating the shared Sikh viewpoint, and little awareness is shown of the fact that his work reflects the intellectual and political milieu of a particular phase of Sikh development.[4] Conversely, the writings of those holding different views tend to be discounted either as ill-informed research by "outside" scholars lacking sympathy for Sikhism or, worse, as a carefully orchestrated attempt to undermine an accurate view of Sikhism.[5]

Over the last several decades a second, contrasting group of historians has gradually emerged, usually trained in and affiliated with Western universities. These scholars question traditional sources and apply the same type of rigorous textual analysis that is used by historians of the Western mode in treating documents that relate to other historical and religious traditions. While respecting the authenticity of Sikhism and supporting the separate boundaries of Sikh doctrine and institutions, Western academicians often cannot accept some of the presuppositions of Sikh historians. They tend to regard Sikhism as an evolving religious and cultural tradition, one that mirrors and in turn affects the environment in which it was evolved. Competing and sometimes conflicting traditions receive attention, as does the process of sorting out and at times creating elements in the common tradition that are consistent with the needs of particular groups within it. The Singh Sabha period has emerged as particularly central in the reformulations that are urged by such historians since it was then that modern Sikhism— the sort espoused by the first group of historians—appeared in response to pressures within and outside the community. It was then that certain symbols, historical events, and records gained legitimacy, while others were rejected or given a secondary status.[6]

The dialogue between the two groups of historians occurs regularly in scholarly journals, newspaper stories, and editorials; in books and conference proceedings; and at annual meetings of professional scholarly organizations. The resulting controversies parallel arguments among groups of historians studying other regions or religions of India and most certainly evoke memories of similar arguments in the record of Western historiography. As to the former, proponents of Muslim separatism and the formation of Pakistan adopted similar approaches to the treatment of historical data and were and are involved in similar controversies with specialists who have other perspectives. The same lines have been pursued by Neo-Hindu historians—both historians such as those who appeared within the Arya Samaj (a Hindu revivalist movement) toward the end of the last century and those whose contemporary writings are designed to foster a Hindu-dominated view of India. Sometimes these Hindu historians cross swords with their Sikh counterparts because the Hindus insist that Sikhism has always been just a small part of the greater tradition of Hinduism.[7] Within a broader context too, one can see that the current upsurge of fundamentalism often seems to require a style of historical reinterpretation that bears a strong resemblance to some of the documentary methods and handling of themes that are prominent among Sikhs.[8]

Another intriguing feature of "insider" Sikh historiography— and one which is paralleled in histories of other regions that came under European control in the nineteenth century—is that it is so dependent upon English-language sources.[9] With the exception of a few books and articles, almost every monograph on the Sikh experience over the last two centuries relies heavily upon Western accounts and/or British official documents. The most striking example is a two-volume history of the Ghadar movement, a Sikh revolutionary group active in the Punjab and elsewhere from about 1910 to 1930. Despite the fact that this history is written by a participant, Sohan Singh Josh, most of the primary sources come from British intelligence records rather than the rich Punjabi sources now readily available.[10]

Yet, historians at large can learn much from recent research on Sikh society, including the research that has emerged from this "insider" faction. Underlying much of Sikh history has been a struggle between competing tribes and castes, and, at times, between regional groupings. Sikh historians know a considerable amount about such divisions and their relevance for historical events. Some, such as Harjot Singh Oberoi (though he would definitely fall in the second, more Westernized group), have evaluated specific trends using the latest sociological theories and taking note of issues prominent in contemporary social historiography. One would have to admit, however, that in much Sikh writing about Sikh history, various divisions and groups are discussed only tangentially and the reason, at least in part, goes back to the basic concern on the part of many Sikhs to demonstrate the unity of their community and the equality of all Sikhs. In fact, some of the loudest criticism of Western scholarship on Sikhism revolves around this point. Non-Sikh scholars are charged with creating divisions, especially pitting Jat Sikhs (the landholding caste group that comprises the majority of Sikhs) and non-Jat Sikhs (especially those from merchant castes) against each other. This has often had the effect of preventing Sikhs from taking seriously the methods and questions that are central to contemporary social historians.[11]

Agrarian and peasant history has been the notable exception. Studies on these aspects of the last 150 years in Sikh history, produced by a group of scholars at Guru Nanak Dev University, Amritsar, have been outstanding and contribute importantly to the "subaltern" movement in recent Indian history.[12] Even in this area, however, the historical research has been uneven. The social basis for the hundreds of organizations linked together in the Singh Sabha movement, for example, has not been explored, nor has an acceptable understanding of the social and political mobilization propelling the massive—and nonviolent—*gurdwara* (that is, Sikh temple) reform movement of 1920 to 1925 been produced. One reason may be the diffusion of documents, primarily in Punjabi; another certainly involves overreliance on British reports, which do not have sufficient data to permit convincing historical treatment at either the broad or the detailed level.[13]

Persistent Sikh attention to the interaction of religious and political traditions puts that area of historical research within the mainstream of Indian and Western historiography. Sikhs regularly address the issue of whether Sikhism can survive independent of a separate Sikh state. They reinterpret the holy scriptures and authoritative traditions of Sikhism to support their arguments, and mount systematic arguments demonstrating the inseparability of state and religion.[14] As with much other scholarly discourse, however, the distinctively Sikh approach to religion and politics is often colored by current political concerns or shaped by pressures to maintain a particular image of Sikh tradition and community. Opponents who emphasize conflicting interpretations of events or major themes are rejected and sometimes charged with sinister motives. The resulting historical record is a mixture of careful scholarship and propaganda—a gold mine for historians who are looking for historical data but at the same time a treasure trove for those who are intrigued by the persistent efforts of groups and communities to legitimize current expectations through their interpretation of the past.

Sikh History in a Western Curriculum

Despite the heat and notoriety of scholarly exchanges in professional settings, the most significant impact of Sikh studies upon the American general public and on American Sikhs themselves will occur within the American education system. Sikhs have increasingly attempted to socialize their children through summer camps and special institutes, and in a less coordinated fashion to arouse public interest through festivals, cultural activities, and occasional seminars. Yet the overall influence of such activities is limited. Both Sikhs and non-Sikh Americans are apt to learn about Sikhism and mold their views about the Sikh religion and its community in educational institutions rather than through sporadic public demonstrations and forums.

Such learning can take place either indirectly, as is now often the case, or directly, and this raises the question of how Sikh history fits into a Western academic curriculum. Perceptions about Sikhs are fostered in the press, on television, and in precollege courses (primarily those in social studies and history), but for the purposes of this discussion, let me restrict my attention to postsecondary education. There, studying and teaching about Sikh history in a critical fashion can serve to illuminate a broad spectrum of issues, such as how and why religions evolve, the relationship between a culture and the ideas and structure of a faith, how religions confront modernity, and the struggle between secularist and fundamentalist tendencies in modern society.

Until a few years ago, Sikh volunteers knowledgeable about their own tradition but without formal advanced degrees could teach *ad hoc* courses in a variety of academic settings. Although this pattern persists in some places, the legitimacy of regular course offerings on Sikh history in North American universities increasingly demands that the instructor have acceptable graduate training, usually a doctorate, as well as a proven ability to communicate effectively with a Western audience. This poses a problem because except for a few students in Western universities and a fresh crop of doctoral candidates from Punjabi University and Guru Nanak Dev University, few academics are qualified by their records of study and published research to teach matters Sikh. Fortunately several specialists on Sikhism are also beginning to be trained in Western universities, where they can be acclimatized to the sorts of perspectives and problems that their students and colleagues will expect them to address.

Approaches to instruction in Sikh subjects, and specifically, Sikh history, will inevitably vary from place to place. One model for introducing Sikh history involves its incorporation within comparative courses on civilization or world history. In the general course on Asian civilizations at the University of Missouri-Columbia, for example, material on Sikhs has been included in sections having to do with the growth of Indian religions, the interaction between political groups and regions in the pre-British period, the creation and maintenance of cultural boundaries, modernization, and responses to regional and national political trends. A related course on colonialism deals with similar issues and also makes use of Sikh materials. "Great Traditions" courses can certainly incorporate a section on Sikhism, especially by making use of the revised edition of *Sources of Indian Tradition* (vol. 1) edited by Ainslie Embree, which contains a short but useful section on the Sikhs and their religion.[15]

Another approach is to incorporate the Sikhs' experience into courses on immigration, on either a global or an American scale. As Arthur Helweg notes in his chapter in this book, the history of Sikh immigration offers numerous opportunities for case studies and comparative discussion. Source materials are readily available for such an effort. For example, the role of Sikhs as immigrants is detailed in a new publication, *South Asians in North America,* as well as in *Continuous Journey,* a book on the social history of South Asians in Canada.[16] Sikh political activities on the West Coast receive excellent treatment in Harish Puri's *Ghadar Movement* and in Joan Jensen's *Passage from India.*[17] Moreover, in December 1986, a group of specialists presented a seminar at the University of Michigan, whose revised proceedings have now been published as *The Sikh Diaspora.* The book contains case studies on Sikh activities in North America as well as essays on economic, intellectual, and political ties between Sikh immigrants and their homeland.[18] While one occasionally finds the Sikhs integrated into broad courses such as those on immigrant history, Sikh history is most frequently taught within curricula that deal specifically with South Asian subjects. Even so, the texts most used in such courses generally give the Sikhs only slight mention. Specialized monographs on Sikh history, early and modern, are now available, but their content and approach mesh poorly with a broader course. Old standbys such as Khushwant Singh's now revised two-volume study or Harbans Singh's *Heritage of the Sikhs* tend to be outdated or too detailed. Fortunately the most systematic collection of source materials, W. H. McLeod's *Textual Sources for the Study of Sikhism,*

is again available in print.[19] This means that instructors have less
to do in the way of generating teaching documents themselves, but
one must still watch to make sure that important subjects are not
ignored.

As for a course on Sikh history per se, there are at least two
possible approaches. The first involves building a syllabus around
specific themes, such as the nature of guruship and the related
matter of who can speak legitimately and with authority about central issues. While intellectually exciting, such a discussion probably
works best as an advanced seminar rather than as an introductory
offering designed for undergraduates. In my experience, undergraduates are more comfortable with the second approach—the standard, chronological review, including sections on the period of the
Gurus, the religious and political era beginning with the *misals*
(Sikh military bands) and ending with the kingdom of Maharaja
Ranjit Singh, the Singh Sabha period and early British rule, and
the Akali and militant phase of Sikh politics that continues until
the present. Within each time period, distinct historical developments need to be highlighted along with controversies over fact and
interpretation, and everything needs to be viewed within the context of Punjab and Indian history generally. The resulting mosaic
would show that Sikhs have had their own unique character and
historical experience while at the same time sharing concerns and
processes that relate them to other religions, groups, and political
networks.

Major Issues in Understanding Sikh History

My research and teaching suggest that several themes run
throughout Sikh history. In the space that remains, I will try to
show how these touch on matters of interest to historians broadly,
and thereby to imply how the study of Sikh history ought to contribute to a general curriculum. Here are the themes I would
emphasize:

1. The evolution of central ideas documented in sacred and historical literature.

2. Struggles over authority and legitimacy: Who should speak
for Sikhs, and with what message? Which institutions came to be

accepted as fundamental, and which families, lineages, and groups were identified with the maintenance of tradition?

3. The formation and institutionalization of Sikh identity, with attention to the structure of Sikh religious, social, and political life, and the transfer of patterns and organizations from central Punjab to the rest of India and, finally, the world.

4. The tension between community solidarity and factional competition. For more than five hundred years, Sikhs have been active in subgroups whose activities have collided with a perceived need for the community to be unified as a permanent minority either within India or as a separate political body.

5. The shifting relationship between religious belief and politics, with attention to varying models of political structure and action and to divergent approaches to protecting a Sikh way of life against internal threats and external danger.

These and other themes cut across particular periods of Sikh history, which raise for consideration their own distinctive concerns. In the time of the Gurus, the need to assess the individual contribution of each Guru and the cumulative achievement of all ten requires sensitive skill. There is also a need to deal with the implied debate between the generally held view that Sikhism was a synthesis between Hindu and Muslim faiths, often promulgated by early Western commentators on Sikhism, and the more recent, more complex understanding of the religious currents found in sixteenth-century Punjab. The *bhakti* (Hindu devotional) movement and related varieties of Islamic ideology were important in the region but recent monographs and collected essays underscore the more persistent influence of the *nath* and *sant* traditions, which celebrated a transcendent, formless deity from more or less within the Hindu tradition.[20] Is this emphasis too in need of revision?

Another issue that arises in relation to early Sikh experience and interests historians generally is the relationship between the oral transmission of the poetry and message of the Gurus and the final construction of an accepted set of scriptures. The issue here is when and how the codification of Sikh scripture actually occurred, and how the written documents related to oral practice, especially since the publishing of a definitive text became imperative only within the increasingly important print culture of British Punjab. That fostered concern over the legitimacy of the *Adi Granth*'s content as well as more mundane matters such as quality of the paper and the arrangement of the poetry found within the text. The determination to remove any perceived Hindu or Muslim elements led some conservative Sikhs to insist that specific passages be excluded or judged less important than others. Similarly the translation of the scriptures into English stirred dissent within official circles as certain Sikhs aligned themselves with foreign scholars active in such efforts.[21] In relation to the formative period of Sikh history, the challenge is to see how these later controversies have shaped our conception of the early years, especially as codified in scripture.

Also central to the ongoing debate about this formative phase is the matter of how key symbols and institutions were defined. The orthodox Sikh view stresses both considerable continuity between the Gurus and the creation of a set of norms and practices through the edicts of the last Guru, Guru Gobind Singh. As historians have attempted to view the process of institution building in context and to weigh the evidence carefully to understand the importance of pivotal episodes, considerable controversy has been aroused among Sikhs. The often uneasy relationship between Jat and non-Jat Sikhs has become enmeshed in the debate, since some of the discussion concerns the prominence of Jat culture in central Punjab and its effect on central Sikh institutions.[22] Similarly, the significance of Jat political activities is a major theme in the scholarly review of the relationship between Sikhs and Mughals. Because these touch on central articles of historical faith that affect Sikhs' sense of their communal identity, such discussions have aroused strong feelings—when and how a distinct Sikh *rahit* (the *khalsa* code of conduct) emerged, for example, or what was the underlying cause for Mughal attacks on Sikh Gurus and their families. In the classroom it is important to try to understand both the facts at issue and the reactions that have been stimulated—on both sides.

The century and a half following the death of Guru Gobind Singh possibly constitutes the most difficult phase of Sikh history to interpret. In the classroom one can discuss specific individuals such as Banda Singh Bahadur or Ranjit Singh, or the politics of competing *misals* and the Punjab state, but one must make students aware that many details are not clear and that often the underlying dynamics shaping this period of Sikh history remain clouded. As with the earlier period, the critical research of W. H. McLeod has aroused strong debate among Sikhs, as one can see from the report he offers in his chapter in this book, but Professor Fauja Singh was the object of similar criticism in the 1970s on charges that he was trying to overturn deeply held convictions about the martyrdom of

Guru Tegh Bahadur. The preparation of critical editions of documents produced in this period—but traditionally held to have been earlier, the work of the Gurus—has been a particularly important feature of this debate.

At least two sets of problems emerge as central. First, what was the nature of Sikh identity? Specific issues such as who perpetuated what traditions, and what constituted distinctly Sikh rituals, customs, and social relationships, require thorough review. Apparently there were different strands and views of the nature of Sikhism in this period. Sikh religious institutions and beliefs were diffuse and mixed with local elements. Brahmanical practice influenced the way in which rites of passage were performed by prominent Sikh families while regional superstitions colored Sikh village life. The sometimes awkward relationship between *kesdharis* (unshorn Sikhs, generally maintaining the five symbols associated with Guru Gobind Singh) and *sahajdharis* (Sikhs who revered the *Guru Granth Sahib* but were not *khalsa* Sikhs following the discipline of Guru Gobind Singh) had not been resolved before the British conquest. Many Sikhs shaved and smoked. Indeed, the boundaries between Hindus and Sikhs were not clearly defined, even by Sikhs who considered themselves orthodox. Harjot Singh Oberoi has written a series of studies on this dimension of the Sikh experience and, in doing so, has stirred reaction from Sikh historians who claim a single line of authoritative practice from Guru Gobind Singh up to the present.

The second set of questions deals with Sikh religion and political expression. The heroism of the Sikhs' struggle to protect their shrines and communal honor are essential elements in the sense of identity felt by many modern Sikhs, so it is disturbing for them to consider, for example, that the regional political strength of the Sikh *misals* may have depended almost entirely on economic and strategic concerns and borne little relationship to Sikhism as a religion. In the classroom one must make it plain that Maharaja Ranjit Singh's being a Sikh ruler did not necessarily cause him to perpetuate any orthodoxy or to favor Sikhs over Hindus and Muslims. Ranjit Singh's policies strengthened the Nirmala sect, with its strong Vedantic leanings, and supported the control of Sikh shrines by those who were not *kesdharis,* that is, who did not wear long hair. These endowments were later perpetuated and given legitimacy by the British. The literature on the Ranjit Singh era is substantial and raises interesting questions about the relationship between doctrine and administrative practice: was there anything "Sikh" about the alliances he developed, the land revenue system he operated, or the modern army he attempted to maintain? Studied primarily by scholars at Punjabi and Guru Nanak Dev Universities, these questions bear on many medieval and early modern states and assume a renewed importance in the era of religious nationalism that many parts of the world now seem to be entering.[23]

The emergence of modern Sikhism resulted primarily from the Sikh encounter with colonial rule—in the burst of reform and revival associated with the Singh Sabha movement. Changed conditions demanded a fresh assessment of tradition, and Sikhs mobilized to meet present dangers and a potentially turbulent future. Historians interested in local responses to imperial or colonial systems can learn much from the Sikh resurgence between 1875 and 1920.

The introduction of British rule into the Punjab marked a new era in the political and religious history of the region. Through a variety of legal and administrative means, the British facilitated communication in the region while reinforcing existing political networks and developing new support groups for colonial power. At the same time, the British presence produced the spread of Western culture and ideological assumptions through schools, expanded communication networks, and, of course, missionary activity. These led Sikhs to rethink cultural patterns and initiate a program of self-strengthening.[24]

Numerous issues emerge in studying and teaching about the period. One is the matter of institutional uniformity, an idea that is often projected into the past once a given group establishes its dominance. Current research suggests that the Singh Sabhas did not constitute a single movement at all but rather an assortment of organizations and individuals with differing commitments and views of history and society. The founding Amritsar Sabha, for example, was led by traditional teachers and aristocrats concerned to spread Western education while preserving Sikh historical documents. This group largely accepted the beliefs and practices current among contemporary Sikhs rather than attempting to define a set of rituals and customs as orthodox Sikhism. Contrariwise the Lahore Singh Sabha, which was drawn from a broader range of classes, championed a *"tat khalsa"* or "true" Sikh faith devoid of popular customs and demonstrably separate from Hinduism.[25] The *tat khalsa* eventually dominated the public life of the Sikh community through its control of the new print culture—journals, tracts, and other means of communication introduced after the 1840s—though Sikhs

still disagreed as to correct ritual *(rahit)* and the appropriate investment of communal resources.

Also important was the struggle between Sikhs who held a conservative view of scripture and perceived tradition, exemplified by
Babu Teja Singh Bhasaur and his followers in the Panch Khalsa Diwan, and a more moderate, accommodative group linked to the
Chief Khalsa Diwan. This struggle provides an opportunity to
stress that "conservative" and "moderate" do not mean the same
thing in every religious debate. While Teja Singh and his fellow activists were committed to protecting a "conservative," unitary vision
of Sikhism, for example, they hoped to do so by spreading female education. Furthermore their conservatism involved a fight—as in
the person of Mohan Singh Vaid of Tarn Taran—to remove images
from Sikh shrines. Similarly Teja Singh challenged untouchability
among Sikhs and helped organize marriages across caste lines. He
crisscrossed the Punjab calling for Sikhs to renounce Hindu practices and return to the teachings of the Gurus *(gurmat),* which he
attempted to clarify by printing the *Guru Granth Sahib* with
certain sections excised. Ultimately these "fundamentalist" views
were rejected by most Sikhs, but the issues raised by this flamboy-
ant leader, such as the role of women in ritual and politics and the
need to dissociate Sikhism from real or imagined contamination by
other religions, helped frame questions that continue to be debated
by Sikhs.

In addition, the conjunction in certain Singh Sabhas between
new forms and ideas and an avowedly revivalist program serves as
an early case study in modern conservative religion. The fusion of
traditional values and modern institutions in new forms of assembly, experiments in education, claims to legal status for Sikh holi-
days, and so forth, parallel what other Indians—Arya Samajis in
particular—were doing at about the same time. The modernizing
efforts of Confucian bureaucrats and Japanese elites also bear some
resemblance to Singh Sabha programs.[26]

The Sikh insistence on continuity from the time of Guru Nanak
onward suggests a theme that interests historians, the reworking of
tradition and the historical record by activists eager to legitimize
current policies and deal with cultural crisis. The Singh Sabha pub-
licists did not create the past through their journals, novels, and
tracts, but in many instances they deliberately or unconsciously
made decisions about what would be emphasized or ignored. In a
variety of public arenas, they promulgated a heightened sense of
loyalty to a heroic past. They also projected a widening sense that

Sikhism was in danger, a threat that served as a powerful motivation for the collection of funds and the rapid spread of political and
religious networks. Much research remains to be done on specific individuals and themes, but already it is clear that the intellectual
roots and concerns of contemporary Sikhism bear the strong imprint of the Singh Sabha movement.[27]

The fusion of religion and politics that occurred in the period
from 1880 to 1920 is an even more fascinating development, and
again one that has left an enduring imprint. Ever since the early
1900s, Sikhs have debated what must be done in public institutions
to protect Sikh values and ensure the survival of Sikhism as a religion. Initially, Sikhs responded to the colonial presence by collab-
orating with the British and relying upon patronage, but with the
gradual decolonization of India, they felt increasingly vulnerable as
a permanent minority community. The colonial power could give
only minimal assistance in a world dominated by votes, majority
rule, and competition. Occasionally loss of elections or inability to
control local policies or organizations was attributed to British bad
faith or the seemingly omnipresent threat of the Arya Samaj, but by
the second decade of this century, Sikhs realized that their fate was
essentially in their own hands. They cried "religion in danger" and
labeled any Sikh seen as cooperating with opponents or promoting
"unpanthic" causes as a major threat to the survival of the religion
and the community.[28]

Like Sikhs today, Sikhs of the early twentieth century disagreed bitterly over the appropriate mix of religion and politics and
over the proper strategy for defending Sikhism and community interests. Some argued for compromise and cooperation with like-
minded individuals from other religions; others insisted on a
solidarity that would be based on self-reliance and a steadfast defense of Sikh cultural boundaries. The Chief Khalsa Diwan attempted the former course and by 1920 lost out in the militant
mobilization surrounding the gurdwara reform protests. Thus, history before the rise of the Akalis mirrors the tension between group
or communal identity and less parochial concerns that was to appear later on, even today.

The Singh Sabha era also reveals many of the sources of dissent
and conflict that were to remain prevalent among Sikhs. The regional split between the areas of Malwa and Majha, the social competition between the rural Jats and the more urban Khatris and
Aroras, the fluctuating relations between *sahajdharis* (Sikhs who
have not received initiation into the *khalsa* but affirm the *Guru*

Granth Sahib) and *kesdharis*—all were active elements in Sikh public life in the Singh Sabha period and can be studied there with a certain historical distance. As the leading Sikh newspapers of the time, the *Khalsa Samachar* and the *Khalsa Advocate,* continually noted, the tendency of Sikhs to fight among themselves made the community vulnerable to attack and slowed the march toward educational and economic advancement. Also unresolved was the issue of which institutions or groups had the authority to lead Sikhs in matters of doctrine and strategy. The heroism of the five-year (1920–25) crusade to rescue the *gurdwaras* and the subsequent rise of the Akali group eventually resolved many issues, at least temporarily, by earning massive community support and enhanced legitimacy for the leadership of *kesdhari* and *amritdhari* Sikhs, that is, for Sikhs who had undergone the *khalsa* initiation.[29]

Heroes and martyrs continued to abound in Sikh history after 1920, first in the *gurdwara* movement and then in events surrounding partition. Books on the Akali struggle often appreciate this facet of history but do not address basic questions such as the political and social backgrounds of participants, the role of the British and their agents in influencing factions, and the different personalities and perspectives shaping the outcome.[30] Teachers of Sikh history should therefore introduce supplementary materials. They might also note that the nonviolent rescue of the *gurdwaras* is a fine case study in the effective application of Gandhian tactics—something that is often downplayed because of current Sikh politics. Until a detailed study of Punjabi documents relating to the Akali campaign appears, however, historians can learn little about its wider implications. Another historiographic gap relates to the tendency to view Sikh politics in the 1920s as isolated events instead of understanding them in the context of a complex legislative system and a series of shifting alliances among Punjabis.

The Akali victories brought to an end the Singh Sabha efforts to preserve tradition and at the same time revitalize the social and intellectual life of Sikhs. Historians concerned with the dynamics of communalism can learn something from the ebb of the Sikh renaissance associated with the Singh Sabhas and a concomitant resistance to dissent and unpopular views among fellow Sikhs. Although Bhai Vir Singh and Bhai Kahn Singh Nabha continued to publish, surrounded by a small band of writers interested in prose, poetry, and drama, the quantity and quality of writings in Punjabi fell short of the richness evident in the pre-Akali period. The eclipse of the *Khalsa Samachar,* the attacks on Sundar Singh Majithia and

the Chief Khalsa Diwan, and subsequent Akali efforts to control independent institutions such as the Sikh Kanya Mahavidyala of Ferozepur (founded by Bhai Takhat Singh and run by his children),
exemplify a growing tendency to distrust and malign Sikhs of different persuasions.[31]

The partition of the Punjab in 1947 affected every Sikh family.
Its horrors and disruptions threatened the social fiber of the community, but arising from the ashes was a revitalized economy and a
concentration of Sikhs within a smaller part of the Punjab. The spe-
cifics of the massacres, mass migrations, and resettlements, and
the reasons they occurred, are difficult to capture in a general
course on Sikh history, but unless some attempt is made, the dyna-
mism propelling Sikhs through the last four decades cannot be explained. Novels such as those by Khushwant Singh help, as do
personal accounts, either recorded in autobiographies or passed
along orally among family members.[32] Once these events receive the
scholarly attention they deserve, historians in other areas will have
a mass of fresh material for understanding processes associated
with communal violence and the rebuilding of social networks and
institutions.

Two themes stand out as major focuses in Sikh history after
1947. The first is the resurgence of Sikh migration and, with a
steady movement beyond the Punjab, the emergence of Sikhs as vi-
tal economic, social, and religious elements in cultures spread
throughout the world.[33] Secondly, and in part as a response, Sikhs
have attempted to protect and consolidate their traditions by set-
tling upon specific rules and rituals that are increasingly viewed as
standard or orthodox and propagating them through tract literature, training camps, and actual practice. The earlier confusion over
rahit and religious doctrine has given way to a series of confident (if
sometimes historically questionable) assertions about fundamental principles.

Yet a sense of confident success has gone hand in hand with a
sense of insecurity. "Sikhism in danger" was a dominant theme in
1890, and it is again today. The Arya Samaj has reemerged as a perceived archenemy of Sikhism, and pamphleteering is common, with
use being made both of fresh material and of truncated versions of
older works.[34] Century-old labels of "enemy of the *panth*" and "back-
slider" again echo in editorials and articles as opponents are
charged with forsaking the will of the community and the teachings
of the *Granth* and the Gurus. Parallels between periods—especially
if one of the periods is the present—provide an excellent focus for

class discussion, and there is much else to bring to the fore. For example, there are strong parallels between the earlier struggles to control *gurdwaras* and other public institutions and recent moves to dominate the symbolic center of Sikhism, the Golden Temple at Amritsar. In the present day, however, dissent meets not just with challenge but with threats of violence. Sometimes opponents are indeed assassinated.

Another familiar theme also appears: Sikhs are continually debating the relationship between religion and politics. In books, journals, and public meetings, scripture and historical evidence are used by those who argue over whether Sikhism can survive independently or only within a theocratic state, a Khalistan (that is, an independent state controlled by the *khalsa*). This in turn affects what can be taught in schools, the content of scholarly research, and the treatment of those who disagree. Similarly, Sikhs openly discuss what sanctions can be used to maintain solidarity and how and when violence can legitimately be employed in the name of religion.[35]

Violence and nonviolence are intertwined within the Sikh tradition. The first Gurus emphasized peaceful existence and love, a theme that reappeared sporadically through the 1920s, when the *gurdwara* reform movement put into action one of the most dramatic and sustained efforts to use nonviolence to produce political change. That thousands of Jat Sikhs would march unarmed into the face of threats, injury, and possible death seems almost unexplainable today. The militant heroism of Guru Gobind Singh and others seems easier to comprehend, as attested in the larger-than-life paintings of Sikh martyrs found in museums and libraries or the vivid illustrations of valor and sacrifice contained in novels and comic books. The question of the legitimate limit to the application of force remains central to the intellectual debate of Sikhs today and to the daily life of Punjabis.

In summary, understanding the major events and themes of Sikh history contributes to a better appreciation of current Sikh concerns—concerns that now have a global impact. Equally important for the historian are the dimensions of Sikh history that throw light on parallel movements and common processes affecting other groups. The conflict between violence and nonviolence, the debate over the meaning of historical events and ideas, the relationship between sacred tradition and scholarly research, the recent strengthening of fundamentalist patterns, and the controversy over correct action and the control of religious and secular institutions—all these are universal themes that can be better understood by knowing how they have affected the life and destiny of Sikhs.

Notes

1. For background on the context of Sikh and Punjab studies, see Barrier, "The Evolution of Punjab Studies in North America," *Panjab Past and Present,* 1983, pp. 398–407, and "The Evolution of Punjab Studies, 1972–1987," forthcoming in proceedings of the Punjab Studies Conference held at the University of Wisconsin in 1988.

2. A major source for such Sikh rhetoric is *World Sikh News,* a journal published in Stockton, California. Two recent volumes highly critical of Western scholarship on Sikhism are Gurdev Singh, ed., *Perspectives on the Sikh Tradition* (New Delhi: Siddharth Publications, 1986) and Jasbir Singh Mann and Harbans Singh Saraon, eds., *Advanced Studies in Sikhism* (Los Angeles: Sikh Community of North America, 1989).

3. This will be a major theme in my forthcoming study of the Singh Sabhas and the Chief Khalsa Diwan. See also Barrier, "Sikh Politics in British Punjab," in Joseph O'Connell et al., eds., *Sikh History and Religion in the Twentieth Century* (Toronto: Centre for South Asian Studies, 1988), pp. 159–90.

4. For background on Macauliffe, see Barrier, "In Search of Identity: Scholarship and Authority among Sikhs in Nineteenth Century Punjab," in Robert I. Crane, ed., *Language and Society in Modern India: Essays in Honor of Professor Robert O. Swan* (New Delhi: Heritage Publishers, 1981), pp. 1–23.

5. For example, the essays by Daljeet Singh in *World Sikh News* (Fall 1989) and in Mann and Saraon, eds., *Advanced Studies.*

6. The best study on the period is Harjot Singh Oberoi, "A World Reconstructed" (Ph.D. diss., Australian National University, 1988). Compare his "From Ritual to Counter-Ritual" in O'Connell et al., eds., *Sikh History,* pp. 135–58.

7. Historical controversies are reviewed in Kenneth Jones, *Arya Dharm* (Berkeley: University of California Press, 1976), and the historiographic issues are summarized in his new book, *Socio-Religious Movements in British India* (Cambridge: Cambridge University Press, 1990).

8. A sensitive treatment of intellectual developments among Sikhs in the last fifteen years is Robin Jeffrey, *What's Happening to India?* (London: Macmillan, 1986).

9. See, for example, the discussion on Subsaharan Africa in Georg G. Iggers and Harold T. Parker, *International Handbook of Historical Studies, Contemporary Research and Theory* (Westport, Conn.: Greenwood Press, 1979), pp. 403–18, and Barrier, "Indian History Since 1945," in *Handbook*, pp. 214–33.

10. Sohan Singh Josh, *Hindustan Ghader Party* (Delhi: Peoples Publishing House, 1972–78). An excellent review of the indigenous literature on the Ghadar movement is Harish Puri, *Ghadar Movement* (Amritsar: Guru Nanak Dev University, 1983).

11. See, for example, Jagjit Singh's discussion of the Jats in Mann and Saraon, eds., *Advanced Studies*, pp. 214–33, and in G. Singh, ed., *Perspectives*, pp. 231–385. The focus of Sikh attention has been on arguments of W. H. McLeod in *The Evolution of the Sikh Community* (Delhi: Oxford University Press, 1975), and, most recently, *The Sikhs: History, Religion and Society* (New York: Columbia University Press, 1989) and *Who Is a Sikh?* Oxford: Clarendon Press, 1989). Also frequently criticized is the discussion of Jat culture by Joyce Pettigrew, *Robber Noblemen: A Study of the Political System of the Sikh Jats* (London: Routledge and Kegan Paul, 1975).

12. E.g., Indu Banga, *Agrarian System of the Sikhs* (New Delhi: Manohar, 1978) and numerous essays in *The Journal of Sikh Studies,* published by the university.

13. For example, the book by Richard Fox, *Lions of the Punjab* (Berkeley: University of California Press, 1985), discussed by Ian Kerr, "Fox and the Lions," in O'Connell et al., eds., *Sikh History,* pp. 211–25. Relevant historiographic issues are reviewed in Barrier, "The Evolution of Punjab Studies."

14. More than a dozen monographs have been published recently on the political views of the Gurus. The articles in *World Sikh News* consistently address this theme, as do recent tracts and polemical works such as S. S. Dharam, *Internal and External Threats to Sikhism* (Delhi: Gurmat Publishers, 1986).

15. A. T. Embree, ed., *Sources of Indian Tradition* (New York: Columbia University Press, 1988), vol. 1, pp. 493–510.

16. Jane Singh, ed., *South Asians in North America: An Annotated and Selected Bibliography* (Berkeley: Center for South and Southeast Asian Studies, 1988); Norman Buchignani and Doreen M. Indra, *Continuous Journey: A Social History of South Asians in Canada* (Toronto: McClelland and Stewart, 1985).

17. J. Jensen, *Passage from India* (New Haven: Yale University Press, 1988).

18. N. G. Barrier and Verne Dusenbery, eds., *The Sikh Diaspora* (Columbia, Mo.: South Asia Publications, 1989). An excellent bibliography of current books and articles on this and other areas of research is in O'Connell et al., eds., *Sikh History,* pp. 457–86.

19. W. H. McLeod, *Textual Sources for the Study of Sikhism* (Chicago: University of Chicago Press, 1990).

20. Karine Schomer and W. H. McLeod, eds., *The Sants* (Berkeley: Berkeley Religious Studies Series, 1987), and numerous books by McLeod. Sikh resistance to these interpretations is reflected in Mann and Saraon, eds., *Advanced Studies* and G. Singh, ed., *Perspectives.*

21. See Barrier, "Trumpp and Macauliffe: Western Students of Sikh History and Religion," in Fauja Singh, ed., *Sikh Historiography* (Delhi: Oriental, 1978), pp. 155–85.

22. First addressed systematically in McLeod, *Evolution,* pp. 51–53, 92–99.

23. Published primarily in *Panjab Past and Present, The Journal of Sikh Studies,* the proceedings of the Punjab History Conference, and in the proceedings of various symposia held at Guru Nanak Dev University, such as J. S. Grewal and Indu Banga, eds., *Maharaja Ranjit Singh and His Times* (Amritsar: Guru Nanak Dev University, 1980).

24. Outlines of major developments are traced in Barrier, *Sikhs and Their Literature;* Barrier, "The Singh Sabhas and the Evolution of Modern Sikhism, 1875–1925," in Robert Baird, ed., *Religion in Modern India* (New Delhi: Manohar, 1989), pp. 189–220; and H. S. Oberoi, "A Historiographical and Bibliographical Reconstruction of the Singh Sabha in the 19th Century," *Journal of Sikh Studies* 10 (1984), pp. 103–30.

25. See H. S. Oberoi, "Bhais, Babas and Gyanis: Traditional Intellectuals in Nineteenth Century Punjab," *Studies in History* 2 (1980), pp. 36–62.

26. See Barrier, "Indian Regionalism and Politics in Historical Perspectives," in Paul Wallace, ed., *Region and Nation in India* (New Delhi: Oxford-IBH and American Institute of Indian Studies, 1985), pp. 111–15; and "Indian History since 1945," in Iggers and Parker, eds., *International Handbook of Historical Studies,* 1979), pp. 280–305.

27. The historical connections are summarized succinctly by Robin Jeffreys in *What's Happening to India?*

28. For example, editorials such as "Our Carelessness on All Sides" or "What We were and What We are Doing Now" *(Khalsa Samachar,* July 11 and September 12, 1906). This issue is highlighted in my paper, "The Sikhs and Politics in the Punjab, 1880–1920," presented at the American Academy of Religion, Anaheim, 1989.

29. See K. L. Tuteja, *Sikh Politics* (Delhi: Vishal, 1984).

30. Fox attempts a social analysis based upon alleged peasant unrest, but the evidence does not support his provocative arguments. As Kerr notes in his review, "Fox and the Lions," however, there have been no other convincing explanations for the movement. A final assessment of the turbulent five years of Sikh militancy would involve at a minimum careful study of newspapers *(Akali* and the Lahore *Tribune)* and work in the All India Congress Committee files and what remains of the Shiromani Gurdwara Prabandhak Committee and Akali papers after the destruction of archival materials in the raid on the Golden Temple in 1984.

31. Almost none of these incidents receives attention in current histories. I appreciate the assistance given by Nahar Singh, M.A., in reconstructing the history of the Sikh Kanya Mahavidyala and recounting the conflict between the Akalis and that institution, as well as with Majithia, for whom he served as private secretary.

32. The finest English novel on partition is *Train to Pakistan* by Khushwant Singh, available in numerous editions. A short book by K. K. Sharma and B. Johri, *The Partition in Indian-English Novels* (Delhi: Vimal Prakashan, 1984), surveys the literature.

33. See Barrier and Dusenbery, eds., *Sikh Diaspora,* passim; Bruce La Brack, *The Sikhs of Northern California, 1904–1975* (New York: AMS Press, 1989); Arthur Helweg, *The Sikhs in England,* 3d ed. (Delhi: Oxford University Press, 1990); and essays on migration in O'Connell et al., eds., *Sikh History.*

34. For example, Kenneth Jones' scholarly article on the Arya Samaj, originally published in *The Journal of Asian Studies,* was edited, given a new introduction, and then reprinted in Punjabi.

35. Within the North American Sikh community, the World Sikh Organization has expanded the popular practice of holding a diwan or large consultative meeting into a series of "panthic conferences" to address immediate problems. The most recent, held in New York at the end of January 1990, came out with many resolutions, including a ratification of Khalistan and a denunciation of McLeod's research.

3

The Study of Sikh Literature

*

W. H. McLeod

There are a variety of ways in which the religious literature of the Sikhs (or indeed of any other religious community with a distinctive canon) may be approached. Three methods of approach may be distinguished.

For fundamentalist believers, the religious literature of the faith will be read or heard as literally inspired, its words possessing a spiritual power that is denied to all other words. The proper attitude is one of devout reverence and the effect upon the person who approaches it in this way is one of deep satisfaction. Questions concerning origin either do not arise or, if they do, they are given an answer in an approved manner. The scriptures are inspired and as such they speak directly to the heart or to whatever faculty illuminates the inner being.

In contrast to this, there is the method of the scholar, who may or may not be a believer. Such scholars should be conscious that they are handling material regarded by the devout as sacred; in their approach to it they will handle it, literally and figuratively, with the utmost delicacy. Their method will nevertheless be distinctively different from the believers'. The purpose of analyzing the literature will be to discover what it reveals as a source for the scholar's particular interest, and as a result, it will be subjected to an examination of the kind that the devout believer would never dream of giving it.

The third method will be that of the person who regards it simply as literature and reads it for whatever it may impart by way of skill or of beauty. In this case also the person who reads the scripture may or may not be a believer; for an adherent, though, there may be an overlap between this mode and the first one. Normally such readers will not be believers but will be attracted to the scripture because they recognize something in it that appeals to their notions of craft or speaks to their sense of beauty.

These are, of course, poles, and there are all shades of difference in the actual approach to the Sikh scriptures. As poles, however, they serve to mark and define general positions, and the principal difference that concerns us in this chapter is the one that separates the attitudes of the fundamental believer from those of the scholar. Here the chances of disapproval or misunderstanding are pronounced, to say the least. For devout believers, the questions that scholars are bound to ask and some of the answers they get to those questions will generate at least irritation and sometimes positive outrage. "How dare such people venture upon sacred territory! The scriptures of the *panth*—the Sikh community—are holy, and none but those who recognize this basic fact is entitled to approach them or to consider them." Even those who acknowledge a certain right to apply scholarly questions to the Sikh scriptures draw strict boundaries when it comes to the answering of those questions. The answers are already known, and anything that carries the discussion away to new and unexplored ground must be resolutely resisted. This indignation and offense bears no relation to the antecedents of the guilty scholar. Whether the scholar be inside the *panth* or on the outside, the reaction will be the same. Such people are the enemies of true religion, and the duty of the devout is clear. They must avoid the works of such people, and they must denounce them before all who share their devotion to truth.

The reaction of some scholars contrasts broadly to this attitude but is equally reprehensible. Confronted by the misgivings of the hesitant faithful or the denunciation of the confident, they respond with a posture that amounts to open scorn. "How absolutely silly these people are! At best their attitude can be described as simpleminded; at worst it is pure bigotry! Probably it is somewhere in between, best described as the pious credulity of a limited mind."

This, needless to say, is taking extreme examples from each end of the scale, but the polarity should not be dismissed as meaningless for this reason. In the first place, there are plenty of people who can be found occupying such extreme positions. And secondly, although most of us would not dream of adopting such extravagant attitudes, we would be dishonest to deny that there are elements of one posture or the other in much of what we say or do. Those who are both scholars and Sikh believers often must acknowledge, when they are really serious, that both attitudes are commonly held and commonly contradict one another. Those who stand outside the *panth,* genuinely and sympathetically seeking to understand it, may well have to acknowledge a similar fact: that there are more than just traces of inherited beliefs in scholarly judgments. Such basic convictions are ever ready to surface if the scholar is not rigorously careful to keep them under control.

So the study of a religious scripture, whether one's own or that of other people, is an enterprise fraught with difficulty. Defended by the ranks of the faithful or closeted within one's study, the problems on either side may not seem to be particularly serious. When, however, one remembers that one's views or reasoning require a larger audience than either the dedicated faithful or the study, and when one ventures to communicate them to this larger audience (which will contain some at least who will regard such views as either dangerous or naive), the task becomes much more demanding.

The problem is much more serious for scholars than for simple believers, the vast majority of whom will never have even glimpsed that there is such a thing as a scholarly view. It may be understandable that scholars too, like believers, often feel that their research and reasoning should properly be confined to the limited circle of those who can appreciate what they are doing. In a scholar's case, this means that one must conduct academic controversy in accordance with the rules of decency and sensible decorum: after all, that is how other scholars do their work. But scholars of religion— and particularly those who work on religious scriptures—are not like other scholars, and they must understand that this is so. Their materials are what other men and women hold sacred, and if the religion they study is a living and vibrant one, there is no means of keeping their research safe from the scrutiny of believers.

Under these circumstances it is necessary that the scholar of religion must tread very softly, and when the field includes a sacred scripture that is profoundly revered, the need becomes altogether compelling. At the same time, every effort must be made to persuade the faithful that a scholar has the right to undertake research and that even though the results of that research may conflict with the traditional view, the scholar has the right to express them, provided always it is done with sensitivity and caution. Just this intention must lie behind an examination of the Sikh scriptures.

What, then, constitutes Sikh scripture? Everyone agrees that the *Adi Granth* (literally, the "primal book") qualifies handsomely for the title. Compiled by Guru Arjan in 1603–1604, the *Adi Granth* occupies for all Sikhs the absolute center of the faith. Believed to represent the eternal Guru for all time, and for that reason known today as the *Guru Granth Sahib* (the Granth which is Guru), the *Adi Granth* clearly can be accepted as scripture.

So too the *Dasam Granth* (the book of the tenth Guru), although in this case a note of hesitation may be detected. The *Dasam Granth* was compiled in the early eighteenth century, and although it is traditionally believed to comprise the writings of the tenth Guru, some doubts have made themselves felt. According to these doubts, some of the *Dasam Granth* does indeed seem to be the work of Guru Gobind Singh, but not the whole collection. Yet this does not prevent the volume from being scripture, and undoubtedly it was regarded as such during the eighteenth century. Today, however, it plainly does not rank with the *Adi Granth,* although the works that the *panth* universally attributes to Guru Gobind Singh are selectively promoted to this level. Other parts of the *Dasam Granth* are largely ignored, and the question of the work's overall scriptural status is left undecided.

At this point we must ask ourselves if we are creating an unnecessary problem by seeking to categorize Sikh writings according to the Western rubric of scripture. I do not believe so. A scripture is a book that is held to be sacred by a particular religion, and if the *Adi Granth* at least is not held sacred by the Sikhs, the word sacred has no meaning. The problem is not whether the Sikhs have a scripture or a canon but what deserves to be included in that category. Is it the *Adi Granth* only, or the *Adi Granth* plus the works attributed to Guru Gobind Singh, or should the whole of the *Dasam Granth* be added in? Are the works of Bhai Gurdas and Nand Lal Goya to be included, and if they are, what about the *janam-sakhis,* the traditional biographies of Guru Nanak? And if the *janam-sakhis* deserve a place, why should the *gur-bilas* literature—traditional accounts about the lives of the Gurus—not find mention? And then there are the *rahit-namas,* the annals of the *khalsa* code of conduct, which deal with that revered subject of religious symbolism, the marks and insignia of the true *khalsa.* There is indeed a problem, but it is not one of whether or not the Sikhs have a scripture.

One indicator of what ought to be regarded as scriptural is perhaps given by the portions of their literature that devout Sikhs learn and recite by heart. This applies to any part of the *Adi Granth,* though there are some portions that command particular affection in this respect. All Sikhs should, of course, know the *Japji*

Sahib, with which the *Adi Granth* begins and which is specified as required recitation for early morning devotions. Not all Sikhs do know it, but a considerable number have learned it and regularly recite it first thing in the morning (after a bath or a shower), sitting quietly or on their way to work. A smaller but still considerable number also know the other passages appointed for devotional purposes, whether for the early evening prayer (*Sodar Rahiras*) or for the prayer before retiring for the night (*Kirtan Sohila*). The devout will also know two lengthy works, *Sukhmani Sahib* of Guru Arjan and *Asa di Var,* which is mainly by Guru Nanak.[1] Beyond these they will know a selection of shorter works, possibly extending to a substantial quantity of the *Adi Granth.* Clearly the whole of the *Adi Granth* is regarded as scriptural, and most Sikhs would wonder why we are bothering to discuss it.

Some of the passages set down for personal devotions, however, come not from the *Adi Granth* but from the *Dasam Granth,* all of them works attributed to Guru Gobind Singh. The early morning order includes his *Jap Sahib* and *Ten Savayyas,* and the early evening specifies his *Benati Chaupai* with *Savayya* and *Dohara.*[2] This seems to indicate that these works should also be regarded as scriptural. All are from the portions of the *Dasam Granth* that Sikh opinion generally regards as the work of Guru Gobind Singh, and they are consequently treated as *gurbani* or "utterances of the Guru." As such they are regarded as scripture, and the same also applies to other works in the *Dasam Granth* that are regarded by the overwhelming majority of Sikhs as compositions of Guru Gobind Singh. They are, in other words, those portions of the *Dasam Granth* which are selectively promoted to equality with the *Adi Granth.* The remainder of the *Dasam Granth* is, however, the subject of doubt, some affirming that it should definitely be regarded as sacred writ and others adopting a more cautious attitude.

Portions of the *Dasam Granth* must therefore be regarded with guarded doubt, and the same applies even more firmly to the poetic works of Bhai Gurdas and Nand Lal. They may be designated as works suitable for recitation in gurdwaras, but most Sikhs, if confronted with the question of whether or not they are canonical, would feel obliged to answer in the negative. With the *janam-sakhis,* this answer becomes a certainty. The *janam-sakhis* are hagiographic anecdotes about the life of the first Guru, Nanak, and although they are believed to be uplifting, they cannot be classified as scripture. The same applies to the *gur-bilas* literature, equally hagiographic in its approach but concentrating on the heroic deeds

of the sixth and particularly the tenth Guru. Also outside the
boundaries of scripture are the *rahit-namas,* prescriptions concerning a *khalsa* Sikh's approved mode of belief and behavior.

The Adi Granth

The first of the examples mentioned above is the *Adi Granth*
and this, as we have seen, we can firmly and without question des-
ignate a scripture. That is not to say, however, that the *Adi Granth*
is without its problems. Most assuredly it has these, and more than
any other range of issues, they set the believer against the scholar.
It is indeed a whole range of issues and not one in particular. The
conspicuous difficulties fall into five categories.

First, there are the questions that relate to the source or
sources that were used by Guru Arjan in compiling the *Adi Granth*.
These concern the Goindval or Mohan *pothis* (a *pothi* is a book or
volume). Secondly, there are those that arise from the manuscript of
what is regarded as the original *Adi Granth*. These questions concern the status of the Kartarpur manuscript. Thirdly, there is the
history of the manuscript during the centuries following its recording until it eventually turned up in the Lahore court in 1849. During these two and a half centuries, its history is obscure, to say the
least. Fourthly, there is the manner in which it came to be trans-
muted into the *Guru Granth Sahib* in the eighteenth century, a subject that demands particular caution and tact. And fifthly, there are
issues that derive from the actual text of the *Adi Granth*. Are the
words it records the authentic compositions of the various authors
to which they are attributed or have they been changed in the period of oral transmission that preceded their copying? This too
raises questions demanding the utmost care. Some of the tasks in
the wider area are those that require the skill of a historian, others
those of the philologist or textual critic. Commonly they will demand both.

It will at once be evident to anyone acquainted with the Sikh
view of the *Adi Granth* that this exercise will involve research of the
most extreme delicacy. Inquiries into the issues listed above will be
attended by the risk of generally ascending uneasiness—ultimately
the danger of grave offense. It will be bad enough questioning the
purity or authenticity of the Goindval *pothis,* but that will not be
nearly as bad as calling into question the status of the Kartarpur
bir (manuscript) or suggesting that the orthodox views of it may be

in some measure astray. The questions concerning the history of the manuscript are perhaps the least likely to cause a serious reaction, but the same cannot be said for the two that remain. Either of them will call forth expressions of outraged indignation and horror. At their peril, scholars question the traditional interpretation of how the *Adi Granth* came to be the *Guru Granth Sahib,* and even more they will create serious disturbance by carelessly broadcasting the view that the text of the *Adi Granth* may be other than the actual words which were uttered by the Guru or *bhagat* to whom they are attributed. It will be a very brave or a very rash person who will venture on the last of these.

Yet this should be precisely the task of scholars in countries such as Canada or the United States, always heeding, of course, the obligation to tread exceedingly softly and always communicating one's findings with the utmost courtesy. To leave these subjects inviolable and untouched may be necessary in some parts of the world, but if that is to be our response everywhere and Sikhs do nothing about it, we necessarily condemn religious Sikhs to stagnation while the world around them rushes on. An unquestioning attitude may suit those whose understanding has already been definitively formed, but it certainly will not accommodate a growing generation who will insist on comparing their faith with the world they find around them. As the world changes, they will find their inherited faith further and yet further out of harmony with it, and that is assuredly a guarantee that many at least will be compelled to relinquish the substance of their faith. Some will remain and lend credence to the voices of those who insist upon no change. They will, however, be a dwindling band.

The first of the general issues involving the *Adi Granth* is the question of origins. Tradition relates that Guru Amar Das had the works of the first three Gurus, together with those of the *bhagats,* copied out by his grandson Sahans Ram. The recording was done in at least two volumes or *pothis,* and as the work is associated with the village of Goindval, the collection is usually known as the Goindval *pothis.*[3] Guru Arjan, having decided to prepare a larger edition for his Sikhs (one to which he added the works of his father Guru Ram Das and his own substantial contribution), is said to have obtained the *pothis* from their current custodian, Baba Mohan. Hence the alternative title of the collection, the Mohan *pothis.*[4]

The Goindval or Mohan *pothis* have received only passing reference in works dealing with Sikh literature. In 1968 Dr. Jodh Singh briefly noted them in his *Sri Kartarpuri Bir de Darashan,*[5] and recently two studies that mention the *pothis* have appeared. The first was an article in English by Nirbhai Singh, "The collection of the hymns of the *Guru Granth*," which appeared in the February–August 1981 issue of *The Journal of Sikh Studies*.[6] This treats the manuscripts in only a summary manner. In 1987 it was followed by a small booklet in Punjabi edited by Gursharan Kaur Jaggi and entitled *Babe Mohan valian pothian*.[7] This introduces the manuscripts and then offers a description of each of them in turn. Although this work is only a brief beginning, it is at least promising, for it does show a certain readiness within the *panth* to explore the matter further. Nirbhai Singh's article does, moreover, mention photocopies that Punjabi University has obtained of what are held to be the original manuscripts.[8] One of the *pothis* was in the possession of the late Baba Dalipchand of Mandi Darapur (near Ahiapur in District Hoshiarpur) and is now held by his family in Jalandhar. Another one is with the family of the late Bhagat Singh of Patiala. This manuscript is now in the town of Pinjore, near Chandigarh.

There are at least four questions associated with this general issue. First, did Guru Arjan actually have the volumes available when he was preparing the text of the *Adi Granth* and did he make use of them? Definitive proof is lacking, but it seems highly probable that the work was at his disposal. Had he not possessed such a collection, the task of compiling the entire *Adi Granth* would have been considerably more difficult. Dr. Jaggi accepts without question the tradition that the manuscripts were available to Guru Arjan,[9] and on the face of it, this seems a likely conclusion to draw.

Secondly, do these two original *pothis* still exist, and if so, are they the manuscripts held by the families of Dalip Singh and Bhagat Singh? As we have noted, Punjabi University has a partial photocopy of one *pothi*, but although the portion of the manuscript photocopied by the university may indeed have been of considerable age, this alone does not definitively establish its claim.

Thirdly, did Guru Arjan have access to more than two such *pothis*? This question has been raised because the two *pothis* in existence do not include any of the material composed by the first three Gurus that is included in the *Adi Granth* in the form of *vars*. These are long works based upon a string of hymns (*shabads*), each hymn preceded by two or more short works or couplets (*shaloks*). Could there have been more *pothis* at Guru Arjan's disposal?[10] The answer appears plainly to be yes, but it still leaves open the question of precisely how many *pothis* were available to Guru Arjan.

And fourthly, what are we to make of the differences in the text that distinguish the Goindval *pothis* from the *Adi Granth*? In some cases, these are minor differences of letters and words; in others, there are whole *shabads* left out of the *Adi Granth* that the Goindval *pothis* contain. In particular there are the differences in the *bhagat bani* (the composition of other *sants* of the preceding and contemporary period) that both collections include but which the *Adi Granth* incorporates in a slightly amended form. This applies particularly to compositions of Kabir and Namdev. The obvious answer is that the actual text was not known (having circulated in oral tradition); it was recorded in Guru Arjan's time in the form then current.[11] This can be glossed with the comment that Guru Arjan supervised the entry of the *bhagat bani* into the *Adi Granth* and where necessary determined the text in ways that would be appropriate to the overall message of his scripture.

It is not the purpose of this article to provide answers to the many questions raised by the Goindval *pothis,* if only because the necessary research has yet to be done. That it needs to be done goes without saying. Dr. Gursharan Kaur Jaggi has made a useful beginning to the task; Gurinder Singh Mann is now preparing a critical edition of the Goindval *pothis.*

The second of the general issues that we raised concerns the status of the Kartarpur *bir* (manuscript). This subject was carefully covered by Jodh Singh in his book *Sri Karatarpuri Bir de Darashan.* More recently Daljeet Singh has drawn heavily upon Jodh Singh's work in producing his *Essays on the Authenticity of Kartarpuri Bir and the Integrated Logic and Unity of Sikhism.*[12] This work attacks me for my contribution to the subject, specifically for the statements I am alleged to have made in my small book *The Evolution of the Sikh Community.*[13] Together with two other writers I

belong to a group of scholars some of whom seem to have exhibited a common belief in repeating, without examining the available writings or materials, the three incorrect suggestions that (a) Guru Granth is not the authentic version of all the *Bani* of the Gurus; (b) *Kartarpuri Bir* is not the *Adi-Granth* prepared by the fifth Guru; and (c) *Kartarpuri Bir* is a copy or the copy of the copy of *Banno Bir* which is first true copy of the *Adi-Granth.*[14]

These suggestions, the book goes on to claim, "appear to give currency to what Jodh Singh calls the poisonous principle of causing confusion by casting doubt on the very authenticity of the scripture of the Sikhs that forms the fundamental pillar of their faith." It adds darkly: "One wonders whether this is being done as a matter of design."[15]

It must at once become clear that the scholar who chooses to work in this area takes some very serious risks. Very firmly and emphatically it underlines for him or her (or me) the paramount need to walk (or tiptoe) exceedingly cautiously. When you are accused of the "poisonous principle of causing confusion by casting doubt on the very authenticity" of what Sikhs hold most sacred and when there is added to it the suggestion that your actions may be deliberate, you see that you have ventured beyond the bounds of safety. And yet you have to venture at least some distance into uncharted waters. None of the three charges leveled against me can be sustained, for in my book I merely raised questions (questions, not answers) with the intention of promoting academic discussion. Even those questions do not point to the three conclusions that have been drawn by Daljeet Singh, conclusions which can be rejected as too simple for the complicate issues being raised.

It will be appropriate if at this point we describe what has been called the Banno *bir* (it figures in the third of the conclusions drawn by Daljeet Singh) and demonstrate something of its bearing upon the subject in question. The Banno *bir* is an old version of the text of the *Adi Granth,* so called because its origin is attached to a person known as Bhai Banno. Bhai Banno is said to have been a resident in Mangat village of District Gujrat who visited Guru Arjan and showed great interest in the recently completed scripture. He requested permission to take the scripture home to his village on loan and the Guru, understandably loath to let the scripture depart from his presence, gave his permission on the condition that the scripture would remain in the village for only one night. Banno circumvented this condition by traveling very short distances each day on the way to his village and then did the same on the way back again. As a result of the lengthy journey (lengthy, that is, in terms of time), he was able to make a complete copy of the large manuscript without breaking his promise. A variant of the tradition claims that he was charged with the duty of taking the manuscript to Lahore for binding and used the opportunity to make his copy.

The copy Banno is said to have made was exactly the same as the original manuscript loaned by Guru Arjan except for certain additions. These were three hymns or parts of hymns by Mira Bai, Sur Das, and Guru Arjan himself together with three portions attached to the end of the manuscript. Of this terminal collection, the most famous is a prose account entitled *Hakikat rah mukam raje shivanabh ki,* "The way to the abode of Raja Sivanabh." The version is known as the Khari *bir,* and perhaps because of the reputation later

earned by this volume, the word *khari* has been construed as meaning "bitter" or "spurious." An alternative etymology derives the
word from *khara,* said to be an earlier name of Mangat village.[16]

The reason for the attack on me was that I had raised the possibility of a useful comparison between the *Adi Granth* and the
Banno *bir,* though never with the intention of suggesting that the
manuscript identified as the oldest version of the Khari *bir* should
be regarded as "the first true copy of the *Adi-Granth.*" The situation
I envisaged was considerably more complex than this simple statement of Daljeet Singh would imply.

The possibility that had occurred to me was that the version
embodying the first three additions to the Khari *bir* might conceiv-
ably have been the text of the Kartarpur *bir;* and this in turn meant
that I had no problem in regarding the Kartarpur *bir* as the *Adi
Granth* prepared by the fifth Guru, Arjan. The difficulty lay in the
existence of numerous deletions in the Kartarpur manuscript, and
at an earlier state in my inquiry, I wondered if there might not be
deletions that served to obliterate these three hymns (or the portion of them which does not appear in the *Adi Granth*). The hymn by
Mira Bai might not create any difficulty were it originally in the
manuscript,[17] nor would the complete composition by Sur Das cause
any serious problem. The hymn by Guru Arjan in *ramkali rag,* however, raised a weightier issue.

This hymn describes the puberty rites that Guru Arjan performed for his son (the future Guru Hargobind), and these rites included the shaving of his head. If this hymn was really in the
original manuscript, it would significantly enlarge our understanding of the earlier Gurus' practice, as distinct from the discipline of
the *panth* following the creating of the *khalsa.* After the *khalsa* had
been founded, it became mandatory for all true Sikhs of the *khalsa*
to keep their hair strictly uncut. Was this hymn telling us that the
fifth Guru had his son's head shaven?

As it turned out, my later research showed that the situation
was not quite as clear as this, for in 1968 Jodh Singh's *Sri Kartarpuri Bir de Darashan* appeared. This made it clear that although
there had been deletion of the Mira Bai hymn,[18] the portions of the
hymns by Sur Das and Guru Arjan were in doubt. Jodh Singh reported that the one line of Sur Das (the line that appears in the
printed editions of the *Adi Granth*) was followed by four blank lines
in the manuscript. This was sufficient space to accommodate the remainder of the hymn, but no attempt had been made to record it.[19]
The same situation was, he wrote, the case with Guru Arjan's

ramkali hymn. The solitary couplet that appears in the *Adi Granth* is duly recorded in the manuscript, but it stands alone with a blank space extending for more than two folios.[20] There is, in other words, no sign of obliteration after these two fragments.

This cast my earlier theory into disarray and I acknowledged this in *The Evolution of the Sikh Community*.[21] Daljeet Singh's treatment of my discussion, however, repeats everything word for word up to the point where I surmised that Guru Arjan's hymn might have been partly obliterated.[22] He then terminates his quotation and begins saying fierce things about me for what he claims are my baseless and misleading arguments.[23] Everything that I subsequently say about having read Jodh Singh's book is overlooked, and although my admission of doubt is implicitly acknowledged, this is scarcely done in a way which will do it justice. In the course of his treatment, he notes how I mislead my readers

> like the way of a biased journalist, first to impress on the reader the fact about the existence of deletions and thereby create a broad suspicion against the genuineness of the *Bir* and then to narrate the story of the presence of the puberty hymn in the *Banno Bir* and its absence in the *Kartarpuri Bir,* knowing full well that there is no deletion in the case either of the puberty hymn or of the hymn of Bhagat Surdas.[24]

This episode has been related at some length because it well demonstrates the dangers awaiting the person who dares to ask questions about the Sikh scripture or to frame tentative theories. Merely gaining access to the Kartarpur manuscript will be difficult for a member of the *panth* in good standing and almost impossible for anyone else. As Daljeet Singh says:

> Nor can it be seriously asserted that the conduct of scholars like Trumpp, G. B. Singh and Mcleod has in any way enhanced the credit of the academic world among the general Sikh Public.[25] At present, the *Kartarpuri Bir* is the property of the Dhir Mal family, and no one is to blame if the custodians want to be sure of the bonafides of a scholar before allowing him access for a study of the *Kartarpuri Bir.* Their exercise of such discretion is natural, understandable and unobjectionable.[26]

Perhaps it is indeed "natural, understandable and unobjectionable," but it prevents me from seeing the manuscript and I venture to suggest that it will prevent any but those whom the custodians can rely on for a thoroughly sound interpretation according to their particular point of view.

Fortunately, Gurinder Singh Mann seems recently to have satisfied these criteria, and his work does apparently confirm the authentic status of the Kartarpur manuscript. Even so several questions still await answer. Why, for example, is the Banno version so prominently represented in the early manuscripts that still survive? Banno copies may not have been present in the Sikh Reference Library at the Golden Temple before its wholly regrettable destruction by the Indian Army in June 1984,[27] but they certainly dominate the collection in the India Office Library and the British Museum.[28] And if Guru Arjan did not write the whole of the hymn in *ramkali rag,* who did write it? This is not to say or imply that he did write it. The fact is that questions remain. Sound advice compellingly dictates that wise scholars will be very cautious in raising them, but raise them they must if our knowledge of the Kartarpur manuscript is not to remain the preserve of those with traditional answers.

The actual possession of the Kartarpur manuscript leads on to the next issue, that of the history of the manuscript between its original recording and the middle of the nineteenth century. The Kartarpur *bir* has been in the hands of the Sodhi family of Kartarpur[29] since the invading British recovered it from the Lahore treasury in 1849,[30] and before its appropriation by Ranjit Singh it was presumably held by the family for most of the period since it was first recorded. But why was this family allowed to retain it? These were the descendants of Dhir Mal, the elder brother of Guru Har Rai and an unsuccessful claimant of the title of Guru, and members of the *khalsa* were required to swear that they would forego all contacts with his followers. The reason may have been simply that the *khalsa* was not much bothered by who possessed the sacred manuscript providing they had access to its copies, but the question remains and it would be very interesting to have it answered.

This, though, we shall forbear to attempt, and likewise we shall not seek here to probe the remaining issues. The questions arising from the acceptance of the *Adi Granth* as the *Guru Granth Sahib* must be left at this point, and so too must the immensely large labor of analyzing the actual text of the various hymns. It is perhaps fortunate that there is no opportunity here to tackle those questions because those are the most delicate of all the issues we might broach and I suspect that with the questions I have raised I have already sailed quite close enough to the wind. I repeat, however, that an attempt must be made to meet the need. It requires extremely delicate treatment, but that treatment is nevertheless required.

The Dasam Granth

For the Sikhs of the later eighteenth century there was no problem about the *Dasam Granth*. When the *Granth* was invoked, it meant that an appeal was made to both the *Adi Granth* and the *Dasam Granth*. Both were present at meetings of the *khalsa* and both received the same reverence. Now, however, it is different. Portions of the *Dasam Granth* are as familiar as any passages in Sikh literature, but the scripture as a whole raises serious questions. These have been settled by placing the *Dasam Granth* on one side. Although it still counts as scripture, there is usually only one volume present to signify the Guru, and that volume is the *Adi Granth*.

The origins of this second scripture of the Sikhs are obscure. The traditional explanation attributes it to the famous Sikh martyr Mani Singh who, during his tenure in charge of Darbar Sahib in Amritsar (1721–34), is believed to have compiled a miscellany known as *Dasven Patshah ka Granth,* "the Granth of the Tenth Master."[31] Following his death in 1734, the *khalsa* debated whether it should be preserved as a single volume or whether the works of Guru Gobind Singh should be held separately. A Sikh called Matab Singh, who was on his way to slay the sacrilegious Massa Ranghar for desecrating the holy Darbar Sahib, proposed that the volume should be divided if he was killed. If, however, he was successful it should remain intact. The plan was accepted, Matab Singh returned victorious, and so there survives this substantial collection of heterogeneous works associated with Guru Gobind Singh.[32]

The *Dasam Granth* presents considerable problems and virtually nothing is being done to solve any of them. The principal reason for this is that whereas the script of the *Dasam Granth* is Gurmukhi (the script in which Punjabi is written and which virtually everyone knows), the language is predominantly Braj (which few Punjabis understand in any detail). Very few people possess the linguistic credentials to study it effectively, and as a result it continues to be largely ignored.

The contents of the *Dasam Granth* may be divided into four groups. First there are two poems that are autobiographical, or at least biographical, both of them attributed to Guru Gobind Singh. These are *Bachitar Natak* or "The Wondrous Drama" (an account of his previous incarnation and early days) and *Zafar-nama* (a defiant letter addressed to the emperor Aurangzeb). Secondly, there are four devotional works attributed to the Guru (*Jap, Akal Ustat, Gian Prabodh,* and *Shabad Hazare*). Thirdly, there are two miscellaneous works (*Savayye* and *Shashtar Nam-mala*); and fourthly, a collection of legendary narratives and popular anecdotes. This fourth group constitutes the bulk of the collection, comprising more than eighty percent of the total.[33]

There are four theories about the authorship of the *Dasam Granth*. The traditional view current amongst the great majority of the *panth* is that the entire collection is the work of Guru Gobind Singh. A second theory, favored by the majority of the *panth's* scholars, is that the first three clusters should certainly be attributed to Guru Gobind Singh, but the remainder must have been the work of writers who belonged to his retinue. The third theory, a more radical view, maintains that only the *Zafar-nama* can be attributed to Guru Gobind Singh. The remainder of the first three sections represent the Guru's views; and the fourth one expresses the ideas and attitudes of his followers. A fourth view is even more radical, holding that even the *Zafar-nama* is not his. It is merely based upon the letter he despatched.

These four theories have been given hesitant currency, but it would be quite wrong to suggest that any controversy has resulted from them. That must await an uncertain future, at a time when scholars with the linguistic and historical credentials are available. In the meantime those portions of the *Dasam Granth* that are already well known will continue to give inspiration to devout Sikhs. *Jap Sahib* and the *Savayye Amrit* are already a part of the regular pattern of daily devotions (*nit-nem*), *Akal Ustat* offers poetry of rare quality, *Bachitar Natak* provides a view of the early life of Guru Gobind Singh, and *Zafar-nama* portrays his defiance.[34]

Clearly these works will continue to exercise a significant influence within the *panth,* with the greater part of the remainder set aside for the foreseeable future. We must hope, however, that the delay will not be too long. The *Dasam Granth* holds within it some very useful perceptions of the early *khalsa,* perceptions it will only yield as research progresses.

The Works of Bhai Gurdas and Nand Lal Goya

Bhai Gurdas was a faithful disciple of several of the Gurus, notably the fifth and the sixth. In his long lifetime, which ended around 1633, he wrote two kinds of poetry: *kabitts* and *vars.* The 675 short *kabitts* are in Braj, and this (as with the *Dasam Granth*) explains their persistent neglect, but for the 39 longer *vars,* there is less excuse. Their language is Punjabi, an annotated Punjabi commentary exists,[35] and as "the key to the *Guru Granth Sahib*" they occupy a place of considerable importance in the Sikh tradition. Although their poetic quality varies, several of them are of a high order, and they include material of considerable interest. Some of them are narrative works that relate episodes from the lives of the earlier Gurus or incidents that occurred during the author's own lifetime. Many more are doctrinal or exegetical.[36] During the past decade little progress has been made on the compositions of Bhai Gurdas, although in the years before that some useful work was done on them by the Punjabi University scholar Rattan Singh Jaggi.

The same is, regrettably, the case with the compositions of Nand Lal Goya. It is in fact much worse, for apart from an edition of his works by Dr. Ganda Singh, there has been virtually nothing for several decades.[37] Nand Lal was a disciple of the tenth Guru and, as with the works of Bhai Gurdas, his poetry has been approved for use in *gurdwaras.* Unfortunately his poetry is little heard nowadays and has been seldom heard for a long time, as a result of its being written in the Persian language. Here too the linguistic capacities, though more common than a knowledge of Braj, are still comparatively rare within the *panth.*[38]

The Janam-Sakhis

The *janam-sakhis* are traditional biographies of Guru Nanak that circulated orally at first and then came to be written down in the centuries following. There are several different accounts of what is regarded as his life story. Amongst the *panth* as a whole, the most popular version is undoubtedly that supplied by the Bala *janam-sakhis,* so named because the narrator is alleged to be a disciple called Bhai Bala. For the educated members of the community, the preference is strongly for the *janam-sakhis* of the *Puratan* tradition because of a much weaker emphasis upon marvels and miracles. The *Puratan janam-sakhis* are by no means without them, however, nor is any of the other *janam-sakhis.* The other important *janam-sakhis* are the *Miharban* tradition, the *Adi Sakhis,* and the *Gyan-ratanavali.* Others borrowed from several traditions and add material of their own. The most important of these individual *janam-sakhis* is the so called *B40 janam-sakhi.*

The usual method of constructing a *janam-sakhi* was to build a narrative around an incident in the Guru's life and then string these anecdotes together in some kind of a coherent sequence. Most *janam-sakhis* are narrative products based upon these anecdotes. The *Miharban Janam-sakhis,* however, give more emphasis to exegesis, using for this purpose the works of Guru Nanak and adding to them commentaries on their meaning. Almost all the *janam-sakhis* feature the works of Guru Nanak, but the *Miharban* tradition is usually the only one to follow it with a commentary.

This treatment, it must be realized, does little to inform us about the actual life of Guru Nanak. The *janam-sakhis* are hagiography, and in any attempt to understand the Sikh tradition, they must be read as such. If, however, they are read as works of popular belief from later periods in Sikh history, they can significantly illumine our understanding of those periods. The form was clearly a borrowing from the Sufis, the anecdotal style being particularly popular amongst their Muslim followers. A beginning has been made on the analysis of the *janam-sakhis.*[39] More, however, needs to be done.

The Gur-Bilas Literature

Works in the *gur-bilas* style concentrate on the mighty deeds of the two later warrior Gurus, Guru Hargobind and particularly Guru Gobind Singh. At the beginning of the seventeenth century, the sixth Guru, Hargobind, is believed to have girded himself with the twin swords of *miri* and *piri* (signifying his adoption of temporal power together with the spiritual authority inherited from his five predecessors) and to have waged a series of wars with the Mughal rulers of the time. These battles ceased under his three successors, but the execution of the ninth Guru, Tegh Bahadur, by order of the Mughal emperor Aurangzeb in 1675 signaled that the *panth* would again have to defend itself. Once he grew to manhood, the tenth Guru, Gobind Singh, fought a number of wars, and these episodes are the ones particularly remembered by the *gur-bilas* writers.

The piety represented by the *gur-bilas* literature is of a distinctively different quality from that of the *janam-sakhis,* emphasizing as it does the heroic deeds of the warrior Gurus. The beginnings of the style are to be traced to *Bachitar Natak,* the poem included in the *Dasam Granth* that is attributed to Guru Gobind Singh himself.

Following his death in 1708 comes the first clear example of the style, Sainapati's *Gur Sobha* ("Radiance of the Guru"). Late in the eighteenth century Sukha Singh produced his *Gur-bilas Dasvin Patshahi* (1791), and during the early or mid-nineteenth century, there followed Koer Singh's *Gur-bilas Patshahi 10* and *Gur-bilas Chhevin Patshahi* attributed to a poet called Sohan. In the same period, Ratan Singh Bhangu completed his *Prachin Panth Prakash* (1841), the climax of the *gur-bilas* style.

In 1844 Santokh Singh produced his *Gur Pratap Suray,* popularly known as the *Suraj Prakash.* This marked a reversion to the *janam-sakhi* style of presentation earlier represented by the author's *Nanak Prakash.* The *gur-bilas* mode was still alive, however, and later in the century was present in the works of Gyan Singh. In 1880 Gyan Singh published his *Panth Prakash,* and between 1891 and 1919 he progressively issued the several parts of his substantial *Tavarikh Guru Khalsa.* This, like its predecessors, represents the history of the *khalsa* in terms that emphasize the heroism of the Gurus.[40]

The Rahit-Namas

The *janam-sakhis* and *gur-bilas* works are obviously beyond the category of canonical scripture, though they would certainly come within any definition of Sikh literature. The same can be said of the *rahit-namas.* The *rahit-namas* are a variety of text that developed after the founding of the *khalsa* in 1699 by Guru Gobind Singh, and each of them seeks to define a *gursikh* (a Sikh of the *khalsa*). What must *gursikhs* believe, and what it proscribed for them? What must they do and what is forbidden? The earliest known example is the *rahit-nama* attributed to Chaupa Singh, which can be traced to the fifth decade of the eighteenth century.[41]

Rahit-namas are much fewer than the *janam-sakhis,* and typically their length is appreciably less than that of the *gur-bilas.* Their effect has nevertheless been immense, and a modern *rahit-nama* has proven to be enormously popular.[42] A beginning has been made on the analysis of the *rahit-namas,*[43] but as in the case of the *janam-sakhis* and *gur-bilas* works, there is much more to be done.

The Place of Sikh Literature in Courses on Indian Civilization

Sikh literature deserves a prominent place in North American courses for at least three reasons. The first is the conspicuous presence of Sikhs today, not just in India but overseas. This has been highlighted since the assault on the Golden Temple and the killings that followed the assassination of Mrs. Gandhi in 1984, but even without those events, the number of Sikhs in North America was sufficiently obvious to be noticeable. Although no one has exact figures, there seems to be little doubt that the Sikhs are the largest of the Indian communities to have immigrated to the United States and Canada, and the same is true for the United Kingdom as well.[44]

Secondly—and this constitutes the major reason—the Sikh faith is a major religion in its own right. There are major features of Sikhism that belong distinctively to it alone, and although the Sikh faith may have grown out of the *sant* movement of the Hindu tradition, it has since acquired characteristics that make it truly unique. No other religion has ever projected an order like the *khalsa,* and none has ever passed through the historical circumstances that produced the Sikhism of today.

Thirdly, there is sufficient material available in translation to provide a beginning student with all that is needed for complete coverage. In this respect the textbook *Textual Sources for the Study of Sikhism*[45] provides a convenient point of departure since it contains an almost complete translation of the Sikh daily prayers and much else besides. Should further resources be desired for an advanced course, there are numerous other books containing modern translations. Sikhism has arrived on the North American scene, and Sikh literature in translation is more than adequate to meet the challenge.

Notes

1. These works are all translated, in whole or in part, in W. H. McLeod, trans., *Textual Sources for the Study of Sikhism* (Chicago: University of Chicago Press, 1990), pp. 86–114.

2. McLeod, *Textual Sources,* pp. 93–95, 99–100.

3. Fauja Singh describes the two volumes as follows:

Fortunately the two *pothis* [manuscripts] prepared by Sans Ram are still extant. One of them is in the custody of Baba Dalipchand of Mandi Darapur in the district of Hoshiarpur while the other is preserved in the family of Bawa Bhagat Singh of Patiala city. The first is displayed for public view on every *Sangrand* [first day of an Indian solar month] and the second on every *Puranmashi* [full moon day]. They are believed to be the same *pothis* for which Guru

Arjan Dev had to proceed to Baba Mohan's house personally and to request him for their loan. Baba Mohan [second son of Guru Amar Das], who had at first declined to part with the *pothis,* was ultimately persuaded by the fifth Guru to lend them for the purpose of compiling the *Adi Granth.* (Fauja Singh, *Guru Amar Das* [New Delhi: Sterling, 1979], p. 138.)

The story of Guru Arjan's proceeding to Goindval and singing a song in praise of Mohan outside his window is plainly apocryphal. It comes from the mid-nineteenth-century work of the Sikh hagiographer Santokh Singh. There are two *pothis* in existence and probably two more (certainly at least one) were also compiled. I owe this information to Gurinder Singh Mann.

4. Baba Mohan was the elder son of Guru Amar Das and the father of Sahans Ram. He had not approved of his father's choice of Guru Ram Das as a successor.

5. Jodh Singh gives two letters from Prem Singh Hoti and a sample folio from one of the *pothis.* (*Kartarpuri Bir* [Patiala: Punjabi University, 1968], pp. 123–25.)

6. Nirbhai Singh, "The Collection of the Hymns of the *Guru Granth*," *Journal of Sikh Studies* 8:1–2 (Amritsar: Guru Nanak Dev University), pp. 9–22.

7. Published by Arshi Publishers, New Delhi. Gursharan Kaur Jaggi worked on the basis of notes taken by Baba Prem Singh Hoti Mardan in the 1940s. A Ph.D. dissertation, which makes extensive use of these *pothis,* by Gurinder Singh Mann of Columbia University is awaited with great interest.

8. Harbans Singh reports that Punjabi University has a photocopy of only one of the *pothis.*

9. Jaggi, *Babe Mohan,* p. 1.

10. Nirbhai Singh, "Collection of the Hymns," p. 20.

11. Nirbhai Singh, "Collection of the Hymns," p. 18.

12. Patiala: Punjabi University, 1987.

13. Delhi: Oxford University Press, 1975, and Oxford: Clarendon Press, 1976.

14. Daljeet Singh, *Essays,* p. 75. *Bani* means the utterance or the compositions of Sikh scripture, normally those of the Gurus. For the Banno *bir* see below pp. 56–59.

15. Daljeet Singh, *Essays,* p. 75.

16. Shamsher Singh Ashok, *Bhai Banno ji te Khare vali bir,* in *Khoj Patrika* (Patiala) 4 (May 1970), pp. 36–37.

17. It could arguably favor idol worship. There is, however, an uncontroversial hymn by Namdev that also can be construed in this sense.

18. Jodh Singh, *Kartarpuri Bir,* p. 106.

19. Jodh Singh, *Kartarpuri Bir,* p. 113.

20. Jodh Singh, *Kartarpuri Bir,* p. 97.

21. McLeod, *Evolution,* pp. 78–79.

22. Daljeet Singh, *Essays,* pp. 50–51. McLeod, *Evolution,* pp. 76–78.

23. Daljeet Singh, *Essays,* pp. 51–59.

24. Daljeet Singh, *Essays,* p. 55.

25. Ernest Trumpp produced a translation of a portion of the *Adi Granth* in 1877, accompanying it with an introduction that was regarded as extremely offensive. G. B. Singh likewise produced a book, *Sri Guru Granth Sahib dian prachin biran,* in 1944 that caused serious offense.

26. Daljeet Singh, *Essays, p. 70.*

27. Daljeet Singh, *Essays,* pp. 54–55.

28. C. Shackle, *Catalogue of the Panjabi and Sindhi Manuscripts in the India Office Library* (London: India Office Library and Records, 1977), pp. 1–5.

29. Kartarpur is a small town on the Grand Trunk Road, a short distance west of Jalandhar City. It should not be confused with the village on the right bank of the Ravi River, opposite Dehra Baba Nanak, where Guru Nanak died.

30. One of the manuscript volumes of the *Adi Granth* in the India Office Library is a copy of the Kartarpur *bir* prepared by Sodhi Sadhu Singh for Queen Victoria and presented to her in 1859 in gratitude for the British government's returning the *bir* to his family's custody (MSS. Panj. E2).

31. Darbar Sahib is today known also as the Golden Temple. It is also known as Harimandir Sahib.

32. Kahn Singh Nabha, *Gurushabad ratanakar mahan kosh,* 2d ed. (Patiala: Languages Department, 1960), p. 461.

33. For further details see D. P. Ashta, *The Poetry of the Dasam Granth* (New Delhi: Arun Prakashan, 1959), pp. 33–168; C. H. Loehlin, *The Granth of Guru Gobind Singh and the Khalsa Brotherhood* (Lucknow: Lucknow Publishing House, 1971), pp. 20–56; and Gobind Singh Mansukhani, *Aspects of Sikhism* (New Delhi: Punjabi Writers Cooperative Industrial Society, 1982), pp. 105–13. See also W. H. McLeod, *Evolution,* pp. 79–81, and

The Sikhs: History, Religion and Society (New York: Columbia University Press, 1989), pp. 89–92.

34. See the brief selection translated in Trilochan Singh et al., *The Sacred Writings of the Sikhs* (London: George Allen and Unwin, 1960), pp. 267–75. Also McLeod, *Textual Sources*, pp. 55–63, 93–95, 99–100.

35. *Varan Bhai Gurdas*, ed., Hazara Singh and Vir Singh (Amritsar: Khalsa Samachar, several editions).

36. For examples in translation see McLeod, *Textual Sources*, pp. 63–69.

37. Ganda Singh (ed.), *Bhai Nand Lal granthavali* (Malacca: Sant Sohan Singh, 1968).

38. For translated examples see McLeod, *Textual Sources*, pp. 69–70.

39. W. H. McLeod, *Early Sikh Tradition: A Study of the Janam-sakhis* (Oxford: Clarendon Press, 1980). See also McLeod, *Guru Nanak and the Sikh Religion* (Oxford: Clarendon Press, 1968; 2d ed., Delhi: Oxford University Press, 1976), chaps. 2 and 3; *Evolution*, chap. 2, and *Textual Sources*, pp. 95–98. For a complete English translation of a *janam-sakhi*, see W. H. McLeod, *The B40 Janam-sakhi* (Amritsar: Guru Nanak Dev University, 1980).

40. The amount of recent work on the *gur-bilas* literature has been small. One important work that deserves to be noticed is, however, Surjit Hans's *Historical Analysis of Sikh Literature* (Jalandhar: ABC, 1988).

41. McLeod, *Textual Sources*, p. 74.

42. *Sikh Rahit Maryada* (Amritsar: Shiromani Gurdwara Prabandhak Committee, 1950 and subsequent editions). Two English translations exist. They are Anon., trans., *Rehat Maryada: A Guide to the Sikh Way of Life* (Amritsar: Dharam Parchar Committee, 1970); and Kanwaljit Kaur and Indarjit Singh, trans., *Rehat Maryada: A Guide to the Sikh Way of Life* (London: Sikh Cultural Centre, 1971). Neither of the translations is completely accurate. A major part is translated in McLeod, *Textual Sources*, pp. 79–86.

43. W. H. McLeod, *The Chaupa Singh Rahit-nama* (Dunedin: University of Otago Press, 1987). See also McLeod, *Who is a Sikh? Problems of Sikh Identity* (Oxford: Clarendon Press, 1989); and McLeod, *Textual Sources*, chap. 5.

44. This is certainly the case in Canada, where Sikhs comprise roughly two-thirds of the East Indian population. Norman Buchignani and Doreen Indra, *Continuous Journey: a Social History of South Asians in Canada* (Toronto: McClelland and Stewart, 1985), p. 128.

45. See note 1.

4

The Sikh Diaspora and Sikh Studies

*

Arthur W. Helweg

While I was doing research in a Sikh village in the Punjab, one of my friends often commented, "Sikhs are like potatoes, they are found all over the world." Although Sikh historians have not extensively chronicled the history of the Sikh diaspora,[1] enough is known to see that the relationship between Sardars residing inside and outside their homeland has been longstanding and on-going. In fact, the tradition of mobility goes back to the inception of Sikhism itself. Thus, overseas Sikhs must be considered if one is to understand Sikhism and the Sikh community fully; for, as this paper will indicate, Sikh theology, philosophy, society, economy, and politics have been influenced by Sikhs residing outside the Punjab.

Overseas Sikhs are rapidly becoming an integral part of social science research and the field of Sikh studies. This is evident from the literature coming out of Australia,[2] Canada,[3] Great Britain,[4] New Zealand,[5] and the United States.[6] In this article I will briefly sketch some themes that have emerged as particularly important in my own study of the Sikh diaspora.

My information comes primarily from an intensive study of one Sikh community—based in Gravesend, England, but with roots in Jandiali, Punjab[7]—but I will situate the experience of the Sikhs I studied in the context of broader patterns of Sikh migration. Several major themes emerge. At the cultural level, there is the Sikh tradition of mobility and its relation to the community's concern for maintaining Sikh identity. Important cultural concepts such as maintaining *izzat* (family honor) and keeping institutions like the arranged marriage system are also important considerations for overseas Sikhs. On the structural level, prominent topics include the interactive relation between Sikh migrant groups, their host societies, and the communities that initially sent them abroad; the place of the *gurdwara* in the life of diaspora Sikhs; and the political processes governing overseas Sikh societies. An examination of these themes will reveal the significance of the expatriate Sikh community not only to Sikh studies but to other fields of inquiry such as the growing field of migration studies.

Gravesend and Jandiali

The Sikhs are an international people.[8] A story goes that when Neil Armstrong first landed on the moon, a Sikh passed him by, plowing the land. Another story says that as soon as he landed, a Sikh taxi driver drove up and said, "Taxi, Sahib?" About 10 percent of the approximate global population of Sikhs—13 million to 16 million[9]—lives outside India, and about a third of the Sikhs in India live outside the Punjab. Members of the *khalsa*, the soldier-saint brotherhood, can be seen in such diverse cities as Bangkok, Hong Kong, London, Los Angeles, Nairobi, Manila, New York, Singapore, Sydney, Toronto, and Vancouver.[10]

The Sikh community of Gravesend, Kent, in the United Kingdom, illustrates some of the themes that are important in understanding Sikh migrant behavior. In the early 1950s, Sikhs began leaving their villages in India to work in the industrial region of Kent. Gravesend is located on the outskirts of London's industrial sector. Like other port cities in England, it had a few Indians living there intermittently. Its paper, cable, rubber, printing, cement, engineering, shipbuilding industries, together with several ancillary enterprises, provided the jobs that attracted immigrants. The 1980 census showed that Indians comprised 5,184 of Gravesend's total population of 94,756. Of these, 70 percent were Jat Sikhs.[11]

By 1980, the Sikh community in Gravesend began to lose its status as a purely immigrant community because 45 percent of its members had been born in England and their class position had changed. A majority of the initial Sikh immigrants had come from agricultural rural Punjab, but within a couple of decades they were making their impact on Gravesend in entirely different spheres. Sikhs owned sixteen chemist shops, four pubs, one automobile repair garage, a number of green grocer shops, two laundromats, a bicycle shop, an electric goods shop, four grocery stores, five driver training schools, three market stalls, one children's boutique, one clothing factory, two construction companies, and a tobacco and sweet shop. By 1985, 20 percent of the wage earners were professionals. The Sikh economy of Gravesend had shifted from one that was dependent on the wider society to a generative economy in which Sikhs were creating jobs and capital for both themselves and the wider English community.

In the 1980s, the Punjab, as the most prosperous region in India, boasted the highest per capita income in the country (Rs. 3,164 or U.S. $420 per year), the highest percentage of irrigated areas (79 percent), the highest agricultural production (82 percent of its total area is under cultivation), the largest number of tractors (60,000), and the greatest milk yield and per capita milk consumption (production averages 2.45 kg and 4.31 kg per day from cows and buffaloes respectively). Life expectancy was 66.8 years for males and 61.9 years for females—by far the best figures in India—and the Punjab was the first Indian state to launch an integrated rural development program.[12]

The village of Jandiali, Punjab, from which many of Gravesend's Sikhs emigrated, is a Sikh community located halfway between the cities of Jalandhar and Ludhiana. This village has sent more than two-thirds of its 1,608 members to England. Other emigrants from Jandiali are scattered in the North Indian states of Rajasthan and Uttar Pradesh. They are also represented in New Zealand, Australia, Canada, the Philippines, and the United States. By 1972, labor opportunities developed in Dubai, Iran, and other Middle Eastern countries, attracting low-caste (*chamar*) males and members of other specialist castes to fortunes in the oil-rich countries, but Sikhs have provided the bulk of Jandiali's emigrant population.

The Nature of Sikh Migration

Since the end of the Second World War, two major changes have influenced the migration patterns of the Sikhs. First, global transportation and communication facilities have enabled people to fly around the world in a matter of days, talk to relatives in their home village in hours or minutes, and transfer money across oceans with electronic rapidity. The effect has been a marked increase in the overseas Sikhs' ability to influence and be influenced by events in the Punjab. Even though Sikhs have lived outside their ethnic region for generations, they, like some other emigrants, have continued to take a keen interest in the village and state affairs of their homeland.

Second, the composition of the migration stream has changed. Before the Second World War, emigration was dominated primarily by people of peasant, merchant, and artisan backgrounds. Jats primarily worked the land in the Punjab but served in the British Army and police forces abroad. There they learned of other opportunities for employment, and often they summoned their relatives once they had jobs themselves. In Canada they went into lumbering, in Australia they cut sugar cane, in the United States they farmed, in Hong Kong they dominated the police force. Ramgarias—Sikhs who were primarily carpenters and tradesmen—were attracted to East Africa as their skills were needed to build and maintain the Ugandan Railroad. The Khatri or merchant segment of the Punjabi Sikh community was noticeable in London, the outback of Australia, and the bush of East Africa.[13]

Following World War II, Commonwealth immigration policy made it possible for Jat Sikhs to go to England in large numbers. The more professionally oriented Khatris (merchant-caste),[14] trained in engineering, medicine, and the sciences, were able to emigrate to the United States, Canada, and Australia because they readily fit into the postindustrial economy of these countries.[15] When the United States revised its immigration laws in 1965, a new system of preferences afforded entrance to the highly educated and technically trained. United States immigration laws emphasizing family reunification allowed less well trained relatives, sponsored by their newly naturalized kinsmen, to obtain entrance as well. The result has been a great deal of diversity among the Sikh community in the United States. In the 1980s the highly educated, professional segment was increasingly overshadowed by a stream of kinsmen who were often not as capable or well educated as their sponsoring relatives. There is yet another segment, the second generation, which is gaining prominence in Canada, England, and the United States by taking advantage of educational opportunities in their overseas homes. The result is a very diverse pattern among overseas Sikh communities: the educated and the uneducated; farmers, business people, and professionals; and groups who sometimes form tight, cohesive communities and sometimes remain residentially dispersed.

Maintaining Culture

Given this diversity, it is understandable that Sikhs abroad are anxious about the cohesive future of their community. In this they resemble Sikhs in India, who fear they may lose their culture and identity because their numbers are not large in relation to the total population. But why do such fears persist, given that Sikhs have successfully transplanted themselves all over the world and have achieved a remarkable record of community survival in a variety of environments?

Part of this insecurity may be traced to a certain anxiety about the erection of social boundaries. Sikhs do not always agree on what constitutes their community.[16] Some maintain that to be a Sikh one must display the classical symbols of the faith; others—*sahajdhari*[17] Sikhs—claim to be members of the Sikh community despite the fact that they ignore these symbols and may or may not be accepted by others. For most Sikhs, it is a combination of symbols and ideology that separates them from outsiders.

Maintaining Sikh symbols and staying distinct are crucial concerns for many in the Sikh community of Gravesend. The "five Ks," as they are called in Punjabi, have a special meaning and are an outward manifestation of an individual's commitment to fight for the right, be holy, and yet live in this world.[18] By taking on these symbols, a male Sikh makes a public commitment to these ideals and shames himself and his faith if he does not uphold the highest teachings of his Gurus. It is not just an idle tenet for Sikh leaders to insist that true Sikhs must don these symbols, thought to have been instituted by Guru Gobind Singh. Wearing the "five Ks" shows a believer's willingness to belong to the Sikh tradition and defend it. What is true in Gravesend is true in many other places as well: this emphasis on maintaining the symbols has been a strong factor in the survival of the Sikh diaspora.

Sikh ideology, too, promotes the maintenance of ethnic boundaries. The emphasis on militancy and martyrdom has not merely given Sikhs a sense of pride and superiority but has also encouraged separateness. Unlike many groups that have had their pride destroyed by not maintaining their ethnic heritage, the Sikhs have not succumbed to outside pressures to be absorbed into the Hindu or Muslim fold in South Asia.

Khushwant Singh and others allege that there is little difference between Sikhs and Hindus except for the "five Ks," but the tradition of militancy, martyrdom, and defending what is right are distinctive tenets that enable even *sahajdhari* Sikhs to perceive themselves as distinct from others, especially the Hindus, with whom they share many common traditions and beliefs. These factors have helped Sikhs develop a fierce pride and a sense of superiority, which was fanned by the British rulers who classified them as a "martial race" and used them effectively in their armed forces. Their dominance in the military continued when India achieved independence, and this valued place in the defense of India has persisted until very recently, when the Sikh role in the Indian military was diminished.[19]

The Sikhs' attention to the maintenance of their culture has not always been uniform. Initially the Sikh communities in England and the United States shed their turbans and other distinctive Sikh symbols at a high rate. But in the next stage the community was characteristically "revitalized" and Sikh values and symbols were reemphasized.[20] The initial settlers of Gravesend, in the early 1950s and 1960s, were primarily Sikh males who had left their wives and children at home in Jandiali with the goal of living frugally in the new land, amassing wealth, and then returning to India to become *barra sahibs,* important men in the village. Their main concern was to maximize their assets, which often entailed working up to ninety hours a week on the job and saving the earnings. Socializing consisted of stopping at a corner pub after work, visiting the Sikh *gurdwara,* and the camaraderie that came from sleeping in common rooming houses. These early years were a time when the men drank together and otherwise interacted with little concern about being good Sikhs, maintaining Punjabi culture, or keeping a proper image among their brethren or their English hosts. As for families—and they were few—their primary aim was to become an integral part of British society. As one person who had been among the scant numbers of Sikh children present in Gravesend at that time remembers it:

> In the early years . . . my mother dressed us in clothes like English children. My brother and I associated with English friends. As our parents did not want us to be different in any way, they assured our learning the English language properly.

In the early sixties, British public resentment against these "coloreds" rose dramatically, no matter what their assimilationist perspective might be. Sikhs and other Asians throughout Great Britain realized that restrictions on Commonwealth immigration

were inevitable, so they sent for their friends and relatives to come
to Britain before the doors to this land of opportunity were closed.
The influx of Asians to England increased considerably as wives,
children, siblings, and mothers arrived to balance out the predominantly male population. The arrival of women and children neces-
sitated that cultural issues be given consideration. The value placed
by Sikhs on female purity came to the fore, as did a concern that
their children uphold the principles of the Sikh faith. Social pressures emerged in full force. As one woman explained:

> When our relatives came, everything changed drastically. The
> women would come to our house and say, "Don't you think Nimi's
> hair should be braided now that she is ten?" or "Nimi should not
> go to school with bare legs [that is, wear dresses like the En-
> glish girls], otherwise she will grow up being immodest." Immedi-
> ately my mother's attitude changed. I was no longer to be like the
> English, but was now to dress and be like Punjabi villagers. I re-
> sented this.

Many Asian males in Gravesend were not willing to maintain the
symbols of their faith, but they pressured their wives and children
to obey the teachings of their Guru. They followed a double standard: lenient values for themselves and stricter norms for their
wives and children. However, practicing the double standard shifted
to a stricter pattern of behavior for themselves as they realized that
the power of example was much greater than verbal admonitions.

There were many reasons for this shift in attitude. Initially,
there was a "colonial mentality" among the Sikh immigrants to England. The English were thought to be fair, honest, and worthy of
emulation, and for many, to identify with British ways was to earn
prestige. Similarly, those in the home village tended to see emigrants as superior simply because they lived in England. Still, this
identification with the British rarely meant a complete rejection of
Sikh identity, and as racism against Asians became a major aspect
of British society, those who had initially hoped to become "Brown
British" often cast their lot with their fellow Sikhs.

Ongoing immigration often has the effect of preserving the culture of the homeland in the overseas community, and this was the
case with the Sikhs of Gravesend. Immigration affected the communal evaluation of family *izzat*. *Izzat* is the prestige given a kin group
because of the favorable evaluation bestowed on it by the community, and it functions among Sikhs in roughly the way that "honor"

defines much of the representative behavior observed in certain Mediterranean cultures.[21] Honor implies a credibility accorded to promises and threats, and a possessive attitude toward individual and familial rights, including certain social privileges and rights having to do with property and women. Rigid expectations about the place and behavior of women is especially crucial to one's honor because the tight control of women in one's own group directly influences others who seek these women in marriage. In this regard Sikh immigrants to Gravesend saw themselves as being evaluated by three different audiences: (1) villagers in the Punjab, (2) other Sikhs in England, and (3) the English host society. Although the first two groups were of primary importance, Sikhs readily projected their own culture onto the British host society in anticipating how the British would react to them.[22]

In Gravesend, women were not only important as the upholders of family *izzat,* however, but because they instituted reliable communications with the home village, Jandiali, the men could no longer behave as if parents and relatives would be unaware of what they did. What they did abroad could shame the family name as easily as if they had remained in the punjab. Men in England did not want their behavior to demean the family name, especially because it might mean that a child, nephew, or niece would have poor chances to establish a good marriage. The arranged marriage system practiced by Sikhs and other South Asians makes it imperative for the family as a whole to maintain *izzat.*

Even in England, a family's *izzat* evaluation was important for the acquisition of a spouse. Emigrants often wanted spouses, especially women, from the Punjab itself because it was perceived that people brought up in the Punjab would be more apt to uphold the true values of their culture. This was a strong concern because elders wanted their children to marry persons who would look after them in their old age. Many feared that if their children were contaminated by the Western value of individualism, they would be foresaken in the twilight years—an issue that weighed heavy on their minds.[23] Furthermore, many Sikhs believed, then as now, that their chief value in life lay with their offspring. If their youngsters forsook the Sikh faith, then they themselves would be shamed.[24]

Such concerns led to a renewed emphasis on Sikh values and institutions in the 1960s. In 1965 The Sikh Missionary Society, U.K., was established in Gravesend. The unofficial leader of this initially small band—about six reformers—was a schoolteacher who had suffered considerably from violent white racism when he moved into council housing.[25] His car tires had been slashed and the windows of his home broken. He felt strongly that his children were being treated unfairly in the local school system and were generally discriminated against.

The primary goal of this leader and his colleagues was the revitalization of the *khalsa*. They were concerned that their children would forget Punjabi and agonized because the Sikh heritage was not being instilled by the British school system. They encouraged men to grow their hair, even if they became less marketable,[26] and condemned the president of the Gravesend Sikh temple because he had forsaken his *kes* (hair)—one of the "five Ks"—to take a job at a paper mill. An even greater anxiety focused on the girls. The reformers and others feared that if their girls started dating English boys and began emulating Western ideas and beliefs, the society would fall apart. Sikhs in Gravesend feared that if their daughters were westernized, they would not be marriageable: eligible men would seek brides from India instead.

The Sikh Missionary Society, U.K., collected money and published pamphlets promoting Sikhism. Its members actively participated in *gurdwara* politics, trying to install a powerful leader who would maintain all the symbols of their faith. In examining the pamphlets published by the society[27] and listening to debates in the *gurdwara* as late as 1986, I found that maintaining the "five Ks," keeping women pure, and instilling Sikh ideology into children continued to remain the great concerns of Sikh men in Gravesend.[28] In general, the revitalization efforts of the Sikh Missionary Society, discrimination from the British host community, the strengthening of ongoing ties with their home region, and the general fear that the second generation would lose its heritage all worked together to produce a resurgence of respect for Sikh ideals and symbols. The *gurdwara* became prominent, instruction in Sikh religion and Punjabi language was instituted, and a successful Gurdwara Sports Federation was developed to build unity among Sikh youth.

In spite of the revitalization of Sikh culture, however, internal conflicts persisted. Many in Gravesend would have seconded the remarks I heard at the Sikh conference held at the University of California, Berkeley, in 1987. One gentleman from the audience stated, "During the day we work in the States, but at night we dream of Punjab." Another said, "Our children are like coconuts, brown on the outside but white on the inside."

If elders feel a certain sense of despair at fighting an uphill battle, young people are prey to a more fundamental sense of confusion.

They see that their parents and grandparents want the arranged marriage system to remain intact, yet their education tells them that Western society considers it barbaric. Sikhs emphasize family honor while the school system emphasizes individualism. And this is not all: differences of food and styles of relationships also exacerbate distinctions within the Sikh community. As a result, the definition of proper Sikh behavior may differ greatly depending on whether a Sikh lives in the United States, India, Kenya, or Britain, while a single, universal standard of behavior and the ideal of a cohesive Sikh unity are publicly maintained. Of course, such unity is not merely fictional. Unified actions among various Sikh communities have had their effect, and there is a history of cooperation between Punjabi and expatriate Sikhs that extends throughout the twentieth century.

Unified Action of Indigenous and Expatriate Sikhs

Currently, expatriate Sikhs are involved in Sikh politics in India as actively as are residents of the Punjab. With modern communication, those abroad can influence Indian, Punjabi, and village politics a good bit more aggressively than in the past, but even at the turn of the century, the desire to do so was sometimes strong, as we see in the formation of the Ghadar Party.

At that time, Sikhs abroad largely upheld the British because, as Khushwant Singh has said, "A large number of Sikh immigrants were ex-soldiers or policemen to whom loyalty to the British Crown was an article of faith."[29] But around 1907, when they were subjected to various forms of discrimination in the United States and Canada, Sikhs were disappointed to find that Britain refused to intercede on their behalf. It was partly owing to this that the Ghadar Party was formed.

Ghadar means "mutiny" or "revolution." The party developed from a newspaper of the same name that started publication in San Francisco in 1913. Under the editorship of Har Dayal and with the financial support of Jwala Singh, a wealthy landowner in California also known as the "Potato King," this paper sought to recruit soldiers to fight for India's independence from British rule. A contingent sailed from San Francisco in August 1914, collecting other groups along the way. They did not get the backing they thought they would in India, however, and by the summer of 1915, virtually all members of the party in India were arrested and the movement was destroyed. The party continued to exist in the United States, but with the deterioration of relations between the United States and Germany, Ghadarites were arrested for violating America's neutrality laws. Nevertheless the newspaper continued publication until India's independence.[30] The Ghadar movement illustrates the concern and active participation of the Sikh diaspora in the local affairs of the Punjab even during the early decades of life abroad.

History repeated itself in 1982, when the Khalistan ("the country of the pure, the nation of the *khalsa*") movement came to the fore and Sikhs abroad served as an influential component of the group that agitated for a Sikh homeland. The idea of Khalistan (an independent state to be controlled by the *khalsa*) started with Kapur Singh, an Oxford alumnus and member of the Indian Civil Service (ICS), who aroused Sikhs to see the need for an independent nation. Gaining support abroad from the emigrant community was significant for the movement. On October 13, 1971, a half-page advertisement in the *New York Times* explained the importance of Khalistan, as Dr. Jagjit Singh Chauhan brought the movement abroad. On June 16, 1980, a press release issued in Britain stated that Khalistan consulates were to be set up in the United Kingdom, Germany, and other West European countries. Sikhs in the United States effectively enlisted the help of such prominent United States senators as Jesse Helms, who in April 1983 helped circumvent the barrier to Dr. Chauhan's entry into the States. When Indian troops stormed the Golden Temple in June 1984, Sikhs around the world united and held mass demonstrations in support of the revolutionary movement. Thousands of dollars a week were collected from *gurdwaras* all over the world to support those who fought for Khalistan.[31]

Emigrant involvement in Punjabi life is not limited to dramatic political events. As the Gravesend study suggests, Sikh communities abroad typically maintain a pattern of ongoing interaction with their villages of origin.[32] In this regard, Gravesend Sikhs went through four phases: premigration, freedom, conflict, and settlement. In *premigration,* before the emigration process developed, information to Jandiali about Gravesend was glorified and stereotypical. Thus, for the potential migrant, England was seen as a place where "streets were paved with gold." In the *freedom* period of initial settlement in Gravesend, communications with Jandiali were limited. Families had not yet emigrated to England, so the males were free of social pressures to maintain Sikh symbols or conform to normative Sikh behavior. The *conflict* phase began as wives and children arrived. On the one hand, the migrant community had to deal with the conflicting dictates of Sikh and Western culture, as made plain by life in England; on the other hand, they had to respond to the perceptions that family and friends in the home village had of their actions abroad. Whatever the tensions, during the freedom and conflict phases, Gravesend Sikhs remitted money to their home villages on a regular basis. Jandiali's overseas population not only provided financial support but actively participated in determining where a new *gurdwara* was to be built, what sort of building it would be, where roads were to be laid, and what style of school building should be constructed. New farming techniques, machinery, capital, seed varieties, and technology were sent back to the Punjab by members of the diaspora to improve agricultural techniques in their homeland.

The *settlement* phase arrives when an immigrant community becomes permanent in its new home. In Gravesend, at this stage, the "myth of return" persisted among some, but most Sikhs came to consider England as their permanent home. Not surprisingly, remittances did drop during this period, but interest and involvement in the homeland remained strong. This interest fairly skyrocketed when the Golden Temple was invaded in 1984 and contributions to Punjabi causes rose similarly—both to the home village and to political groups that the emigrants felt worthy of financial support. Thus the interactional relationship between Gravesend and the Punjab has remained important, though not invariant, in all phases of the Sikh community's settlement in Britain.

The Gurdwara

The *gurdwara* has always been a crucial institution for knitting together the Sikh community, whether at an international or local level. Traditionally, it has been a multipurpose institution: a place of worship, a political center, an educational institution, and a center for hospitality and service. Although it is a place of worship, the *gurdwara* is also the symbolic center for Sikh temporal and political authority. The term *gurdwara* means "the gateway of the guru" and refers to the fact that its central object is the *Guru Granth Sahib,* where the teachings of the ten Gurus are enshrined. A canopy is kept over the *Guru Granth Sahib* and an attendant uses a brush of yak's hair to whisk off dust and insects; both canopy and brush symbolize royalty. The worshiper comes to the *Guru Granth Sahib* with all the respect that would be appropriate if one were in the presence of royalty or divinity. In the *gurdwaras* shoes are removed, feet are washed, money is offered in proximity to the Holy Book, and supplicants drop to their knees and perform obeisance by rubbing their foreheads on the ground. Worshippers understand that by behaving in this way they are humbling themselves before an authority that is both temporal and spiritual,[33] and the *gurdwara* as a whole communicates the combined spiritual and temporal orientation of the Sikh faith.

In Gravesend the *gurdwara* is used for all the above-mentioned functions and plays a crucial role in the Sikh community. As a center of worship, it has provided solace to the Sikhs of Gravesend ever since immigration began. Initially, it was but a small room in the home of a Sikh who had brought a *Guru Granth Sahib* from the Punjab. Weekly Sunday services were held in this house for all who wished to attend, whether Sikhs or adherents of other faiths. The ecumenical spirit was prominent. For the Sikhs in Gravesend, life in England was hard, and being apart from family and friends created psychological tensions. To be able to pray and associate with fellow Sikhs in an atmosphere of equality, community, and support was comforting. The local *gurdwara* served to alleviate the loneliness, heartache, and sense of unease that came from being in an alien land. Although the community grew and the location of the *gurdwara* changed after a former church was purchased to house it, the weekly Sunday services remained a prominent communal function.

When the revitalization phase began, it was strongly manifest in the life of the *gurdwara*. It was in the competition for *gurdwara* leadership that the Sikh Missionary Society, U.K., and other groups began to insist that the president of the Gurdwara Committee be an unshaven Sikh. During the weekly service at the *gurdwara,* women learned about the community. The *gurdwara* was a forum, a place where rumors and gossip were exchanged and information was sent back to the Punjab, informing elders and friends of any deviant behavior in Gravesend. People shared experiences, learned of job and investment opportunities, and heard of means by which they could do better in England. The *gurdwara* also served as the platform where religious and community issues were debated. When the Gravesend Sikhs felt that their children were receiving unfair treatment in the British schools, they debated the idea of forming their own *khalsa* school in the *gurdwara*. British politicians and bureaucrats also turned to the *gurdwara* when they wanted support from the immigrant community or communication with the Asians in

Gravesend. Sikhs who felt oppressed in the Punjab or were visitors from India used the *gurdwara* forum to share their concerns. Debates for and against Khalistan were passionately presented in the Gravesend *gurdwara,* as they were in *gurdwaras* throughout the world.

The *gurdwara* was not just an arena to obtain information and launch action, it became the representative institution for the Asian element of Gravesend. Although many immigrant organizations, such as a branch of the Indian Worker's Association, competed for the leadership of Gravesend Asians, it was the Gurdwara Committee that became the recognized representative for Sikh and non-Sikh alike.[34] The *gurdwara* also took on many welfare and social-service functions for the Asian community in Gravesend. In 1985, the Gurdwara Committee obtained a government grant to create a social center for the elderly. Previously, elderly Sikh males had gathered in the center of town during the warm months but had been housebound during the winter period. Now they could socialize at the *gurdwara* center, watch television, play games, read newspapers, and catch up on village news. The *gurdwara* has also become a social service agency, not only looking after the elderly, but also helping poor Sikhs of the community, and in general providing utensils and helping with weddings, funerals, and *akhand paths* (that is, uninterrupted recitations of the *Guru Granth Sahib*).[35] It became the sponsor of Sikh youth clubs and the Sikhs Sports Federation, providing a place where young people could play *kabaddi,*[36] cricket, and other sports and compete against *gurdwara* teams throughout England.

In addition it became the primary educational center used for promoting Sikh and Punjabi culture. Punjabi language classes were held there, along with instruction in the Sikh faith. Although the idea of a *khalsa* school has not yet been realized, the *gurdwara* debates serve an educational function.

The *gurdwara* is where Sikhs gain esteem. A Sikh does not necessarily have to be a political figure or hold a position of leadership to gain community respect. All he or she needs to do is perform *seva* (service) to others. This concept goes back to the teaching of Guru Arjan, who in the *Adi Granth* emphasized the idiom "servant of the servants" (*das dasan ke*). He taught that one must do social service to achieve spiritual realization.[37] In fact, according to him, social obligations ought to precede prayer.[38] In Sikh culture, *seva* (service) is used in the communal evaluation that determines the honor (*iz-*

zat) of a Sikh family.[39] Thus one can gain meaning in life by serving
in the *gurdwara*—by cooking, cleaning, serving food, or performing
other needed tasks to support the community.

The *gurdwara* is thus a multifunctional institution, even more
so in the Sikh diaspora than at home in the Punjab. It is a place
where a Sikh can always go to make a meaningful contribution to
community and Guru. It is a crucial institution for Sikh survival in
an alien land.

Sikh Political Organization

With their continuous need for mobility and flexibility, Sikhs
have not found it advantageous to adopt a centralized administrative system like that of the Catholic Church, where authority is
ultimately vested in the pope. Sikhs are independent and autonomous, and local communities may have their own rules. As was
shown above, there was a time in the life of the Gravesend community when shaven (*sahajdhari*) Sikhs led the *gurdwara,* a practice
that would have been regarded as deviant back in Jandiali. Conditions then seemed to demand it: jobs were more important than
maintaining the "five Ks," and a justification could be provided. As
the leaders stated, "Guru Nanak did not wear a beard, so why
should I?" Thus the lack of centralized control among Sikhs allowed
rules to be adapted to local conditions. What supplanted such centralized authority in the Sikh community was an operating principle similar to the one that animated the *misal* system in earlier
Sikh history,[40] that is, loyalty to family and kin alliances and to
those who were able to give, help, and/or protect. As with the pe-
rennial ruling families of the *misals,* loyalty in Gravesend was
based on a person's or family's power to lead and look after any
charges. And, as with a *misal,* it was very unusual for an individual to have power without a strong kin group to provide a core
of support.

The political parties that developed in Gravesend were organized to meet the needs of the constituency. Although these parties
were informally organized and did not put up candidates and con-
test elections in Gravesend proper, they were recognized groupings
that developed a slate for leadership positions in the Gravesend
gurdwara. Though not formally acknowledged in public meetings,
each group was regularly referred to as a "party." There were two

such parties, both centered on a prominent leader and held together by loyalties based on kinship and services rendered, especially to the more recently arrived brethren.

In each party there were six identifiable roles: kingmaker, core of advisers, broker, social worker, sympathizer, and member.[41] The "kingmaker" usually was a former president of an organization such as the Gurwara Committee who, though politically strong, had made enemies and could not gain sufficient strength to obtain or hold office. Nonetheless, his following provided a strong core of support for any candidate he chose, so the kingmaker could remain in the background, supporting, advising, and determining the policy of his candidate. The kingmaker had a core of advisers with whom he met and discussed local politics and strategy. These advisers were politically astute and knew their community, but they generally lacked sufficient numbers of relatives to build a core following on their own.

The "social worker" selflessly helped his fellow Asians, whereas a "broker" bridged the cultural gap between the British and Punjabi communities. The latter was bilingual and knew enough about English ways to help immigrants with their income tax, their medical and social service forms, their jobs, and their general survival in Britain. He was therefore in a position to exploit his fellow immigrants. By contrast, those who helped their fellow Gravesend Asians selflessly were termed "social workers" by others in the community. They too interpreted for their fellow Sikhs and helped with forms, but they neither asked for anything in return nor sought political office; they simply befriended those in need.

The "sympathizer" was not active in any party, but because he had friends or relatives in one, he was considered sympathetic toward that party. Since he was not actively committed to any group, he gained the confidence of both parties and mediated conflicts and disagreements, yet his position was precarious since his neutrality was often suspect. Unlike sympathizers, "members" actually aligned themselves with one party or another. Membership was informal, but recognizable, and unless there was a split, kinsmen and those who had been neighbors back in the Punjab tended to remain unified.

This organization served the community admirably. It was informal and flexible, and it enabled people to receive help when it was needed. All that was required was loyalty to a political group and the party provided protection against exploitation, helped to decipher complicated forms, and afforded social support.

Conclusions for Sikh Studies and Migration Studies

An examination of the Sikh diaspora has obvious—but too often overlooked—consequences for understanding Sikhs and Sikhism, and at the same time it provides a rich reservoir of material to aid in developing an understanding of migrant adaptation in general. The literature about Sikh studies in India seems to neglect the diaspora almost entirely, hewing to a focus on the ideology, history, and social structure of Sikhs living in India and in the Punjab.[42] Abroad, however, the story is different. In 1979 Juergensmeyer and Barrier recognized the importance of the overseas community and placed a strong emphasis on it in the collection of essays they edited.[43] Even so, the essays on overseas Sikhs in their book focused primarily on two themes, motivation for emigration and adjustment to life in America. As such, they reflected the interests of a time where emigrant behavior was perceived as purely a bilateral interaction between the host society and its migrant enclave. It was a time when knowledge of the Sikh diaspora was still in its infancy.

Since then much has changed. Dusenbery, writing a decade later, emphasized the diverse experiences of Sikhs in the diaspora as well as the different patterns of emigration that characterized different time periods.[44] While acknowledging the ongoing importance of kinsmen, the classic process of "chain migration,"[45] and key concepts such as *izzat* and the institution of arranged marriages, Dusenbery's collection went a step further and considered the factor of remittances and the political involvement of overseas Sikhs.[46] Implicitly this meant abandoning a total reliance on the bilateral model of analyzing immigrant behavior.

Parallel developments in the field of migration studies support such a shift. Traditionally, scholars in this field concentrated on four broad topics: (1) causes of population shifts, (2) social psychological concerns of immigrant adaptation, (3) social problems caused by immigration, and (4) the nature and dynamics of migrant groups and their social networks. This meant that they focused on the dyadic interaction between host and immigrant societies, usually in a rather static way.[47] With the worldwide communications revolution, however, the ongoing interactional relationship between migrant societies and the home societies that had spawned them became both more evident and more efficient. Migration was no longer self-evidently a one-way process that made it unnecessary to take the home society into account. In fact it has become increasingly plain that the interaction is not always limited to just host,

home, and a single migrant group. It may involve a more complex
dynamic that relates a given migrant group to other, similar migrant communities in other host societies that share a common
identity, as is the case with the Sikhs.

During the last fifteen years, migration studies have begun to
assume this level of complexity in analyzing population movements,
and as they have done so, many issues that once seemed separate
processes now demand more intricate theoretical formulations.[48]
Take, for example, the theme of maintaining culture and identity
through the erection and preservation of ethnic boundaries, a task
that is of utmost importance in immigrant societies. If a culture is
not maintained, social and psychological breakdown occurs. People
become shiftless, directionless, even victims of substance abuse in
response to the sense of inferiority that an alien environment fos-
ters, especially as the immigrants' own children outpace them in
adapting to the new society. Emphasizing their ethnicity is a way to
recover from this process while at the same time creating institutions helpful in distributing the economic, educational, and social
resources available within the immigrant community itself.[49]

We have already seen that the Sikhs of Gravesend adopted different approaches to ethnicity at different stages of their history,
but it is worth adding that while in England discrimination had
much to do with stimulating a revitalization of Sikh culture—this
was a clear case of bilateral interaction between host and migrant
communities—no parallel rise in discrimination was responsible
for the reassertion of Sikh ethnicity in the United States during
roughly the same period.[50] The two countries are alike, however, in
that revitalization occurred in correlation with a surge of immigration by women and children, which contributed to an increase in
real interaction between immigrant Sikh communities and the
home societies that sent them abroad. Communal pressure increased and forced deviants to conform to the cultural dictates of
the ideal type of Punjabi Sikh. The revitalization also had a financial aspect, as a scholar such as Michael Banton would be quick
to observe.[51]

Finally, as we have hinted, events in the Punjab played an enor-
mous role in shaping the definition and maintenance of ethnic
boundaries in overseas Sikh communities during the 1980s, something the old bilateral frame of analysis is ill equipped to describe.
Since 1984, especially abroad, Sikhs have emphasized the distinction between Sikh and Hindu—not, say, the boundary between Sikh
and white American.[52] The literature on ethnic relations and migration is having to stretch well beyond its old mold to deal with a

people interested in creating ethnic boundaries between themselves
and a group residing on the other side of the globe rather than between themselves and the society that borders them in an immediate geographic sense. A complicating factor is that Hindus too, not
just Sikhs have newly become integrated. The theoretical literature
in migration studies has a good way to go before it can make sense
of the significant role played by emigrant Sikhs in supporting the
Khalistan movement, though similar patterns of advocacy and interaction can certainly be brought to bear from other ethnic groups
such as Poles, Jews, and Armenians.

The issue of boundary definition and identity formation suggests many other ways in which scholars of Sikhism can learn from
students of other groups, and vice versa. Like Sikhs, many immigrant groups in the United States have developed associations to
look after their own, provide psychological and social security, and
advance the welfare of the group. Jewish groups had their mutual
aid societies,[53] the Irish dominated urban politics through political
bosses such as flourished under Tammany Hall, while other groups
like the Germans and Scandinavians had mutual-aid associations
and voted in blocks according to their ethnic interests.[54] In a similar
way, Gravesend's Sikh "parties" centered on an individual and fulfilled many of the functions of social support. One apparently distinctive aspect of the Sikh party, however, is the role played by
kinship ties and village origins in determining support, and another is the specialization of roles within the party structure itself.
In organizations like those found in Tammany Hall, many of the
welfare functions were centralized in the boss or head of the unit
rather than distributed to other "specialists" within the party.[55]

Another seemingly distinctive aspect of overseas Sikh society is
the *gurdwara*. Undoubtedly religious centers such as churches and
synagogues have helped their ethnic congregations and generously
contributed to social aid. However, the combined temporal and spiritual roles of the *gurdwara* have made it a uniquely multipurpose
institution. A spiritual institution such as a church may perform
welfare functions to advance its spiritual causes, but in the *gurdwara* these two are integrally interrelated. One of the frontiers in
the field of comparative ethnicity is to determine whether such differing ideological constellations result in different patterns of behavior, even when superficial appearances suggest sameness, and if
so, how.

There is much yet to learn about the Sikh diaspora, but already
it is clear that a holistic and dynamic perspective must be used if
one is fully to understand the behavior of immigrant Sikhs, with its

record of changing relationships between host, immigrant, and sending communities. Further research is needed to determine if the generalities set forth above are valid for all diaspora Sikh communities and to see if they apply to other migrant communities as well. And further study is also needed to gauge more adequately the ways in which recent developments in the study of other immigrant communities can enrich our understanding of the Sikhs.

Notes

1. The term "diaspora" has its origins in Deut. 28:25 (Septuagint), which states, in referring to the Jewish people, "thou shalt be a diaspora," that is, "dispersed." In the New Testament, the term was used to refer not only to the body of Jews being dispersed among the Gentiles but to the body of Jewish Christians outside of Palestine. More recently the term diaspora has come to refer to any group of people residing outside their land of origin. See Glenn Hendricks, *The Dominican Diaspora* (New York: Teachers College Press, 1974); Gabriel Sheffer, ed., *Modern Diasporas in International Politics* (London: Croom Helm, 1986); and N. Gerald Barrier and Verne A. Dusenbery, eds., *The Sikh Diaspora* (Columbia, Mo.: South Asia Publications, 1989).

2. Marie M. de Lepervanche, *Indians in a White Australia* (Sydney: George Allen & Unwin, 1984).

3. Norman Buchignani and Doreen M. Indra, *Continuous Journey* (Toronto: McClelland and Stewart, 1985); James G. Chadney, *The Sikhs of Vancouver* (New York: AMS Press, 1984); and Hugh Johnston, *The Voyage of the Komagata Maru,* (Delhi: Oxford University Press, 1979).

4. Roger Ballard, "Family Organization Among the Sikhs in Britain," in *New Community* 2, no. 1 (1978) pp. 12–24; Parminder K. Bhachu, *Twice Migrants* (London: Tavistock, 1985); Arthur W. Helweg, *Sikhs in England,* 2d ed. (Delhi: Oxford University Press, 1986); Raj Madan, *Colored Minorities in Great Britain* (Westport, Conn.: Greenwood Press, 1979); Vaughan Robinson, *Transients, Settlers and Refugees* (Oxford: Clarendon Press, 1986); and Darshan Singh Tatla and Eleanor M. Nesbit, *Sikhs in Britain: An Annotated Bibliography* (Coventry: Centre for Research in Ethnic Relations, 1987).

5. W. H. McLeod, *Punjabis in New Zealand* (Amritsar: Guru Nanak Dev University, 1986).

6. Margaret A. Gibson, *Accommodation Without Assimilation* (Ithaca: Cornell University Press, 1988); Joan M. Jensen, *Passage From India* (New Haven: Yale University Press, 1988); Bruce La Brack, *The Sikhs of North-*

ern California 1904–1975 (New York: AMS Press, 1988); and Jane Singh, *South Asians in North America* (Berkeley: Center for South and Southeast Asia Studies, University of California, 1988).

7. Research in Jandiali and Gravesend was supported in 1970–71 by an NDFL Fellowship and in 1977–78 by the Faculty Research Program of the Fulbright-Hays Program, U.S. Department of Education. Fieldwork in 1981–82 was financed by the Smithsonian Institution. Study in Gravesend was further supported by a Faculty Research Grant and Fellowship from Western Michigan University in 1985, and by travel grants in 1986 and 1987.

8. W. H. McLeod, *The Sikhs: History, Religion, and Society* (New York: Columbia University Press, 1989), pp. 102–112.

9. Exact figures are hard to state because the issue of "who is a Sikh" is not definitively answered, even by the Sikhs themselves, and "Sikh" is seldom a category of enumeration in countries hosting the diaspora. See Barrier and Dusenbery, *The Sikh Diaspora,* p. 20.

10. Arthur W. Helweg, "Sikh Identity in England: Its Changing Nature," in Joseph T. O'Connell et al., eds., *Sikh History and Religion in the Twentieth Century* (Toronto: Centre for South Asian Studies, University of Toronto, 1988), p. 356; and Iqbal Singh, *Punjab Under Siege: A Critical Analysis* (New York: Allen, McMillan, and Enderson, 1986), p. 3.

11. These numbers are an underrepresentation of the South Asian contingent because the census only identified ethnic groups by place of birth. The actual figure may be 40 percent higher.

12. Iqbal Singh, *Punjab Under Siege* pp. iv, 3, 8, 9; and Paul Wallace, "The Sikhs as a 'Minority' in a Sikh Majority State," *Asian Survey* 26, no. 3 (1986), pp. 363–77.

13. For a treatment of South Asian emigration in which the story of the Sikhs is included, see Hugh Tinker, *The Banyan Tree* (Oxford: Oxford University Press, 1977); Hugh Tinker, *Separate and Unequal* (London: C. Hurst, 1976); and Hugh Tinker, *A New System of Slavery* (London: Oxford University Press, 1974).

14. H. A. Rose categorizes the *khatris* as merchants, yet they are also prominent in the professions. Many members of that caste identify with the *kshatriya* castes, are professionals, and claim superiority over the merchant element. Only *khatris* who emigrated to Gujarat were primarily merchants. See H. A. Rose, *A Glossary of the Tribes and Castes of the Punjab and North-West Frontier Province,* vols. 1 and 2 (Patiala: Languages Department, Punjab, 1970), pp. 501–26.

15. A postindustrial society is one in which the emphasis is on knowledge, information processing, and managerial and bureaucratic control.

See Krishan Kumar, "Post-Industrial Society," in Adam Kuper and Jessica Kuper, eds., *The Social Science Encyclopedia* (London: Routledge & Kegan Paul, 1985), pp. 633–35.

16. Barrier and Dusenbery, *The Sikh Diaspora,* p. 20.

17. There are two kinds of Sikhs: *sahajdharis,* who neither grow long hair nor adopt the discipline of the "five Ks," and *kesdharis* or *khalsa* Sikhs, who proudly wear these symbols.

18. Among the "five Ks," the uncut hair symbolizes saintliness, but if it is not orderly, it symbolizes insanity, so Sikhs keep a comb in the hair. The steel bracelet was used to protect the vulnerable right wrist in sword fighting; it and the sword symbolize militancy. The undershorts are designed to provide the freedom of movement essential for fighting, as well as to remind men to use their life-giving fluids properly. Sikhs are admonished to treat women with respect, even women of conquered people. Thus Sikhs have a reputation for treating both Sikh and non-Sikh females with dignity.

19. See Arthur W. Helweg, "India's Sikhs: Problems and Prospects," *Journal of Contemporary Asia* 17, no. 2 (1987), p. 148.

20. See Helweg, *Sikhs in England;* La Brack, *The Sikhs of Northern California;* Anthony F. C. Wallace, *Culture and Personality* (New York: Random House, 1961), pp. 188–99; and Anthony F. C. Wallace, *Religion: An Anthropological View* (New York: Random House, 1966), pp. 30–39, 163–66, 209–15.

21. J. G. Peristiany, *Honor and Shame: The Values of Mediterranean Society* (Chicago: University of Chicago Press, 1966).

22. Helweg, *Sikhs in England,* pp. 12–21.

23. In Gravesend, the emphasis on obtaining spouses from India began to diminish by 1988. Families found that bringing a village female for marriage was not the panacea they originally thought. Such a bride was not as adept at making money as a woman raised in England would have been. If marriage was arranged with a middle-class Punjabi woman who was used to servants, moreover, she generally neither knew housework well, nor obedience and submissiveness. Similarly there was disappointment when males were brought over, because they were not employable in England, especially if they came from the village. A village man would often try to assert himself as patriarch of the household, which did not sit well with women influenced by British cultural values.

24. See Helweg, *Sikhs in England,* pp. 58–61.

25. This is the British term for public housing projects.

26. Long hair was considered to be dangerous in areas where fast-moving machinery was present. Thus English employers were reluctant to hire long-haired Sikhs in their factories.

27. Kirpal Singh, *The Sikh Symbols (Kesh-hair)* (Gravesend: The Sikh Missionary Society, U.K., 1971); G. S. Sidhu, *The Apostle of Peace* (Gravesend: The Sikh Missionary Society, U.K., 1970); G. S. Sidhu, G. S. Siva, and Kirpal Singh, *Guru Nanak (For Children)* (Gravesend: The Sikh Missionary Society, U.K., 1969).

28. Helweg, *Sikhs in England,* pp. 98–115.

29. Khushwant Singh, *A History of the Sikhs,* 2 vols., (1963; rev. ed. Delhi: Oxford University Press, 1991), vol. 2, p. 175.

30. M. V. Kamath, *The United States and India, 1776–1976* (Washington: Embassy of India, 1976), pp. 104–6; and Khushwant Singh, *History,* pp. 185–92.

31. Aseem Chaabra, "Thousands of Sikhs Protest," *India Abroad* (June 15, 1984), pp. 1, 14; John Barber, "A Troubled Community," *Maclean's* 99, no. 25 (1986), pp. 10–13; Ramesh Chandran, "United Kingdom: Tackling Terrorism," *India Today* (November 30, 1985), pp. 28, 29; and Aseem Chaabra and Ramesh Gune, "3,000 Sikhs in N.Y. Meeting Demand 'Khalistan' Creation," *India Abroad,* August 10, 1984, pp. 1, 5.

32. See especially Arthur W. Helweg, "Indians in England: A Study of the Interactional Relationships of Sending, Receiving, and Migrant Societies," in M. S. A. Rao, ed., *Studies in Migration* (Delhi: Manohar, 1986), pp. 363–94.

33. See Surinder Singh Kohli, *Outlines of Sikh Thought* (New Delhi: Munshiram Manoharlal, 1978), p. 14, and Harbans Singh, *The Heritage of the Sikhs* (New Delhi: Manohar, 1985), pp. 107–11.

34. In essence, this was what happened on the west coast of North America. In North America there were various Indian organizations, but since *gurdwaras* were the only public place where Indians could meet, they became the centers of political activity. See Khushwant Singh, *History,* vol. 2, p. 175.

35. An *akhand path* is an unbroken, continuous reading of the *Guru Granth Sahib.*

36. A competitive Indian sport that is prominent in the Punjab.

37. The sect of *seva panthis,* social workers, can be traced back to Bhai Ghanahia, a Sikh contemporary of the ninth and tenth Gurus. He is said to have served water not only to wounded Sikh soldiers but to their opponents, and did so with the blessings of the Gurus. See Avtar Singh, *Ethics of the Sikhs* (Patiala: Punjabi University, 1979) p. 196.

38. Avtar Singh, *Ethics,* p. 195.

39. *Izzat* or *man* is the sum of an individual's social credit. The evaluation is linked not only to the action of the person but also to the communal

appraisal given to his kin group through the *jati* system. See Helweg, *Sikhs in England,* pp. 14–15, and David G. Mandelbaum, *Society in India* (Berkeley: University of California Press, 1972), pp. 468, 626.

40. The *misal* was a unit of organization developed by the Sikhs during the first Afghan invasions (1747–1748). The *dal,* or Sikh army, was divided into eleven *misals* under the leadership of prominent men and their families. Sikhs were free to join any *misal* they wanted. The system provided flexibility and freedom, while unifying the units under a single king. See Khushwant Singh, *History,* vol. 1, pp. 132–33.

41. The terms "kingmaker" and "broker" are analytical categories used to explain what was observed. The other categories were used by the Punjabis themselves.

42. Jagjit Singh, *Perspectives on Sikh Studies* (New Delhi: Guru Nanak Foundation, 1985).

43. See Mark Juergensmeyer and N. Gerald Barrier, eds., *Sikh Studies: Comparative Perspectives on a Changing Tradition* (Berkeley: Berkeley Religious Studies Series, 1979).

44. Verne A. Dusenbery, "Introduction: A Century of Sikhs Abroad," in Barrier and Dusenbery, eds., *The Sikh Diaspora,* pp. 1–28.

45. "Chain migration" is a term used to identify the common situation in which an individual emigrates, then tells relatives and friends in his home region of his new situation, and they subsequently follow.

46. Bruce LaBrack, "The New Patrons: Sikhs Overseas," pp. 261–304, and Arthur W. Helweg, "Sikh Politics in India: The Emigrant Factor," pp. 305–6 in Barrier and Dusenbery, eds., *The Sikh Diaspora.*

47. Roy Simon Bryce-Laport, ed., *Sourcebook on the New Immigration* (New Brunswick, N.J.: Transaction Books, 1980); S. N. Eisenstadt, *The Absorption of Immigrants* (Westport, Conn.: Greenwood Press, 1954); J. A. Jackson, ed., *Migration* (Cambridge: Cambridge University Press, 1969); Clifford Jansen, ed., *Readings in the Sociology of Migration* (London: Pergamon Press, 1970); Leonard Kasdan, "Introduction," in Robert F. Spencer, gen. ed., *Migration and Anthropology* (Seattle: American Ethnological Society and the University of Washington Press, 1970); and R. Paul Shaw, *Migration: Theory and Fact* (Philadelphia: Regional Science Research Institute, 1975).

48. George Gmelch, "Return Migration," *Annual Review of Anthropology* 9 (Palo Alto, Calif. Annual Reviews, 1980); William Petersen, Michael Novak, and Philip Gleason, *Concepts of Ethnicity* (Cambridge: Belknap Press of Harvard University, 1982), p. 21; and Rosemarie Rogers, "Return Migration in Comparative Perspective," in Daniel Kubat, ed., *Politics of Return: International Return Migration in Europe* (New York: Center for Mi-

gration Studies, 1984). Nancy B. Graves and Theodore Graves, in writing about internal migration, emphasized the need for the three-way interaction model ("Return Migration," *Annual Review of Anthropology* 3, [Palo Alto, Calif.: Annual Reviews, 1974] pp. 117–52). Similar work is in its infancy concerning international migration, however.

49. Michael Walzer, Edward T. Kantowicz, John Higham, and Mona Harrington, *The Politics of Ethnicity* (Cambridge: Belknap Press of Harvard University, 1982), pp. 12–18.

50. See Gibson, *Accommodation Without Assimilation,* p. 85.

51. Michael Banton, *Racial and Ethnic Competition* (Cambridge: Cambridge University Press, 1983).

52. The distinction between Sikh and Hindu is prominent in writings contained in *World Sikh News,* especially in negative reactions to the work of W. H. McLeod. See also S. S. Dharan, *Internal and External Threats to Sikhism* (Arlington Heights, Va.: Gurmat Publishers, 1988); Gobind Singh Mansukhani, "Mostly Old Material With Many Inaccuracies," in *World Sikh News* (September 22, 1989), p. 2; Gurtej Singh, "McLeod's Work Propagandist," in *World Sikh News* (September 15, 1989), p. 2; and Daljeet Singh, "Casual Vague, Generalised," in *World Sikh News* (September 29, 1989), p. 2, and *World Sikh News* (October 6, 1989), p. 2.

53. Arthur A. Goren, *The American Jews* (Cambridge: Belknap Press of Harvard University, 1982), p. 63–8.

54. Walzer et al., *The Politics of Ethnicity,* pp. 29–68.

55. See William L. Riordon, *Plunkitt of Tammany Hall* (New York: E. P. Dutton, 1963).

5

Sikh Studies and the Sikh
Educational Heritage

*

Gurinder Singh Mann

This chapter is concerned with the relationship between Sikh studies and the Sikh community. It is divided into two sections: the first deals with the historical background of the Sikhs' understanding of their educational heritage and the community's role in building its educational institutions; the second section analyzes the Sikh community's effort to replant this heritage in North America. I see the recent acceleration of these efforts not so much as a consequence of the need to respond to Operation Bluestar after 1984 but as a general indication of the Sikh community's coming of age in its adopted land. The last several years in particular have provided an extremely fertile environment for fostering an alliance between the Sikhs and the academic community in North America. The Sikh community's strong resolution to promote its heritage has coincided with the commitment of leading North American universities to teach Sikhism as a tradition that has made a significant contribution to the history of the Indian subcontinent and the history of religion in general. The chapter concludes with concrete suggestions for strengthening this happy alliance.

I. The Sikh Educational Heritage

I begin with the Sikh educational heritage, which is deeply rooted in Sikh religious thinking. After all, the very word Sikh literally means a disciple, a learner. A Sikh is one who learns the truth of life by reflecting upon the ideas of the Gurus.[1] Hence, not

95

surprisingly, the theme of knowledge (*gian*) is greatly emphasized in Sikh scriptures. The *Japji,* a Sikh morning prayer, regards the realm of knowledge (*gian khand*) as the foundation for any spiritual elevation.[2] And Guru Nanak describes the centrality of knowledge in human life by likening it to the oil that is needed to light a lamp:

> How can a lamp be lit without oil?
>
> Crush through the holy books to yield that oil;
> Take as your wick a godly fear,
> Place it in your lamp, your body,
> And light it with the spark of truth.
>
> This is the oil that lights the lamp;
> It makes the light that lets you meet
> the Lord.[3]

Other images are also used. Knowledge is frequently described not only as the oil in a lamp but as the lamp itself, the source of light (*dipak*).[4] It can also be called an eye cleanser (*anjan*), something that clarifies and sharpens one's vision.[5]

This emphasis on knowledge as a prerequisite to spiritual elevation has important implications for active day-to-day living. In this arena, knowledge is called the sword (*kharag*) Sikhs need to cut their way through the snares of life in the world. With the help of the sword of knowledge, Sikhs grapple with the inner instincts that would divert their attention from the real goal of life. With such a sword, Sikhs are expected to succeed in destroying the five enemies (*panch dut*), thus cleansing the heart and preparing it for the light of the Lord.[6]

In the Sikh vision of life, knowledge is not inert. Rather it creates a natural and powerful yearning to do good for others (*parupkar umaha*). Knowledge helps the person who possesses it, but at the same time it ought to create a strong sense of responsibility for others (*vidia vichari tan parupkari*).[7] A Sikh is constantly warned against the intellectual arrogance that knowledge sometimes brings.[8] Knowledge is expected to result in humility (*saram*), not pride (*haumai*).[9]

As the Sikh tradition evolved, it consciously developed its own scripture, the *Adi Granth,* and held the knowledge and understanding of that scripture to be crucial. Guru Arjan declared the *Adi Granth* to be the very dwelling place of the Lord (*pothi parmesar ka thanu*) in that it was the repository of Sikh religious knowledge.[10] The exegesis of the *Adi Granth* began in earnest immediately after its compilation: this was a document not just to be praised or recited but studied and understood. The traditional claim is that Bhai Gurdas was given the duty of exegeting the *Adi Granth* so that all Sikhs could understand the knowledge it contained. The literary structure of his *vars,* where he takes one or another important theme and goes on to explain it on the basis of the compositions of the Gurus (*gurbani*), reveals his commitment to providing a clear interpretation of the tenets of Sikh thought.[11]

With Bhai Gurdas another important dimension of Sikh learning entered the field, namely, the history of the Gurus (*guru itihas*). As Dr. Taran Singh has pointed out, each Sikh Guru is understood to have lived out the content of his teaching; consequently it was considered important to know the life history of the Gurus.[12] Bhai Gurdas composed an entire *var* on the life of Guru Nanak, and the later *janam-sakhi* literature expanded on this theme in a major way. Bhai Gurdas also offered details about the life of other Gurus and their relationship to the contemporary community. At this early stage, then, Sikh knowledge took shape in two ways: through the exegesis of the *Adi Granth,* which shaped the new *panth's* theology, and through an outline of the lives of the Gurus, which shaped its history.

These two thrusts in Sikh education continued to develop as the tradition matured. In theology, the early emphasis on the interpretation of the *Adi Granth* was strengthened by the rapprochement that took place between the Sikh tradition and the Udasi followers of Baba Srichand, the elder son of Guru Nanak, in the early seventeenth century. The Udasis joined the mainstream during the period of Guru Hargobind. But asceticism continued to play an important role in the lives of Udasi Sikhs, who were instrumental in the establishment of the Sikh missionary centers known in the tradition as the four *dhuain* (literally the big burning logs around which ascetics would sit and talk), and the six *bakhshishan* (bounties).[13] In addition, at the time of Guru Gobind Singh, the Nirmala ascetics who emerged within the community claim to have been sent to Banaras to learn Sanskrit by the Guru himself.

These Nirmala and Udasi ascetics were responsible for introducing a Vedantic interpretation of the Gurus' teaching into the broader stream of Sikh theology. In their effort to show that Sikhism was part of a broader Hindu context and that the *Adi Granth* was to be regarded as the fifth Veda, they translated the key Sikh texts into Sanskrit. In similar fashion they also rendered a number of basic Hindu texts into a Braj Bhasha that was written in *gurmukhi,* so that Sikhs could understand what the Nirmalas and

Udasis saw as their broader heritage. By the second half of the eighteenth century, the zeal of scholars like Pandit Gulab Singh and Pandit Nikka Singh had added new texts to the corpus of Sikh learning. Pandit Gulab Singh was responsible for introducing the influential works entitled *Adhyatam Ramayana, Bhavarasamrita, Karam Vipak, Mokh Panth,* and *Prabodh Chandar Natak.*[14] The Udasi *mahants* (abbots) Santokh Das and Pritam Das established the important Braham Buta and Sangalawala *akharas*— "institutes," one might say—where ascetics gathered near the Golden Temple for instruction and other activities. They used these *akharas* to transmit their version of Sikh theology.[15] As Sikh theology proliferated and developed during the seventeenth and eighteenth centuries, so too did the hagiographical literature classified in the community under the heading of *janam-sakhi* and *gurbilas,* and again in large part at the aegis of the Nirmalas and Udasis. Whatever one may think of the accuracy of the theological contribution made by the Nirmalas and Udasis and however one may evaluate the historical details of the *janam-sakhi* and *gurbilas* literature, one must acknowledge that they contributed importantly to the growing body of knowledge that an educated Sikh was expected to master.

Similarly it was the Nirmala and Udasi ascetics who kept the Sikh educational program going through the violence and turmoil of the eighteenth century. It was they who staffed the seminaries (*taksals*) established at Amritsar and Damdama where Sikhs could be educated in scripture and history. Both these places expanded their work during the Sikh *raj* (1799–1849) and were primarily responsible for the training of *bhais* and *gianis* who could teach in the *gurmukhi* schools that were established in Sikh villages as part of local *gurdwaras* toward the end of the eighteenth century. At the time of the arrival of the British, then, Sikh education was already well developed. The Amritsar and Damdama seminaries provided many Sikh villages with trained teachers of *gurmukhi* and *gurbani,* who conveyed to the wider community the tools and primary content of religious education.

G. N. Leitner, the first principal of Oriental College, Lahore, has made a series of interesting references to what was taught in these seminaries. In his *History of Indigenous Education in the Punjab,* he gives a detailed account of the training of a Sikh teacher (*bhai*), saying that it included the learning of *gurmukhi* grammar and the following texts: the *Adi Granth,* the *Dasam Granth,* selections from the *janam-sakhi,* and the *gurbilas* literature, Bhai

Gurdas' *vars,* the *Adhayatam Ramayana,* the *Hanuman Natak,* the *Ramcharitmanas,* the *Vishnu Purana,* and the *Vasishtha Purana,* all available in *gurmukhi* script. The *bhais* were also expected to master elementary Sanskrit. As for *gianis,* they were trained in the *nyaya* system of logic and in Vedantic philosophy.[16] At this time, rest houses (*bungas*) that had been founded in the vicinity of the Golden Temple also became centers of considerable learning, as one can see from the fact that several influential works were produced there, for example, Rattan Singh Bhangu's *Prachin Panth Prakash,* Bhai Santokh Singh's *Suraj Prakash,* and Giani Sant Singh's commentary on the *Ramcharitmanas* of Tulsidas.[17] Fields such as musicology (*rag vidya*), calligraphy, and medicine (*ayurveda*) were also taught in the *bungas.*

To sum up, while fighting for the Sikh *raj* and afterward, the Sikh community managed to support a fairly sophisticated educational program. Many Sikh villages had a *gurmukhi* school, which was part of the local *gurdwara,* and supported a *bhai* qualified to offer the basic tools of Sikh education. While these schools were sustained by local Sikhs, larger centers of learning, the *akharas, bungas,* and *taksals,* ran on royal patronage and the support they received from various Sikh chiefs. Apparently the network was sufficiently dense that in several instances large donations of land were offered to the Nirmala ascetics for setting up new centers of Sikh learning, but these were refused as unnecessary.[18] Other donations, of course, were accepted, and the tradition of establishing new centers continued. Dharamdhuja, for example, the famous Nirmala *akhara* at Patiala, was created in 1861 through the support of the Sikh chiefs of Patiala, Nabha, and Jind.[19]

With the annexation of the Sikh *raj* by the British in 1849, modern Western education was introduced into the Punjab. As it interacted with local patterns of Sikh education, the results came in two stages. At first British models tended to cause a breakdown in indigenous Sikh education at the village level, though the foreign impact was not sufficient to damage such central institutions as the Damdami Taksal, which is still functioning today.[20] Then, however, a more positive result ensued: a system of modern education for Sikhs that was a curious blending of the old Sikh tradition and the new Western system. This amalgam is prominently represented by such institutions of learning as Khalsa College, Amritsar.

This new blend of educational traditions was endorsed by Sikh leaders of the time because it opened doors to such opportunities as employment in the British police force and civil service. More importantly, however, it was seen to provide a congenial and healthy environment for the inculcation of Sikh principles and social values in the younger generation. In this regard, Gerald Barrier has rightly highlighted the emphasis placed by founders of the Singh Sabha upon the boarding school as an instrument for training future Sikh leaders.[21] The residential setup of Khalsa College provided an opportunity for teachers to mingle with students and make them aware of what Singh Sabha leaders considered to be the degraded state of Sikhism, and consequently work for restoring Sikhism to its pristine purity. Thus from the founders' point of view, the Khalsa College and the new system of Sikh education were a continuation of genuine Sikh education, if in a changed environment. Western subjects and methods were not thought to conflict with traditional ideals; they were added on as ways to stimulate the further progress of the community.

In this new framework, the indigenous Sikh system and the Western educational system worked closely together. One must remember that it was a command (*hukamnama*) issued from the Golden Temple that initiated the fund-raising drive that made possible the establishment of Khalsa College in Amritsar.[22] Keeping with the tradition of sponsoring the religious cause of Sikh education, Sikh chiefs and common folk alike contributed handsomely, and the college was founded the very same year, 1892. This support for Khalsa College continued whenever the need arose, and the role of the British in urging on local chiefs was always of great consequence. A significant juncture was reached in 1904 when a Conference was called under the presidentship of Maharaja Hira Singh. It led to the establishment of an endowment fund for the college that soon reached Rs. 1,530,477. In addition to this, 300,000 rupees were collected for the building fund.[23] Sikhs wholeheartedly supported the college and in return expected it to nurture the religious and political leadership of the community.

Khalsa College, Amritsar, was for men, but female education was also given due attention. The first Sikh college for women, another community-supported project, was established at Ferozepur in 1892, the same year in which Khalsa College was brought into being. Bhai Takhat Singh, the leading light behind the project, and his wife were interested in giving a religious education to Sikh women that would prepare them effectively to nurture Sikh children and provide general guidance within the context of Sikh family life. As with the Khalsa College, the motive behind this Sikh Kanya

Mahavidyala was an emphasis on the correct transmission of Sikh values to the younger generation. At least in the mind of Bhai Takhat Singh, the project took a logical place in the history of Sikh educational efforts, and he went out of his way to keep the college a community venture, by refusing government grants. He traveled to Singapore and Hong Kong to acquaint the Sikh communities there with his work and collect funds to keep the college financially viable. When returned from his trip, he reported that he had "Rs. 50,000, and the goodwill of the Sikhs overseas."[24]

As Sikhs moved into the twentieth century, other institutions of higher learning were founded along the same lines and with the same and similar supporting agencies. Among them, Sikh National College, Lahore, was built on land donated by Dera Sahib, the historic Sikh *gurdwara* in Lahore. And Khalsa College, Bombay, was built at the request of Dr. B. R. Ambedkar. This time funds came from the main *gurdwara* located at Guru Nanak's birthplace in Nankana Sahib.[25]

During this period the Chief Khalsa Diwan, the prime Sikh organization to emerge from the Singh Sabha revival, developed the Sikh Educational Conference and used it effectively as a forum for focusing the Sikh community's concern for education. Its mode of operation was simple but extremely successful. When the Sikh Educational Conference started in 1908, there were only seven Khalsa Schools, but, by 1947, 340 Sikh schools had been founded with its help.[26] Typically the educational committee of the Chief Khalsa Diwan would call a meeting under the auspices of a local *gurdwara,* where Sikh intellectuals would make speeches emphasizing the need for Sikh education, and an appeal for funds would be made to the congregation (*sangat*) of the *gurdwara.* The *gurdwara* would add the required amount to donations that had already been collected by the Sikh Educational Conference, and a school would be started. The number of schools that were founded by this method indicates the vigorous response given by local communities to these appeals in the cause of Sikh education.

In the postpartition phase of Sikh history, this concern for education was translated into the founding of some of the preeminent centers of modern-day university education in the Punjab: Punjabi University, Patiala, and Guru Nanak Dev University, Amritsar. Whatever the official understanding of these places, Sikhs saw them as Sikh institutions. The credentials of the first vice chancellors—Bhai Jodh Singh at Patiala and Bishan Singh Samundari at

Amritsar—clearly suggest as much. Both these men had a long and fruitful association with Sikh education before they assumed the leadership of these new universities.

Sikhs saw the founding of Guru Nanak Dev University, in particular, as a major Sikh event. It was understood as the fulfillment of the dream that Khalsa College could develop into a full-fledged university. This idea was first floated in the 1920s by G. A. Wathen, a British principal of the Khalsa College.[27] Although the Khalsa College was to continue to function independently with a separate governing board, the university was seen as the concretization of the dream that it should be expanded. The physical proximity of the two institutions and the appointment of Bishan Singh Samundri, who at that time was the principal of Khalsa College, as the first head of the university supported the Sikh community's general perception of the close relationship between the two.

In addition to these major universities, numerous Khalsa colleges and schools were established with the help of the local *gurdwaras* and grants from rich Sikhs. Such grants were not confined to the Punjab itself. Principals of colleges in the Doaba region, which sent so many Sikhs overseas, commonly made trips abroad to collect donations from Sikhs who had previously resided in their particular areas or had been students at their colleges. Between 1966 and 1975, the centenaries of the births of Guru Nanak and Guru Gobind Singh and of the martyrdom of Guru Tegh Bahadur provided appropriate occasions for the opening of new Sikh educational institutions. Many Sikhs saw the building of a college or a school as the best tribute to the memory of their Gurus. Although often overlooked, the significance of these twentieth-century educational institutions and of the forums that created them is immense.

It was, in fact, at such a forum—the Sikh Educational Conference of the Chief Khalsa Diwan, held in March 1981—that a naturalized American Sikh made the claim that the Sikhs were to be understood as a distinct nation and were therefore entitled to an independent state, which he called Khalistan.[28] Similarly it is the Khalsa colleges, as places of religiopolitical learning, that have served as the major setting in which the Sikh Student Federation has developed over the past few decades. Of course, not all of the formidable Sikh resistance to the present political structure in the Punjab can be attributed to forces that grew up as a consequence of the educational legacy established by the Singh Sabha and its successors. The indigenous Sikh system that preceded the colonial period survived in all its purity in the *taksal* of Sant Jarnail Singh

Bhindranwale at Chowk Mehta. This institution represents the continuity of more than two and a half centuries of Sikh learning, and Sant Bhindranwale found his direct descent from Baba Dip Singh, the first head of the Damdami Taksal, to be a major source of inspiration. Yet Sant Bhindranwale could never have achieved what he did if he had not become closely associated with the Sikh Student Federation, which grew up not in a seminary (*taksal*) setting but in the Sikh colleges of the Punjab that fulfilled the Singh Sabha's dream of blending modern education with *khalsa* beliefs. Had these two visions of Sikh education not coalesced, we might not have seen the current drive for greater Sikh autonomy in modern Punjab.

Sikh Studies in a Western Academic Environment

When Sikhs began to emigrate from the Punjab they, like any other first-generation immigrant group, were initially concerned with establishing themselves in basic ways. This meant financial viability and the bringing of wives and families from the Punjab. With the arrival of families, the issue of the passing on the Sikh heritage to the children in an alien environment became a pressing one, and by the 1970s in Britain and North America, there was a concerted effort to think about ways and means to accomplish this goal.

The first indication of the establishment of a Sikh community, however small, was the founding of a *gurdwara*. Once established, the *gurdwara* served as the major center where communal thinking and action took shape. It also served as the central place for social activity and provided a natural environment for the transmission of the Sikh heritage to each new generation. I remember the *gurdwara* atmosphere in Southall, England, in the mid-1970s, where vehement appeals were made to the parents after the *bhog* (the completion of the service) to speak Punjabi at home and to teach *gurmukhi, gurbani,* and Sikh history to their children. It always reminded me of the Singh Sabha days; after all, the aims of the *Khalsa Samachar,* an important Sikh newspaper at the turn of the century, were no different. As stated in its opening issue, the *Khalsa Samachar* aimed to "propagate Sikh religion, education, Punjabi language, and Gurmukhi."[29] There were other parallels too. Just as the Singh Sabha worked to reclaim and reorient Sikh identity by shedding brahmanical accretions to Sikhism, so modern Sikh communities like the ones in Southall were trying to resist the cultural incursions that now came into their homes from a newly adopted alien environment.

The issue of maintaining the Sikh heritage has been a high priority with several private Sikh organizations. In this regard the Sikh Foundation of Palo Alto, California, under the leadership of Dr. Narinder Singh Kapany, deserves special mention. It has for some time attempted to "disseminate information regarding religion, culture, history, philosophy, literature, and art of the Sikhs"[30] by organizing lecture series and sponsoring publications related to Sikh themes. The Sikh Foundation was the first organization to support programs in Sikh studies at American institutions of higher education. These were, coordinately, the University of California, Berkeley, and the Graduate Theological Union, with whom the foundation co-sponsored conferences on Sikh studies in 1976 and 1987. Both conferences were held in Berkeley. As the Sikh population in other parts of the United States has become denser, other foundations and organizations have also gone to work at imparting Sikh education in a Western environment.

The basic forum for Sikh education in North America, however, remains the *gurdwara,* where Sikh children are taught *gurmukhi* and *gurbani.* In most large congregations, these programs are a permanent feature of the *gurdwara* routine. Many devoted individuals have offered their service to this cause, but the general feeling persists that more disciplined training is required. This has resulted in the organization of residential summer camps, which offer an opportunity to teach young Sikhs a complete Sikh way of life. Each day begins with the morning recitation of the *Japji* and closes with the *Kirtan Sohila,* the traditional evening prayer. All through the day, children are taught Sikh history and the religious ideas of Sikhism. The Sikh children I have spoken to seem to enjoy these camps. They easily make friends with other Sikhs—friendships for which they have often yearned in local schools where no other Sikh children are in attendance. They return home having learned much more in a group environment than their parents could teach them in individual family settings.

The most ambitious project of this sort is the Khalsa school at Vancouver, where a total immersion in Sikh education is made possible for local Sikh children during the regular school year. The school has expanded from small beginnings to the point where it now runs classes from kindergarten to the ninth grade and has two hundred students.[31] Recognized by the British Columbia Ministry of Education, it offers a regular academic program that is supplemented by an extra hour of Sikh teachings (*gurmat*) daily. The film that has been produced about the school makes one point abundantly clear: Sikh boys are very happy there.[32] From filmed interviews, it emerges that these children were uncomfortable in the Canadian public school system because of their fellow students' inability to respond positively to the Sikh religious symbols of uncut hair and the turban. This school is an important Sikh response to the issue of Sikh education in North America, but it remains to be seen how effectively its graduates will be equipped to handle their lives in Canadian society.

The period following 1984 in the life of the Sikh diaspora is often seen by outsiders as a time when overseas Sikhs took a leading role in demanding a separate state for the Sikhs and publicized issues of human rights in the Punjab in international forums. This view rightly emphasizes their initiative but fails to take full account of the ways in which such Sikhs responded to new events in the Punjab. It needs to be pointed out that the single most significant result of those happenings was the incredible boost they provided to overseas efforts to articulate, define, consolidate, and perpetuate the religiopolitical identity of Sikhs. The work of earlier decades has gathered considerable momentum since 1984 as new ways and means to improve the teachings of a Sikh way of life to Sikh children have been devised.

The dramatic events of the 1980s also demanded the projection of a clearer image of the Sikh community to non-Sikh Canadians and Americans. This deeply felt need forced the Sikh community to look beyond its own boundaries. In consequence it began to establish liaisons with leading North American universities, prodding them to introduce Sikh studies into their academic programs. Such efforts have met with considerable success. Within a brief span of few years, the teaching of Sikhism and Punjabi has been introduced at the University of British Columbia, Columbia University, the University of Michigan, and the University of Toronto.

Of course, there have been some difficulties along with the successes. The first outburst of enthusiasm, which resulted in the establishment of an independent program at the University of British Columbia, has not always been maintained, owing to the relatively unstable state of local Sikh communities, on the one hand, and the large amounts required by American universities to establish such programs, on the other. Furthermore the construction of new *gurdwaras* and the expansion of old ones that followed 1984 have pushed many Sikh communities into financial commitments that are hard to sustain. In addition there is the fact that the University of British Columbia project was partly financed by the Canadian government, while most American universities would have to fund a program of the same nature with their own monies or those donated by interested Sikhs. Financial issues, then, are an important aspect in the starting of a curriculum for teaching Sikh studies in North American universities, but other aspects deserve to be recognized as well.

After the British Columbia experience, it emerged that a key issue for the Sikh community would be its inability to influence the process of decision making that would go into the appointment of a teacher of Sikh subjects, the establishment of a Sikh curriculum, and the determining of its approach. Universities are emphatic about maintaining their authority to appoint persons who meet proper academic criteria and are often felt to be entirely unresponsive to the sentiments of the Sikh community on this question. If the issue is handled sympathetically, however, I believe it can be resolved to the satisfaction of both parties: some place can be given to the community in this shared venture without compromising the academic integrity of the university.

No one aware of the tradition of Western academic life can question that the right to make an academic appointment should remain the prerogative of the university, but in this instance it seems sensible to insist that some provision be made whereby it would be expected that an incumbent scholar of Sikh studies would spend some part of his or her time with the community that raised funds for the endowment supporting the position. Such an involvement would be of benefit not just to the surrounding Sikh community but to the university itself in that it would form an aspect of its program in outreach and development. Of course, some scholars might resist taking on this dual role, but to others it undoubtedly would seem a worthwhile challenge. Even from a purely academic point of view, after all, what could be more appropriate for a teacher than to spend time with the community of his or her scholarly interest? At present, this can perhaps most effectively done by a Punjabi-speaking Sikh scholar, but I foresee a time—and not far off—when non-Sikh scholars will also be able to go to *gurdwaras* and talk profitably about the Sikh tradition with community members. On many occasions such interchanges have already occurred.

A second problem to be dealt with is the feeling that seems to have been generated of late among university-based scholars to the effect that religious scholarship within the Sikh community is out of tune with the way religion is taught at North American universities. The conference held at Los Angeles in December 1988[33] and the review articles in *World Sikh News* condemning the results of a historical approach to Sikh studies[34] do give that impression. But it would be a great mistake to conclude that this view represents the mainstream Sikh academic outlook.

Since the establishment of Punjabi University, Patiala, and Guru Nanak Dev University, Amritsar, Sikh studies have moved comfortably into university departments. These departments have produced such leading scholars of Sikhism as Professors Fauja Singh and Ganda Singh at Patiala and Professor J. S. Grewal at Amritsar, to name but a few. They have demonstrated their strong commitment to the assumptions and methods of the Western academic approach to historical scholarship while maintaining their identity as Sikhs. The tradition of critical scholarship among Sikhs can be traced back further, too—especially to the early part of the century when Karam Singh was raising basic questions relating to the *janam-sakhi* literature.[35] In addition, Professor Taran Singh points to the debt to Western modes of thought that was displayed by such major Singh Sabha scholars as Bhai Jodh Singh, Principal Teja Singh, and Professor Sahib Singh, all of whom introduced Western styles of scriptural interpretation into the Sikh context and went on to do important analytical work in Sikh theological thought.[36]

It is true that Professor W. H. McLeod's works have been criticized in *Sikh Review*[37] and, more recently, in *World Sikh News*,[38] but the reception often accorded his works in the universities of the Punjab shows that this is only part of the picture. Professor Ganda Singh, for example, wrote a forthright editorial defending the rigorous approach and controversial findings of McLeod's *Guru Nanak and the Sikh Religion* in *Panjab Past and Present*, the major historical journal published by Punjabi University.[39] The same issue carried a long review of the book in which it was observed that "the unique attempt by the author has been generally lauded [in] rationally minded Sikh circles." The reviewer hoped that this pioneering and monumental work would form a permanent part in the annals of studies of Guru Nanak and Sikhism.[40]

Of at least equal significance to a review such as this is the fact that Guru Nanak Dev University published a Punjabi translation of the second section of the book, under the title of *Guru Nanak de Udesh* ("Teachings of Guru Nanak").[41] This translation carried forewords with glowing tributes from Professor J. S. Grewal and Bishan

Singh Samundari, the vice chancellor of the university. Similarly, a major review of Professor McLeod's *Early Sikh Tradition* in Guru Nanak Dev University's *Journal of Regional History* began with the following words: "Professor W. H. McLeod's scholarship is formidably impeccable. A man has never carried such a numerous collection of Janamsakhis in his head since the first one was written. His achievement is likely to stand unrivalled in the future too."[42] More recently, I. J. Singh of New York University found McLeod's writing to be "refreshing and lucid in its brevity and clarity, and free of the conceptual cobwebs and convoluted verbosity that often define religious writing."[43]

There is no doubt that it is disturbing to many Sikhs to have deeply held convictions put under the critical microscope and found wanting in historical truth, but Sikhs are not alone in having to deal with that discomfort. My personal belief is that if other traditions have survived the onslaught of critical scholarship for more than a hundred years and are reasserting themselves effectively, the Sikhs have very little to be worried about.

For that to happen, though, Sikhs who see the value of historical, critical scholarship need to participate more effectively in the debate within the community. They cannot simply be silent and allow others to shape the understanding of these issues in forums that extend beyond the university. It may be time-consuming for university-based Sikh scholars to invest their energy in explaining the motivations and methods of a critical point of view, but the long-term benefits are great. On the basis of my experience with local Sikh communities, I am sure that a sympathetic hearing is possible. I have discussed this issue in great detail with Amarjit Singh Grewal, Baldev Singh, Jagjit Singh Mangat, and Rabinder Singh Bhamra, influential Sikh leaders in the New York area, and with many others. All understand the tension between the requirements of scholarly inquiry and those of religious faith, yet strongly support historical scholarship.

It is important for leaders of the Sikh community to understand that a distinction can and must be made between the teaching of Sikhism in a university setting and its promotion at the *gurdwara* level. The one is teaching *about* the Sikh tradition in the hopes of making possible a dispassionate understanding of it; the other is the act of actually teaching the tradition, with all the passion that belief and commitment require. These are distinguishable activities, but they are not mutually exclusive. After all, in the very act of teaching about a tradition, one promotes it; one shows how it could have claimed the allegiance of so many people for so long. As Sikh subjects are taught in American universities, American students will understand Sikhs better, and Sikh students who take these courses will emerge with a more profound understanding of their tradition. They will then be in a position to act as responsible interpreters of it and to serve as agents of change when the need arises.

If universities are open to the suggestion that contacts with local Sikh *gurdwaras* can in some way represent part of the academic load of a scholar of Sikh studies, it will be of benefit to many. At Columbia, I have been involved in arranging to send students from a Sikhism class to spend a weekend with local Sikh families, and the experience was one of great satisfaction. The students returned happy to have had a firsthand chance to learn Sikh tradition by spending time in a family environment and visiting the *gurdwara* with them. Sikh families, for their part, were thoroughly gratified to participate in this modest venture and were eager to offer assistance to young Americans attempting to understand their religion. The cultivating of such relationships ought to stimulate further the Sikh community's participation in conferences and other outreach activities sponsored by the university and will attract bright Sikh students to the university concerned, thus helping it achieve a culturally diverse student body.

With every passing year it becomes clearer that the Sikh community resident here is part of North American society first and foremost. It looks not to Amritsar or Patiala for its primary educational guidance but to educational institutions on this continent. It should therefore support the cause of Sikh studies by establishing programs in leading universities where a new generation and new breed of scholars and teachers of Sikhism can be trained. Such programs, in their routine functioning, will generate up-to-date translations of Sikh scriptures and produce other source material required for teaching Sikhism. They will also build documentation centers and other library collections related to the field. As this happens, the Sikh tradition will move quickly toward becoming a major actor on the stage of world religions, a status it now demands and rightly deserves.

The Sikh community thus stands at an historic juncture, for North American universities are now open to the prospect of initiating programs in Sikh studies. In harmony with their vigorous tradition of supporting education, Sikhs should seize the opportunity and become creatively involved. That will be the best gift Sikhs in North America can give to their own generation and generations to come, and it will serve as a fitting way to honor the memory of those tireless Sikh scholars who worked to establish the major educational institutions of the modern Sikh community a century ago. Sikhs have been in the diaspora for about a hundred years. What better way to celebrate that centennial than by opening the way to teaching and research in Sikh studies at the leading universities of North America? A commitment to do so would symbolize at once the Sikh community's coming of age in the modern world and its keenness to preserve and propagate a priceless heritage from the past.

Notes

1. *Sikhi sikhia gur vichari. Asa di var, mahala* 1. *Adi Granth,* p. 465. All references given here are from *Shabdarth Sri Guru Granth Sahib Ji* (Amritsar: Shiromani Gurdwara Prabandhak Committee, 1969). The pagination being uniform, the reference would apply to any standard edition of the *Adi Granth.*

2. *The Japji, Adi Granth,* p. 7.

3. *Sri ragu, mahala* 1, *gharu* 5, *Adi Granth,* p. 25.

4. *Gur gian dipak ujiara. Ragu gauri cheti mahala* 5, *Adi Granth,* p. 210.

5. *Gur gian anjanu sachu netri paria. Majh mahala* 3, *Adi Granth,* p. 124. *Gian anjanu guri dia agian andher binasu. Gauri sukhmani, mahala* 5, *Adi Granth,* p. 293.

6. *Gian khargu le man siu lujhe. Maru mahala* 1, *Adi Granth,* p. 1022. *Gian khargu kari kirpa dina dut mare kari dhai he. Maru solahe mahala* 5, *Adi Granth,* p. 1072.

7. *Asa mahala* 1, *chaupade, Adi Granth,* p. 356.

8. *Vaid parahi te vad vakhanai binu Hari pati gavai. Sorathi mahala* 1, *gharu* 1, *tituki, Adi Granth,* p. 638.

9. *Japji, Adi Granth* pp. 1–8.

10. *Sarag mahala* 5, *Adi Granth,* p. 1226.

11. Gursharan Kaur Jaggi, ed., *Varan Bhai Gurdas* (Patiala: Punjabi University, 1987) is the standard edition of the text.

12. Taran Singh, *Gurbani Dian Viakhia Pranalian* (Patiala: Punjabi University, 1980), p. 47.

13. Taran Singh, *Gurbani Dian Viakhia Pranalian,* pp. 455–58.

14. For this information I am indebted to a conversation with Dr. Mrigendra Singh, a well-known scholar of the Nirmal *panth.*

15. Fauja Singh, ed., *The City of Amritsar* (New Delhi: Oriental Publishers, 1978), p. 218.

16. G. W. Leitner, *History of Indigenous Education in the Punjab Since Annexation and in 1882* (1882; reprint, Patiala: Language Department, 1971), pt. 1, pp. 34–35, and pt. 4, p. 2.

17. Giani Sant Singh, *Ramayana* (Bankipur: Kharag Vilas Press, 1897). This edition was printed in *devanagari;* the original *gurmukhi* edition was published in Lahore in 1894.

18. Giani Gian Singh, *Nirmal-Panth-Pradipka* (Kankhal: Nirmal Panchaiti Akhara, 1962), pp. 67–68. I am indebted to Dr. Mrigendra Singh for a photocopy of the book.

19. Bhai Kahn Singh, *Gurushabad Ratnakar Mahan Kosh* (1931; reprint, Patiala: Language Department, 1981), pp. 38–39.

20. G. W. Leitner, *History of Indigenous Education,* pt. 1, p. 36.

21. N. Gerald Barrier, "In Search of Identity: Scholarship and Authority among Sikh in the Nineteenth Century Punjab," in Robert I. Crane and Bradford Spangenberg, eds., *Language and Society in Modern India* (Delhi: Heritage, 1981), p. 21.

22. Khushwant Singh, *A History of the Sikhs,* 2 vols. (1963; rev. ed. Delhi: Oxford University Press, 1991), p. 144.

23. *Panjab Past and Present* 7, no. 1 (1973), p. 78.

24. *Panjab Past and Present* 7, no. 1 (1973), p. 106.

25. Durlab Singh, *The Valiant Fighter: A Biographical Study of Master Tara Singh* (Lahore: Hero Publishers, 1942), pp. 153, 157.

26. *Panjab Past and Present* 7, no. 1 (1973), p. 68.

27. *Panjab Past and Present* 7, no. 1 (1973), p. 81.

28. Paul Wallace and Surendra Chopra, eds., *Political Dynamics and Crisis in Punjab* (1981; rev. ed. Amritsar: Guru Nanak Dev University Press, 1988), p. 37.

29. Joginder Singh, "Khalsa Samachar: Some of its Major Concerns and Approach, 1899–1920," in *Studies in Sikhism and Comparative Religion* 6, no. 1 (1987), p. 172.

30. *Activities Report* (967–68) of the Sikh Foundation, 586 College Avenue, Palo Alto, Calif. 94306.

31. Prospectus of the Khalsa School, 6010 Fraser St., Vancouver, B.C. (not dated).

32. I am grateful to Joginder Singh Kalsi of Toronto for sending me a videotaped version of this film.

33. The published proceedings of the conference are available in Jasbir Singh Mann and Harbans Singh Saraon, eds., *Advanced Studies in Sikhism* (Irvine: Sikh Community of North America, 1989). I am grateful to Dr. Mann for sending the book to me.

34. *World Sikh News,* July 8, 1988; July 22, 1988; September 15, 1989; September 22, 1989; September 29, 1989; June 29, 1990.

35. Karam Singh Historian, *Katak ke Visakh* (Ludhiana: Lahore Book Shop, 1912).

36. Taran Singh, *Gurbani Dian Viakhia Pranalian,* p. 15.

37. W. H. McLeod, *Guru Nanak and the Sikh Religion* (Oxford: Clarendon Press, 1968).

38. *Sikh Review* (Calcutta), February–March, 1970.

39. *Panjab Past and Present* 4, no. 2, (1970), pp. l–x.

40. Gurcharan Singh and Karamjit Singh, "Guru Nanak and the Sikh Religion," in *Panjab Past and Present* 4, no. 2 (1970), pp. 435–41.

41. Mohanjit Singh, trans., *Guru Nanak de Udesh,* (Amritsar: Guru Nanak Dev University Press, 1974), pp. 1–115.

42. Surjit S. Hans, "Early Sikh Tradition," in *The Journal of Regional History* 1 (1980), pp. 175–88.

43. *South Asia in Review* 16 (1992), p. 54.

6

Sikh Studies in North America: A Field Guide

*

Joseph T. O'Connell

Sikhs and their way of life have been studied in some of the better American and Canadian universities for most of the current century, but largely from such perspectives as British imperial history or the Indian nationalist struggle. Likewise, many textbooks and courses on religion still treat Sikh religion as a subtopic of their Hindu chapter, or as a Hindu-Muslim hybrid. One major exception, it should be noted, was the 1934 volume by the American scholar, John Clark Archer, *Faiths Men Live by,* which devoted a chapter to "The Sikhs and Their Religion."[1]

Unlike Great Britain, neither the United States nor Canada has had a longstanding engagement in the study of the Indian or South Asian subcontinent. What study of Asian religion there was in North America before the 1960s sometimes was carried out in church-related institutions. The quality of scholarship on non-Christian religion in such institutions could be very high—as, for example, at the Hartford Theological Seminary, where Clinton H. Leohlin and H. A. L. Gleason taught Sikh religion and Punjabi language respectively some years back—but often the treatment of such subjects was neither rigorous nor sympathetic.

With the exception of a very few major universities, there was little intensive language-based study of South Asian civilization in North America before the establishment of a number of South Asian language and area centers at certain American universities in the 1950s and 1960s. These are financed in part by the federal government through the National Defense Education Act and by Public Law 480 counterpart funds for study and research in India. What older programs there were, for the most part, concentrated on classical Indic studies, effectively removing from serious attention the religion and history of peoples such as the Sikhs, whose scriptural and literary traditions are recorded in vernacular languages.[2]

In Canada likewise, there never has been a national commitment to South Asian scholarship based on the vernacular languages. This is so despite the Shastri Indo-Canadian Institute programs and despite substantial classical Sanskrit and Indian historical scholarship going back many years in certain universities.[3]

Thus, the meager development of Punjabi language and area scholarship (and likewise of Sikh history and religion) is hardly an isolated phenomenon nor an indication of anti-Sikh, anti-Punjab bias in academia. In part the problem lies in the sheer multiplicity of vernacular languages such as Punjabi (and their respective cultural regions) in South Asia, and in part it stems from the relatively low political and economic priority of South Asia for both Canada and the United States. This situation makes it all the more crucial that there be cooperation between scholars who are concerned about South Asia and persons outside academia who share such concern. This chapter discusses some major attempts to build up resources for Sikh and Punjabi studies at American and Canadian universities, in an effort to provide a brief account of progress that has been made to date and problems that have been encountered along the way.

Sikh Studies in the United States

Pioneering work in the development of Sikh Studies in the United States began in California, home to the earliest concentration of immigrant Sikhs in the country. The University of California, Berkeley (UC Berkeley hereafter), through its Center for South and Southeast Asia Studies and its successor, the Center for South Asia Studies, and the Graduate Theological Union (GTU hereafter), also at Berkeley, have been the main academic focuses for this development.

Among the early Sikh settlers in California were members of the politically radical Ghadar Party, which for many years sponsored efforts to end British rule in India. Its center was in San Francisco; papers relating to the Ghadar party are in the library of UC Berkeley. In 1970 the university's Center for South and Southeast Asia Studies began a research project based on these documents and additional Ghadar material, including oral histories.

Independently of the university, there came into being in San Francisco the Sikh Foundation, headed by Dr. Narinder Singh Kapany. Though by profession a physicist and laser scientist, Dr. Kapany became director of the Sikh Foundation and publisher of its journal, *Sikh Sansar*. Through cooperation between the Sikh Foundation and scholars at the GTU and UC Berkeley, significant developments in Sikh studies have come about, including the first major scholarly conference on Sikh religion and history in North America. Held in 1976, this Sikh studies conference featured several distinguished scholars from overseas, including the historian of Sikh and Mughal relations, J. S. Grewal (then of Guru Nanak Dev University, Amritsar; later director of the Indian Institute of Advanced Study) and W. H. McLeod. The volume of papers from the 1976 Sikh Conference at Berkeley, edited by Mark Juergensmeyer and N. Gerald Barrier under the title *Sikh Studies: Comparative Perspectives on a Changing Tradition,* quickly became a point of reference and source of encouragement for scholars.

In 1987 UC Berkeley, the GTU, and the Sikh Foundation hosted a second international conference, drawing scholars from India, England, the Netherlands, Australia, Belgium, Mexico, Canada, and the United States. Like its 1976 predecessor, this conference took up the fundamental task of assessing the current status of scholarship in all fields of Sikh studies. It treated history, literature, religion, Sikhs abroad, contemporary issues in Sikh studies, and "an agenda for Sikh Studies in the next decade."

In April 1989, UC Berkeley hosted a series of lectures on Sikh and Punjabi studies by Christopher Shackle, the well-known scholar of Punjabi and Urdu at the University of London's School of Oriental and African Studies. The GTU had made a more substantial effort at introducing instruction on Sikhism a decade before— at the time of the first Berkeley conference—by inviting W. H. McLeod to teach there for a term. Nonetheless, there are at present no courses on Sikh religion or religion per se, nor on Punjabi language, at the GTU or UC Berkeley, although one doctoral student at the GTU, Gurudharam Singh Khalsa, has completed a dissertation on Guru Ramdas. The departure in 1989 of Mark Juergensmeyer from UC Berkeley and the GTU has been a serious loss to the cause of Sikh studies in Berkeley. Only very recent events suggest that UC Berkeley may be reconsidering its stance, in response to a proposal that Punjabi language be taught.

The one university in the United States that has made significant progress toward an endowment for a chair in Punjabi and

Sikh studies is the University of Michigan at Ann Arbor. The main initiative for the drive has come from Sikh donors, but with close cooperation from the university's side. A committee of three Sikhs bears primary responsibility for fund raising, which has extended beyond Michigan into the rest of the United States, and even Canada.

The first University of Michigan course supported by interest from the endowment was offered in 1988–89: elementary Punjabi language. It was followed in 1989–90 by a course in intermediate Punjabi. Students so far are mostly of Sikh family background and number about a half dozen per class. The current plan is to alternate these two courses on a two-year cycle. In addition to the language course, Michigan offered in the summer of 1989 a course on Sikh religion instructed by Surjit Singh Dulai of Michigan State University. Michigan has now appointed Pashaura Singh a visiting Assistant Professor with its endowment for Sikh studies. He will be integrated into other programs sponsored by the Center for South and Southeast Asian Studies by teaching a certain number of courses that extend beyond Punjabi and Sikhism as such.

The University of Michigan has organized three conferences in conjunction with local Sikhs; and papers from the second conference were published in 1988 as *The Sikh Diaspora: Migration and the Experience beyond Punjab,* a book edited by N. Gerald Barrier and Verne A. Dusenbery. The last of these conferences was, in contrast with the preceding two events, not a strictly academic affair. It included, along with the more professional academic papers, talks more on the order of testimonials or tributes to Guru Nanak and his teachings. All but one of the fifteen speakers were Sikhs; not all were university scholars. The kinds of issues that academics choose to address and the ways they treat them are not necessarily interesting to the public at large nor are they expressly designed to be inspirational. Hence it proved more feasible for all concerned that Sikh leaders in Michigan organize conferences like this on their own. Importantly, though, the university did extend its cooperation, by way of providing university facilities, formal sponsorship, and professors to serve as moderators of sessions.

Columbia University in New York is the first East Coast university to offer courses in Sikh religion; it also offers courses on Punjabi language and literature. Since 1988–89 the combined religion departments at Columbia and Barnard have annually offered a course specifically on Sikh religion. In addition, Columbia's Department of Middle East and Asian Languages and Cultures now offers basic and intermediate Punjabi and an advanced sequence comprising "Introduction to the Sacred Language of the Sikhs" and "Major Texts of Sikhism." The instructor for all these courses is the versatile and acute Gurinder Singh Mann (M.T.S., Harvard), who has completed his doctorate at Columbia with a dissertation on the earliest collections of Sikh sacred literature.

While there are able and sympathetic senior scholars at Columbia, it would not have been possible to mount most of these courses were it not for substantial and timely financial support by Sikh donors in the greater New York area. What makes this tangible support all the more noteworthy is that contributions have been coming from a rather large number of individuals. To date, these have been coordinated through the Sikh Cultural Society associated with the Richmond Hill *gurdwara*, in Queens.

Columbia has demonstrated its interest in scholarship on the Sikhs in other ways as well: invitations to such scholars as W. H. McLeod to lecture there; publication of the latter's recent book, *The Sikhs: History, Religion, and Society;* and the conferences on "Sikh Studies: The American Agenda" (March 1989), from which the present book comes, and on major themes in Sikh theology, a year later.

In ways such as this the Columbia program is raising—and thinking out loud about—fundamental issues in the academic study of Sikh religion. Through its conferences and publications and by arranging for the participation of Gurinder Singh Mann at a number of meetings of the American Academy of Religion, Columbia has begun to be a major force in building up Sikh studies in the United States. If an endowment can be secured for the creation of a permanent position there—a current goal—such efforts promise to be a continuing part of the development of Sikh studies on this continent.

As a way of concluding this section on the development of Sikh studies in the United States, I wish to acknowledge that other American scholars not associated with the three main centers have done important work in the field. The sort of approach taken by N. Gerald Barrier to the subject of Sikh history can nicely be judged by his contribution to this volume. He is joined at the University of Missouri by Paul Wallace, a political scientist specializing in matters Punjabi. Harvard University's Center for the Study of World Religions has served over the years as a magnet for scholars affiliated with Punjabi University, Patiala, especially through Harvard's special relationship with Professor Harbans Singh, who has lectured at Harvard and served as a visiting scholar on more than one occasion. Professor Darshan Singh, a younger scholar, has also been a visiting scholar at the Harvard Center, and one doctoral student, Nripinder Singh, has been trained there. Notable among other American scholars of Sikhism are Professors Bruce LaBrack of the University of the Pacific, Verne Dusenbery of Reed College, Jane Singh and Margaret Gibson of UC Berkeley, Karen Leonard of UC Irvine, Joan Jensen of New Mexico State University, and Arthur Helweg of Western Michigan University—all specialists on the Sikh diaspora; and Guninder Kaur (a.k.a. Nikky Singh), an interpreter of Sikh scripture at Colby College, and Gene R. Thursby in religious studies at the University of Florida. Finally, a summer course on Sikhism has twice been offered at Richard J. Daley College in Chicago. The instructor is Robert Engles of the Department of Sociology, who organized this course with the help of Balwant Singh Hansra of the Department of Education.

Sikh Studies in Canada

Similar resources exist in Canada. At McGill University, political scientist Baldev Raj Nayar has published on twentieth-century Punjab political history, emphasizing relations between the Sikhs and the Arya Samaj, and at the University of Ottawa, Amarjit Singh Sethi has published works on *nam-simaran* and edited the *Journal of Comparative Sociology and Religion,* which has a Sikh emphasis.

Ian Kerr of the University of Manitoba does research on Sikhs in relation to nineteenth- and twentieth-century Punjab economic and social history. In addition to these students of Sikhs in the Punjab, several Canadian scholars have taken an interest in the experience of Sikhs abroad. Among them are Josephine Naidoo, a social psychologist at Wilfrid Laurier University, whose research on immigrant women in Canada has included many Sikhs; John Spellman, an historian at the University of Windsor, who has published on the Ghadar movement; and Norman Buchignani and Doreen Indra at the University of Lethbridge, who have, with Ram Srivastava, recently published a book prominently treating Sikh ethnic experience in Canada: *Continuous Journey: A Social History of South Asians in Canada.* Hugh Johnston, a historian of the British Empire at Simon Fraser University, is the author of *The Komagata Maru Incident;* he teaches a course on Sikh history.

Two universities—the University of British Columbia and the University of Toronto—have made efforts to supplement these scattered resources by creating full academic programs in Sikh studies, and much of the rest of this chapter concerns what they have done.

It is fitting that the first chair of Punjabi and Sikh studies in Canada—indeed North America—should be based at the University of British Columbia (hereafter UBC) since Vancouver has served as port of entry for Sikh immigrants to Canada since 1903 and has been the scene of epic struggles between Sikhs and their sometimes less than willing hosts. The more immediate history of the chair at UBC, however, goes back only to 1984, when students there expressed interest in Punjabi language study and in an eventually wider range of related Punjabi and Sikh topics. Contact was made with the Federation of Sikh Societies of Canada, based at Ottawa, which was interested in establishing at some university a center for Sikh studies in Canada. Student initiative, university cooperation, and indications of community financial support all concentrated at UBC, which quickly became the favored site.

Coincidentally, the government of Canada (through the Multiculturalism Division of the Office of the Secretary of State—an office that in the Canadian government deals with domestic cultural matters, not foreign relations) was implementing a policy of contributing up to $350,000 each toward the cost of endowing ethnic studies chairs at Canadian universities. An ethnic community desiring such support would itself have to raise a comparable amount and a university would have to be willing to design and manage such a chair. The requisite amount was raised rapidly by a federation from Sikh donors—most, though not all, from British Columbia—and in 1984 a formal agreement was signed by the government, the university, and the Federation of Sikh Societies establishing a chair of Punjabi and Sikh studies in the Department of Asian Studies at UBC. Its mandate includes Sikh religion, history, and philosophy, the Sikh experience in Canada, and Punjabi language and literature.

There then ensued a tantalizing delay of about two years as the fate of the Punjabi and Sikh studies chair evidently became linked to considerations quite other than academic ones. Traumatic events of 1984 and 1985—the assault on the Golden Temple, the assassination of Indira Gandhi, the massacre of Sikhs in Delhi, the crash of an Air India flight from Toronto—and continuing controversies over Khalistani separatism, Canada-India trade and diplomatic relations, alleged human rights violations in India, and alleged terrorist activity in Canada created a climate in which any official gesture relating to Sikhs could be considered sensitive. The chair was put on hold. Only in 1987, when an extradition treaty between India and Canada was signed, did the government of Canada release the funds it had pledged.

UBC moved quickly to recruit the first incumbent of its new chair, opting for a younger scholar rather than a seasoned veteran. What they could expect to gain by that kind of choice was energy, training in the most up-to-date methods of scholarship, generational affinity with the bright young men and women who would be his/her students—and all this for half the cost in salary of a more renowned senior scholar. If the initial choice proved to be a happy one, the position could be converted to a tenure-stream appointment, and the individual would then become the prime architect of the program in Punjabi and Sikh studies at UBC.

The selection fell upon Harjot Singh Oberoi, a native of Delhi who was just finishing his doctorate in history at the Australian National University in Canberra. Oberoi's primary expertise is in historical and social scientific research on Sikhs in relation to Hindus in the late nineteenth and early twentieth centuries. His first book, on the restructuring of Sikh institutions and beliefs in the nineteenth century, is expected to be published in 1993. At UBC, he teaches an undergraduate course on the history of the Sikhs from the time of Guru Nanak to the Akali movement of the 1920s. He also offers a graduate course on religion and nationalism in modern Indian history and teaches two courses in Punjabi language.

Few teaching materials exist for elementary Punjabi, so those that Oberoi and other scholars in his position (Elena Bashir and Pashaura Singh at Michigan, Gurinder Singh Mann at Columbia) develop will be an important contribution to the field. In the future, Oberoi plans to collaborate with Professor Kenneth Bryant, a specialist on medieval and other forms of Hindi, to offer a course that would concentrate on the language (or cluster of dialects) of the *Guru Granth Sahib*. At present Bryant himself reads with advanced students selections from the *Granth*. A substantial gift from an anonymous local donor enabled the university to hire a part-time language-teaching assistant in Punjabi.

UBC's program has several other aspects. Its newly donated Asa Johal fellowship (worth $9,000 a year) supports a Ph.D. or M.A. candidate in the field. Its library now has more than five thousand volumes in Punjabi and on Sikh religion and history, thanks in part to a large consignment of books acquired from the University of Washington when the latter closed out its Punjabi collection. As with the Library of Congress's Public Law 480 program in the United States, the Shastri Indo-Canadian Institute provides a regular input of books in Punjabi and English that are printed in India. The UBC library also has an arrangement with the India Office Library in London for duplicating a supply of nineteenth-century publications. And in 1988 UBC held a small conference on "Sikh Literature and Language: Text and Transmission." It seems clear by all academic indicators that the Chair of Punjabi and Sikh Studies at the University of British Columbia, in its short period of operation, has been making solid progress.

Toronto is the other Canadian focal point for Sikh studies. A large, growing, and economically successful population of recent Sikh immigrants lives in the area. Scholarly contact between the University of Toronto and the Sikhs goes back at least to 1969, the 500th anniversary of Guru Nanak's birth, when Dr. Jarnail Singh of Toronto brought visiting Sikh scholars to meet scholars at the university. It was not until 1983, however, at a Sikh students' anniversary celebration in honor of Guru Nanak, that students requested that a university course on Sikh religion be offered. The Department of Religious Studies agreed that upon my return from a 1984–85 sabbatical leave I would offer such a course on a trial basis and under the "Special Topics" rubric. In the following year (1986) the presence of W. H. McLeod as Visiting Commonwealth Fellow made it possible to offer three courses on Sikh religion taught by an expert in the field. That Commonwealth visit was crucial for giving impetus to Sikh studies at Toronto in several respects. It exposed numerous undergraduate and graduate students to Sikh studies; and subsequently two doctoral candidates (one a Sikh, one a non-Sikh) took Sikh religion for specialization. Even the noncredit evening course had the unanticipated value of fostering face-to-face exchange between the Sikh men and women enrolled in the course and another group of students, officers of the Metropolitan Toronto Police seeking to understand the cultural background of the Toronto Sikhs! McLeod's presence was the catalyst for a major conference in February of 1987 and its companion volume, *Sikh History and Religion in the Twentieth Century*. This conference, apart from its scholarly contribution, had considerable impact on Canadian perceptions of the Sikhs, as typified by the request of the Canadian Secretary of State for External Affairs, the Honorable Joe Clark, to address the gathering. The activities of 1986–87 led to an initiative by the university and private donors, mostly Sikhs, to fund the appointment in subsequent years of visiting professors of Sikh religion and history and instructors in the language of the *Adi Granth.*

During his Commonwealth visit to Toronto, McLeod was invited to speak at other Canadian and American universities, thus raising the profile of Sikh scholarship across the continent. He was the first scholar of Sikh religion to be asked to deliver the annual American Council of Learned Societies' Lectures on the History of Religion, subsequently published as *The Sikhs: History, Religion, and Society,*[4] but while participating in a conference at New York in early February 1987 (virtually on the eve of the Toronto conference that was to have been the culmination of his Commonwealth visit) McLeod was felled by a nearly fatal stroke. Timely assistance by friends and doctors in New York and the dedicated support of his wife Margaret fortunately resulted in gradual recovery of speech and mobility over many difficult months. By 1988 he was able to return to Toronto as the second Visiting Professor of Sikh History and Religion, though with restricted activities at first. In the fall of 1992 he is serving his fifth term as Visiting Professor at Toronto.

The Visiting Professorship in Sikh History and Religion at Toronto has been based on an informal understanding among those in the university most concerned to foster Sikh and Punjabi studies and those individuals beyond the university (notably Gary Singh and his associates, Suresh Bhalla and Amrik Singh) most committed to fund-raising for this cause. The understanding was to try bring a distinguished scholar to Toronto for one term for five years—if availability of scholar and funding would permit—and then review the experience and decide what to do next.

This arrangement has enabled two eminent scholars, J. S. Grewal and W. H. McLeod, to train up doctoral candidates at Toronto, assist doctoral candidates elsewhere on the continent, and foster in many Sikh and non-Sikh students respect for scholarship on the Sikh tradition. The first Visiting Professor of Sikh History and Religion (January–April, 1988), J. S. Grewal, organized a seminar on "Religious Identity and Political Articulation in the Punjab," in which Indian, American, and Canadian scholars participated. He also introduced a new course on "Sikh History: 16th to 18th Centuries" while teaching the graduate and undergraduate courses on Sikh religion. McLeod then added a course on "The Sikhs in the 19th and 20th Centuries." Both have lectured widely, precipitated and helped organize conferences and seminars, written and edited publications, and provided expert consultation within and beyond academia.

In 1991 the teaching of "classical Punjabi" (i.e., the language of the *Adi Granth*) as a credit course within the university's Department of Linguistics was begun, with Pashaura Singh as first instructor; Mrs. Jugraj Baath succeeding him in 1992–93. Once again it was a combination of Sikh student urging and generous response by Sikh donors that made this course possible.

There have been other facets of Sikh and Punjabi studies in the University of Toronto, including a symposium (April 1986) on "Evolution of the Sikh Community: in India and in Canada" featuring W. H. McLeod and Norman Buchignani of the University of Lethbridge, cosponsored by the Rabindrananth Tagore Lectureship Foundation (Toronto) and St. Michael's College. The university's School of Continuing Studies offered in 1987 a noncredit course (mounted in collaboration with T. Sher Singh and the Toronto-based Macauliffe Institute of Sikh Studies) on "Sikh Religion and the Arts" by Guninder Nikky Singh of Colby College. Pashaura Singh taught a noncredit course (1988) on the "Sacred Language of the Sikhs" offered by the Macauliffe Institute in collaboration with the university's Centre for South Asian Studies. Senior tutors in French at St. Michael's College have assisted Dr. Jarnail Singh in his translation of the *Guru Granth Sahib* in French, and individual professors have participated in Sikh conferences and other functions over the years.

Toronto, contrary to a widely shared impression, does not have a chair in Sikh and/or Punjabi studies. One option to be considered in the current review of the Toronto initiative in Sikh and Punjabi studies, of course, would be commitment to raise an endowment for a permanent chair or professorship. A drive designed to be completed in time for the tercentenary of Guru Gobind Singh's formulation of the *khalsa* might be especially fitting. But there are many other options, including more modest ones. The main sustaining or constraining factor will the extent of support by those private donors who want to see Sikh and Punjabi studies at the core, not on the periphery, of Canada's largest university.

Beyond—and Against—the University

There is a network of quite vocal Sikhs who are evidently troubled by the thrust of rigorous critical scholarship as it bears upon the religious history of the Sikhs. The main voices—some quite strident, others more modulated—are from Delhi and the Punjab, but they have like-minded associates in the United States who have influence in Sikh associations and access to community publications.

Their point of view was recently expressed at a conference on Sikh studies convened on the campus of California State University at Long Beach. Though it met on university grounds, the conference seems not to have been organized by university staff on an academic basis, but by volunteers—notably orthopedic surgeon Jasbir Singh Mann and Harbans Singh Saraon—on a community basis. Of those participants whose papers appear in the swiftly published conference volume, all but two are Sikhs. Several, but not all, of the Sikhs are (or were before retirement) academics in Indian colleges or universities. The two American Sikh contributors have professional academic qualifications, but not directly related to Sikh studies. Others write on Sikh matters, though not as professional academics.

The conference had two objectives: "presenting a clear image of Sikhism and its institutions" and "evoking interest in the community for the urgent need of organizing a Center of Higher Learning and Research in Sikh Studies."[5] The second proposal, it would seem, does not refer to a university-based center but to one owned and controlled by Sikhs. Plans for such a center, to be located in the Los Angeles area and directed by Dr. Mann, are in their seminal stage.

One can hardly fault the principle of there being such a center, or several such, to project what Sikhs consider to be the truth about Sikhism and its institutions. Christian denominations and groups in North America have established many centers, schools, colleges, theological institutions, and even universities over the years. Within such religiously oriented institutions, it has been customary for the sponsoring group to exercise close control over the content of teaching and even research on the group's religious heritage. What is noteworthy, however, is that, apart from the theological institutions (and in some respects they too), those denominational schools and centers that have grown in academic stature have tended to transform themselves into precisely the kind of multidisciplinary institutions of critical scholarship (where believers and nonbelievers, adherents and nonadherents work—and argue—side by side) from which the Long Beach group seem to wish to distinguish their proposed center.

To build an accredited Sikh institution of higher learning complete with professors, students, and degrees would be a demanding and costly enterprise, all the more so if done independently of any existing theological school or university. The Long Beach proposal presumably envisages a more modest entity. Such a center might do all sorts of constructive things: produce instructional and inspirational books, booklets, course outlines, audio-visual resources; assemble archives for immigration history; offer language instruction; commission translations. It might be a haven for thoughtful conferences and retreats; if in the right surroundings, it might serve as a youth camp. If done well, any number of such centers—indeed existing *gurdwaras* themselves—could provide much positive service for the local Sikh *panth* and for the wider communities within which Canadian and American Sikhs reside.

Such a center, however, for all its potential for community service, is not apt to have much impact on international academic work about the Sikhs. If one wants "higher" or "advanced" scholarship on Sikh history and religion—and all the more so if one wants to have any positive impact on the direction of mainline North American scholarship on the Sikhs—then the universities are where one must expect to look. That is where Canadian and American scholars get their training and where they find professional employment. That also is where bright young Sikh men and women get their higher education—including whatever higher education they may receive in Sikh religion and history—not in community centers, not in colleges and universities in Delhi or the Punjab.

There was also, however, a negative side to the Long Beach agenda, as perusal of the conference volume will confirm. What seems to unite the various papers is not so much a vision of what constructive work an independent Sikh center for learning and/or research might do, but the negative bond of being united against contemporary academic research on Sikh history and religion. One scholar, Noel King, expresses dissatisfaction with modern critical scholarship as a whole as it bears on religion, but others seize upon the work of McLeod, Grewal, or Oberoi. Criticism of scholarship is, of course, a legitimate scholarly exercise, if done fairly and competently, and some important issues deserving further discussion and research are highlighted.[6] Unfortunately, however, some of the Long Beach writers fail to distinguish between criticizing views and imputing motives or otherwise attacking the personal integrity of those with whom they disagree—or just do not fathom.

As many contributors to the present book have emphasized, there is always some degree of tension between those committed to scholarly inquiry and those committed to preserving and fostering a religious way of life. The tension may be located within the same person, who in one respect is a man or woman of religious faith and in another respect a rigorous scholar examining his/her own religious heritage. The tension may also emerge between scholars who are not adherents of the religious tradition they study and scholars who are.[7] Finally, it may appear between scholars—whether adherents or not—and nonscholar believers. Human life is complex. The challenge for human maturity is to understand and manage such tensions in constructive and creative ways.

Let us hope that through reasonable encounter and intelligent goodwill the tensions inherent in the relationship between scholarship and the religious experience of Sikhs in North America may prove to be creative ones. If so, we may anticipate a maturing of understanding and cooperation among all concerned with building up Sikh studies and enhancing the Sikh way of life in Canada and the United States.

Notes

1. For observations on the parallel situation in Britain see W. Owen Cole, "The Sikh Diaspora: Its Possible Effects on Sikhism," in Joseph T. O'Connell, Milton Israel, and Willard G. Oxtoby, eds., with W. H. McLeod and J. S. Grewal, visiting eds., *Sikh History and Religion in the Twentieth Century* (Toronto: South Asian Studies, University of Toronto, 1988), pp. 388–402.

2. For an outline of the past and present state of South Asian studies in the United States (mostly), see the brochure edited by Joseph E. Schwartzberg, *South Asian Studies in North American Higher Education* (Ann Arbor: Association for Asian Studies, 1989).

3. For a thorough account of the state of Indian studies in Canadian universities, see Edward C. Moulton, *Indian Studies in Canada* (Calgary: Shastri Indo-Canadian Institute, 1984). For Sikh Studies in Canada, see Joseph T. O'Connell, "Sikh Studies and Studies of Sikhs in Canada," *Studies in Sikhism and Comparative Religion* (New Delhi) 5, no. 2 (October 1986), pp. 154–73, or his "Sikh Studies in Canada," in Bhakshish Singh Samagh and Gurcharan Singh, eds., *Proceedings of the Sikh Conference 1980* (Ottawa: National Sikh Society of Ottawa, 1985), pp. 49–92. For the Shastri Institute, see Michael Brecher's historical review and assessment of the institute published as an occasional paper by the Centre for South Asian Studies, University of Toronto.

4. *The Sikhs: History, Religion, and Society* (New York: Columbia University Press, 1988).

5. J. S. Mann and H. B. Saraon, eds., *Advanced Studies in Sikhism* (Irvine, Calif.: Sikh Community of North America, 1989), Preface, p. viii .

6. McLeod, in fact, provided a point by point rejoinder to a set of objections, but the editor failed to include it in the conference volume or in any other Sikh community publication to which he had access. McLeod's essay in this volume gives readers a fair sense of the tone—and some of the substance—of his response.

7. For a classic statement of the subtle (and constructive) implications of involving both the adherent/believer and critical observer in the academic study of religion, see Wilfred Cantwell Smith, "Comparative Religion: Whither and Why?" in Mircea Eliade and Joseph Kitagawa, eds., *History of Religions: Essays in Methodology* (Chicago: University of Chicago Press, 1966), reprinted (with minor revisions) in Wilfred Cantwell Smith, *Religious Diversity,* essays edited by Willard G. Oxtoby (New York: Harper and Row, 1976).

7

Teaching the Sikh Tradition:
A Course at Columbia

*

Gurinder Singh Mann

In 1988 an interesting situation emerged when Columbia University decided to introduce a course on Sikhism into its curriculum. I had moved to Columbia the previous year to work for a doctorate in Indic religion and history, and the idea that I would be called upon to teach Sikhism had not even crossed my mind. Although I had four years of formal work in comparative religion behind me, I had never had the opportunity to take courses on Sikhism myself. Nonetheless I was offered the chance to teach it, and I took up the challenge, convincing myself that at least my lack of formal training would free me to arrive at an independent understanding of what I think is most valuable in my own tradition. Also, of course, I would have to think through the question of how that tradition could effectively be communicated to students of comparative religion and history, and in a Western setting.

Preliminary Concerns

I began planning the syllabus with three matters in mind: the possible constitution of the class, the various approaches that would do justice to the Sikh tradition, and the basic resource materials available to study Sikhism in English. Given the rich diversity of the student body at Columbia, I hoped that the class would attract undergraduates in two broad groups: (1) students with a faint newspaper idea of Sikhism, who would come out of general interest and would need to acquire basic factual information to

understand the tradition; and (2) those whose parents or grandparents had been immigrants from South Asia and who could be
expected to come with a set of presuppositions that would need to be
consistently addressed. I also hoped to have a few advanced students of Indology and wanted to make sure they would receive material of sufficient depth to find the class a worthwhile experience.
I was aware that Sikh students, if any, would require special handling: they would be expected to grow beyond their inherited perceptions toward a more critical way of looking at their religion.

In weighing a thematic approach against a historical one, I
chose the latter, for several reasons. Most important, perhaps, was
the fact that Sikhs themselves have tended to see their tradition in
historical terms. Sikhs are one of the very few religious communities to emerge from Indian soil that possess an acute self-
consciousness of their communal history. This dimension of Sikh
thinking manifests itself in the prayer (*ardas*) offered twice a day in
Sikh *gurdwaras* and homes. The prayer is a straight record of the
historical memories of the community, with all its trials and tribu-
lations, and the record is constantly updated. In 1947, for example,
when the Punjab was partitioned, new references to historical Sikh
shrines now separated from the community were added to the
prayer, along with an appeal for divine sanction in opening free passage to them. In the mid-1980s, memories of "Operation Bluestar"
were similarly introduced, complete with references to the martyrs
(*shahid*) who had sacrificed their lives for the future of the community. As the readings in the course would demonstrate, Sikhs understand these events not just as historical data but as sacred
memories that emerge from history and show Sikh history to be
part and parcel of a divine design.

Fortunately, the Sikh emphasis on history fits in well with
Western modes of thinking. At Columbia, in particular, there is a
strong historical orientation to studies in religion, and the history
department is large and influential. I could therefore expect most
students to come to a course on Sikhism with some basic interest in
history. Sikhism lends itself to being treated in this fashion since it
originated in the full light of history. So I took a straightforwardly
chronological approach, presenting the tradition as an almost ideal
case study of how religious communities originate and generate
their central institutions—doctrine, loci of authority, holy places,
scripture. At the same time I pursued a sort of counterpoint, showing how theological and historical symbols, once evolved, exerted a
strong force on later history.

As for the readings, I hoped they would work at two levels. Some would present more or less straightforward statements of the tradition's self-perception—its religion, literature, and major historical events and personages. Others, both ancillary source materials and theoretical essays, would enable us to address certain specific issues in all their complexity. The overall attempt was to offer a critical reconstruction of the tradition by placing it firmly in the socioreligious context of the Punjab, where it grew up. This meant giving special attention to the distinct elements in the Sikh tradition, while at the same time looking at Sikh ideas and institutions in relation to those of Hinduism and Islam.

At first I used Harbans Singh's *Heritage of the Sikhs* (Delhi: Manohar, 1983) and Khushwant Singh's *A History of the Sikhs,* 2 vols. (Princeton: Princeton University Press, 1963, 1966) as basic texts. Recently, however, I have replaced them with J. S. Grewal's *The Sikhs of the Punjab* (1990), which forms a part of the new Cambridge History of India. *The Sikhs of the Punjab* enables a teacher of Sikhism to provide students with a rigorous critical overview of Sikh religious history. W. Owen Cole and Piara Singh Sambhi's *The Sikhs: Their Religious Beliefs and Practices* (Boston: Routledge and Kegan Paul, 1978), being written for Western students, fills in important introductory information. Finally, W. H. McLeod's *Textual Sources for the Study of Sikhism* (1984; reprint, Chicago: University of Chicago Press, 1990) supplements both these books by presenting accurate and readable translations of the most valuable primary sources.

To pursue the course's second level—greater detail and fuller context—I selected position papers on various controversial issues and constructed my lectures around them. These readings offered me an opportunity to present to students the complexities of the problems addressed and to show that just because Sikhism has a relatively well defined point of origin in the early sixteenth century does not mean its history is cut and dried, with clear answers available for all basic questions. These readings tended to come from recent books on confined topics and from scholarly journals.

Course Outline

The following is an updated version of the syllabus I used in 1989, with a schedule of lectures, readings, and topics for reflection and discussion.

A. LECTURE OUTLINE

Week 1. I. Introduction to the course.
    II. Medieval Punjab: its socioreligious milieu.
   2. I. Guru Nanak: his life and teachings.
    II. Guru Nanak: teachings (continued).
   3. I. The consolidation of the early Sikh community.
    II. The *Adi Granth.*
   4. I. Beginnings of Sikh militancy.
    II. The institution of the *khalsa.*
   5. I. Early Sikh literature.
    II. Early Sikh literature (continued).
   6. I. Evolution of the community during the eighteenth century.
    II. Maharaja Ranjit Singh.
   7. I. Anglo-Sikh wars and the fall of Sikh kingdom.
    II. The British and the Sikhs.
   8. I. The Singh Sabha, and the Chief Khalsa Diwan.
    II. Sikh literature of the turn of the century.
   9. I. The Gurdwara Reform Movement.
    II. The Gurdwaras Act and diversity within the Sikh *panth.*
  10. I. The Sikhs and national politics.
    II. The partition of the Punjab.
  11. I. The place of women in Sikhism.
    II. Sikh ceremonies and festivals.
  12. I. Sikh art and architecture.
    II. Sikhs in the diaspora.
  13. I. & II. Sikhs in independent India.
  14. I. & II. What is happening in the Punjab?

B. READING ASSIGNMENTS

Week 1.

I. Ainslie T. Embree, "Locating Sikhism in Time and Place: A Problem for Historical Surveys," and Mark Juergensmeyer, "The Forgotten Tradition: Sikhism in the Study of World Religions," in Mark Juergensmeyer and N. Gerald Barrier, eds., *Sikh Studies: Comparative Perspectives on a Changing Tradition* (1979), pp. 13–24; 55–64.

Consider: How is Sikhism perceived by historians of religion? How can these perceptions be explained? What special use can the study of Sikhism serve in the study of religion?

II. Fauja Singh, ed., *History of the Punjab,* vol. 3 (1972), pp. 1–20.

J. S. Grewal, *Guru Nanak in History* (1969), pp. 62–140.

J. S. Grewal, "Historical Geography of the Punjab," *Journal of Regional History* 1 (1980), pp. 1–14.

Consider: What impact did the continuous invasions have on life in the Punjab? How was Hindu society affected by the advent of Islamic rule? What were the key religious beliefs prevalent among different communities and how did these varied beliefs interact with each other?

Week 2.

I. John S. Hawley and Mark Juergensmeyer, *Songs of the Saints of India* (1988), pp. 63–88.

W. H. McLeod, *Guru Nanak and the Sikh Religion* (1969), pp. 148–226.

Consider: Guru Nanak's understanding of the nature of God, the world, and human beings in it. What, according to McLeod, are the major components of the "Sant synthesis"?

II. Fauja Singh, "Guru Nanak and the Social Problem," in Harbans Singh, ed., *Perspectives on Guru Nanak* (1975), pp. 141–50.

J. S. Grewal, *From Guru Nanak to Maharaja Ranjit Singh* (1982), pp. 6–30.

Bruce B. Lawrence, "The Sant Movement and North Indian Sufis," in Karine Schomer and W. H. McLeod, eds., *The Sants: Studies in a Devotional Tradition of India* (1987), pp. 359–73.

S. A. A. Rizvi, "Indian Sufism and Guru Nanak," in Harbans Singh, ed., *Perspectives on Guru Nanak* (1975), pp. 191–222.

Charlotte Vaudeville, *Kabir* (1974), pp. 81–110.

Consider: How do you understand Guru Nanak's emphasis on ethical and moral values, and how can this be related to the description of Sikhism as a religion of interiority? How does the Sikh theological vision relate to that of Islam?

Week 3.

I. Fauja Singh, *Guru Amar Das: Life and Teachings* (1979), pp. 106–42.

J. S. Grewal, *Guru Nanak in History* (1969), pp. 287–313.

Surjit Hans, "The Sikhs of the Early 16th Century," *Journal of Sikh Studies* 10, no. 1 (1983), pp. 33–41.

W. H. McLeod, *The Evolution of the Sikh Community* (1975), pp. 1–19.

Consider: the evolution of key doctrinal concepts like that of the *guru* and the *shabad*. What socioreligious institutions developed during the sixteenth century and what is their relation to the doctrinal content of Guru Nanak's teachings? What developments took place in the social constitution of the Sikh community during this period?

II.   Frits Staal, "The Concept of Scripture in the Indian Tradition," in Mark Juergensmeyer and N. Gerald Barrier, eds., *Sikh Studies: Comparative Perspectives on a Changing Tradition* (1979), pp. 121–24.

W. H. McLeod, *The Evolution of the Sikh Community* (1975), pp. 59–82.

Consider: the theological status of the *Adi Granth* by relating it to the concept of *shabad* in Guru Nanak. How does one relate its status in Sikh worship to parallel concepts in Hinduism and Islam?

Week 4.

I.   Fauja Singh, "Development of Sikhism under the Gurus," in Fauja Singh et al., *Sikhism* (1969), pp. 1–39.

Ganda Singh, trans., " 'Nanak Panthis' in *Dabistan-i-Mazahib*," *Panjab Past and Present* 1, no. 1 (1967), pp. 47–71.

Jagjit Singh, "The Jats and Sikh Militarization," in his *Perspectives on Sikh Studies* (1985), pp. 85–102.

Consider: the factors responsible for bringing the Sikh community to the path of militancy after the death of Guru Arjan. How does Guru Tegh Bahadur's success in the Malwa region relate to his martyrdom in Delhi?

II.   Fauja Singh, "Foundation of the Khalsa Commonwealth—Ideological Aspects," *Panjab Past and Present* 5, no. 1 (1971), pp. 197–210.

J. S. Grewal, *From Guru Nanak to Maharaja Ranjit Singh* (1982), pp. 78–88.

W. H. McLeod, *Who is a Sikh?* (1989), pp. 23–42.

Consider: the historical circumstances surrounding the institution of the *khalsa* and its effect on the Sikh community's self-understanding and history. What is the nature of the relation between the teachings of the early Gurus and the *khalsa*?

Week 5.

I. W. Owen Cole, *Sikhism and its Indian Context, 1469–1708* (1984), pp. 166–212.

Fauja Singh, "The Image of Guru Nanak in Bhai Gurdas," *Proceedings, Punjab History Conference* (March 1969), pp. 68–76.

Surjit Hans, *A Reconstruction of Sikh History from Sikh Literature* (1988), pp. 178–220.

W. H. McLeod, trans., *The B40 Janam-Sakhi* (1980).

W. H. McLeod, *Early Sikh Tradition* (1980), pp. 237–69.

Consider: the nature and purpose of early Sikh literature. Why are these documents problematic for the reconstruction of the life of Guru Nanak? What do these writings tell us about the beliefs of the early Sikh community?

II. Gopal Singh, *Thus Spake the Tenth Master* (1978), pp. 148–61.

Surjit Hans, *A Reconstruction of Sikh History from Sikh Literature* (1988), pp. 245–65.

W. H. McLeod, trans., *The Chaupa Singh Rahit-Nama* (1987), pp. 31–49.

Consider: the theology of the *Zafar Nama*. What do you think is the main complaint of Guru Gobind Singh against the Emperor? Under what circumstances does he find the use of violence justified? What do you understand by the *khalsa rahit*? What are its implications for Sikh identity?

Week 6.

I. Mazaffar Alam, *The Crisis of Empire in Mughal North India* (1986), pp. 134–203.

Bhagat Singh, *Sikh Polity in the Eighteenth and Nineteenth Century* (1978), pp. 45–155.

Ganda Singh, *Baba Banda Singh Bahadur* (1976), pp. 1–40.

J. S. Grewal, *From Guru Nanak to Maharaja Ranjit Singh* (1982), pp. 100–6; 127–38.

W. H. McLeod, *Who is a Sikh?* (1989), pp. 43–61.

Consider: the community's adjustment to the absence of the living spiritual mentor after the death of Guru Gobind Singh. What were the heroic ideals developed by the *khalsa*? How was political power understood by Sikhs, and how did it shape their conception of the state?

II. Bhagat Singh, *Sikh Polity in the Eighteenth and Nineteenth Century,* (1978), pp. 156–92.

Fauja Singh, *Some Aspects of State and Society under Ranjit Singh* (1982), pp. 36–79.

J. S. Grewal, *The Reign of Maharaja Ranjit Singh* (1981), pp. 1–37.

B. Hasrat, *Life and Times of Ranjit Singh* (1977), pp. 374–438.

Consider: the factors that brought Maharaja Ranjit Singh to the forefront. What was his attitude toward other religious communities? What was the importance of the institution of the *khalsa* army in the Sikh kingdom?

Week 7.

I. Fauja Singh, *After Ranjit Singh* (1982), pp. 1–19; 244–90.

B. Hasrat, *Anglo-Sikh Relations 1799–1849* (1968), pp. 240–346.

Consider: whether British intrigue or inner dissension among the Sikh aristocracy was responsible for the fall of the Sikh kingdom. How is this period perceived in later Sikh history?

II. Ganda Singh, "Indian Mutiny and the Sikhs," *Panjab Past and Present* 12, no. 1 (1978), pp. 103–20.

I. J. Kerr, "The British Relationship with the Golden Temple, 1849–90," *Indian Economic and Social History Review* 21 (1984), pp. 139–51.

Nazer Singh, "Early British Attitude Towards the Golden Temple," *Journal of Regional History* 3 (1982), pp. 87–98.

Consider: the Sikh role in the mutiny of 1857 and its result on the British attitude toward Sikhs. What components of Sikh society were given special attention by the British and why? What were the major development projects assigned to the Punjab and what effect did these have on Sikh masses?

Week 8.

I. G. S. Dhillon, *Researches in Sikh History and Religion* (1989), pp. 69–98.

Ganda Singh, ed., *The Singh Sabha and the other Socio-Religious Movements in the Punjab 1850–1925* (1984), pp. 23–94.

W. H. McLeod, *Who is a Sikh?* (1989), pp. 62–81.

Surjit Singh Narang, "Chief Khalsa Diwan—An Analytical Study of its Perception," in Paul Wallace and Surendra Chopra, eds., *Political Dynamics and Crisis in Punjab* (1988), pp. 70–86.

Harjot S. Oberoi, "From Ritual to Counter-Ritual: Rethinking the Hindu-Sikh Question, 1884–1915," in Joseph T. O'Connell et al., eds., *Sikh History and Religion in the Twentieth Century* (1988), pp. 136–58.

Consider: the factors that shaped the early history of the Singh Sabha. What group provided the movement with its leadership? Did the Singh Sabha revive and redefine an earlier Sikh identity or create one anew? How did the Chief Khalsa Diwan strive to consolidate the community and protect its rights in a fast-changing political environment?

II. N. Gerald Barrier, *The Sikhs and the Literature* (1970), pp. 1–45.

Jarnail Singh, trans., *Ham Hindu Nahin* (1984).

Joginder Singh, "Resurgence in Sikh Journalism: Early Decades of the Twentieth Century," *Journal of Regional History* 3 (1982), pp. 99–115.

Joginder Singh, "Bhai Kahan Singh's Ham Hindu Nahin: Polemic or a Social Document?" *Journal of Sikh Studies* 14, no. 1 (1987), pp. 65–74.

Consider: the key religious and historical concerns of the literature of this period. How did this literature emphasize the distinct character of Sikh doctrine? How did it contribute to the political awakening of the community?

Week 9.

I. Richard G. Fox, *Lions of the Punjab: Culture in the Making* (1985), pp. 79–104.

Kamlesh Mohan, "The Babbar Akalis: An Experiment in Terrorism," *Journal of Regional History* 1 (1980), pp. 142–74.

Mohinder Singh, *The Akali Struggle: A Retrospect* (1988), pp. 1–65.

D. Petrie, "Secret C. I. D. Memorandum on Recent Developments in Sikh Politics (1911)," *Panjab Past and Present* 9, no. 2 (1970), pp. 300–79.

Teja Singh, *Essays in Sikhism* (reprint 1989), pp. 133–75.

Consider: the central effort on the part of the Sikh leadership to confront the *gurdwara* issues. What were the reasons for the breakdown of communication between the Sikh leadership and the British administration? What was the actual relationship of Sikhs with the Indian National Congress?

II. Text of the Gurdwaras Act (1925).

Rajiv K. Kapur, *The Sikh Separatism* (1986), pp. 1–35.

Bhagat Singh, "The Kuka Movement," in Ganda Singh, ed., *The Singh Sabha and the Other Socio-Religious Movements in the Punjab 1850–1925* (1984), pp. 170–79.

Darshan Singh, "How did Nirmalas Preach?" *Journal of Sikh Studies* 5, no. 1 (1978), pp. 147–52.

Kashmir Singh, *Law of Religious Institutions-Sikh Gurdwaras* (1989), pp. 161–216.

W. H. McLeod, *Who is a Sikh?* (1989), pp. 82–98.

Sulakhan Singh, "Udasi Beliefs and Practices," *Journal of Regional History* 4 (1983), pp. 77–98.

Teja Singh, "Are There Sects in Sikhism?" *Panjab Past and Present* 12, no. 1 (1978), pp. 130–41.

John C. B. Webster, *The Nirankari Sikhs* (1979).

Consider: the legal definition of Sikh identity as set out in the Act and its practical implications for diversity within the Sikh community. What is the importance of the Shiromani Gurdwara Prabandhak Committee as the new principal religious institution of the community?

Week 10.

I. Indu Banga, "The Crisis of Sikh Politics (1940–47)," in Joseph T. O'Connell et al., eds., *Sikh History and Religion in the Twentieth Century* (1988), pp. 233–55.

Fauja Singh, "Akalis and the Indian National Congress (1920–1947)," *Panjab Past and Present* 15, no. 2 (1981), pp. 453–70.

Stephen Owen, "The Sikhs, Congress, and the Unionists in British Punjab, 1937–45," *Modern Asian Studies* 8, no. 3 (1974), pp. 397–418.

K. L. Tuteja, *Sikh Politics* (1984), pp. 135–207.

Consider: the tension between the vision of the future that was dominant in the Indian National Congress and the one held by Sikh leaders of the time. What options did the Sikhs have, and how can one understand their decision to join India?

II. Kushwant Singh, *Train to Pakistan* (1956).

S. H. Munto, *Tobha Tek Singh* (1953).

Amrita Pritam, selected poems to be circulated in class.

Division of Hearts, a film on the partition of the Punjab, will be shown.

Consider: the literary response to the tragedy of partitioning of the Punjab. Does the literature help us to understand the sources of intercommunal fury?

Week 11.

I. R. L. Ahuja, "The Education of Girls at the time of Annexation," and Sardul Singh Caveeshar, "The Sikh Kanya Mahavidyala," in Ganda Singh, ed., *The Singh Sabha and the Other Socio-Religious Movements in the Punjab 1850–1925* (1984), pp. 80–85; 110–24.

Beryl Dhanjal, "Sikh Women in Southall: Some Impressions," *New Community* 1, no. 2 (1976), pp. 109–114.

Harbans Singh, "Place of Women in Sikhism," *Khera* 9, no. 3 (1990), pp. 64–71.

Teja Singh, "Woman in Sikhism," in his *Essays in Sikhism* (reprint 1989), pp. 44–49.

Consider: the possible reasons for the discrepancy between the doctrinal position on the status of women and their actual role in Sikh society.

II. Davinder Kaur Babraa, *Visiting a Sikh Temple* (1981)

W. Owen Cole, "Sikh Festivals," in Alan Brown, ed., *Festivals in World Religions* (1986).

Jogendra Singh, *Sikh Ceremonies* (reprint 1968).

Madanjit Kaur, "Ceremonial Practices and Celebrations," *The Golden Temple, Past and Present* (1983), pp. 118–41.

Short films on *armit sanskar* and a Sikh wedding ceremony will be shown in class.

Week 12.

I. Mulk Raj Anand, ed., *Maharaja Ranjit Singh as Patron of Arts* (1981), pp. 2–8;109–20.

W. G. Archer, *Paintings of the Sikhs* (1966).

Darshan Singh, ed., *The Sikh Art and Architecture* (1986), pp. 1–46.

Kanwarjit Singh Kang, "Art and Architecture of the Golden Temple," *Marg* (1977), pp. 23–41.

W. H. McLeod, "The Development of Sikh Art," in his *Popular Sikh Art* (1991), pp. 3–31.

Pritam Singh, "Keertana and the Sikhs," *Journal of Sikh Studies* 3, no. 2 (1976), pp. 5–9.

II. W. Owen Cole, "The Sikh Diaspora: Its Possible Effects on Sikhism," in Joseph T. O'Connell et al., eds., *Sikh History and Religion in the Twentieth Century* (1988), pp. 388–402.

Verne A. Dusenbery, "A Century of Sikhs beyond Punjab," and Arthur W. Helweg, "Sikh Politics in India: The Emigrant Factor," in N. Gerald Barrier and Berne A. Dusenbery, eds., *The Sikh Diaspora: Migration and the Experience Beyond Punjab* (1989), pp. 1–28; 305–36.

Harish K. Puri, "Ghadar Movement: An Experiment in New Patterns of Socialization," *Journal of Regional History* 1 (1980), pp. 120–41.

K. S. Sandhu, "Sikhs in Singapore," *Khera* 9, no. 3 (1990), pp. 54–63.

Manjit Singh Sidhu, *The Sikhs in Kenya* (n.d. [1980?]), pp. 1–99.

Consider: What part of the Sikh community moved out of the Punjab and why. What problems did the early Sikh immigrants have in their adopted lands? What future do Sikhs foresee for themselves in these new lands?

Week 13.

I. Gurnam Singh, *A Unilingual Punjabi State and the Sikh Unrest* (1960), pp. 26–88.

B. R. Nayar, "Sikh Separatism in the Punjab," in Donald E. Smith, ed., *South Asian Politics and Religion* (1966), pp. 150–75.

Joyce Pettigrew, "The Growth of Sikh Community Consciousness 1947–1966," *South Asia* (December 1980), pp. 43–62.

Consider: the emergence of the demand for a Punjabi state. Why was it opposed both by the national leadership and by Punjabi Hindus? What was the attitude of different segments within the Sikh community to this demand?

II. The text of the Anandpur Sahib Resolution.

Paul R. Brass, *Language, Religion and Politics in North India* (1974), pp. 277–336.

G. S. Dhillon, *Researches in Sikh History and Religion* (1989), pp. 127–48.

Harish K. Puri, "Akali Politics: Emerging Compulsion," in Paul Wallace and Surendra Chopra, eds., *Political Dynamics and Crisis in Punjab* (1988), pp. 299–321.

Consider: the reasons given to prove the secessionist nature of the Anandpur Sahib Resolution. How have scholars understood the apparent secularization of Akali politics at this time? How did the Green Revolution influence this political stance?

Week 14.

I. and II.   Amrik Singh, ed., *Punjab in Indian Politics: Issues and Trends* (1985), pp. 1–28.

K. R. Bombwall, "Sikh Identity and Federal Polity: A Critique of [the] Akali Position," in Gopal Singh, ed., *Punjab Today* (1987), pp. 156–66.

Paul R. Brass, "The Punjab Crisis and the Unity of India," in Atul Kohli, ed., *Democracy: An Analysis of Changing State-Society Relations* (1988), pp. 169–213.

Surendra Chopra, "Ethnicity, Revivalism and Politics in Punjab," in Paul Wallace and Surendra Chopra, eds., *Political Dynamics and Crisis in Punjab* (1988), pp. 465–501.

M. S. Dhami, "Punjab and Communalism: A Survey," in Gopal Singh, ed., *Punjab Today* (1987), pp. 123–55.

Ainslie T. Embree, *Utopias in Conflict* (1990), pp. 113–32.

Joyce Pettigrew, "In Search of a New Kingdom of Lahore," *Pacific Affairs* 60, no. 1 (1987), pp. 1–25.

Consider: Sikhs' understanding of themselves as a nation. Is the current Punjab crisis a product of postpartition confrontational politics or do its roots go further back into Sikh history and religious thinking? How far does the label "Sikh fundamentalism" go in explaining the source of current tensions in the state? What are the possible solutions to the present situation and their implications for the future of the Sikh community in the Punjab?

Major Currents in the Course

Many of the broad concerns of the course will be evident simply from a reading of the syllabus, but in other cases it may help to draw out key strands that are only implicit in the general structure of the course. The format was this: I began my lectures with a summary of scholarly positions presented in the assigned readings and then went on to give my views on the issues under discussion. Students were encouraged to ask questions during the lecture itself, and there was frequent and lively discussion. In what follows I will give a review of the positions that tended to emerge on key issues in the study of Sikhism, beginning with its origins.

Starting with McLeod's *Guru Nanak and the Sikh Religion,* we reconstructed Guru Nanak's core theological categories—his emphatic assertion of the unity and uniqueness of God as a personal Lord and Master (*patishahu, sahibu*) who creates and runs the world by his command (*hukam*), principles of justice (*nian*), and grace (*nadar*); and his insistence that the world is not divine, but not illusory either—instead, a place that provides human beings with an opportunity to achieve union with God, which is the goal of all human life. For Guru Nanak, human self-centeredness (*haumai*) is the main obstacle on the way to this union, a flaw that can be overcome by submitting to the command of God (*hukam*) at the personal level while at the social level claiming one's rightful share of things (*haq halal*) and performing service (*seva*) to God and others.

Building on Grewal and Rizvi, however, we departed from McLeod's position on the marginal role of Islam in understanding Guru Nanak's theological and social vision. How else to explain the clarity of Guru Nanak's theocentric universe and his emphasis on a stern ethical code—aspects of his thought that set him apart from contemporaries who were either immersed in the rich texture of the Hindu polytheistic imagination (the *sargun bhagats*) or were monotheists (*muwahids*) with little inclination to cultivate a constructive social vision, like Kabir? In any case, the strong dimension of moral code and personal piety in Guru Nanak's theological vision was clearly determinative as he spent the last twenty years or so of his life at Kartarpur nourishing a community with an all-encompassing texture of spiritual, social, and ethical concerns. This enterprise was not just an attempt to immerse believers in meditation on the name of God (*nam*), but a self-conscious effort to found a community disciplined by formative institutions: a liturgy of collective prayers, a shared community kitchen (*langar*), an ethic of hard work (*ghal khai*) and of sharing its results with others (*dan*), and an emphasis on living a life of honor (*pati*) as an indivisible part of one's social and spiritual obligation. Guru Nanak's care to select a successor before his own death also reveals his acute consciousness of communal needs.

The relation of this upcoming community with the Nath Yogi centers (*tillas*) spread all over the Punjab can best be seen as one of absolute mutual rejection. Yet, by the same token, Guru Nanak's community was not a replica of Vaishnavas gathering in the presence of their God to sing his praises. Sikhs under Guru Nanak's care apparently had a set of theological and communal assumptions quite different from those ordinarily available in medieval Hinduism. Contemporary Sufi centers (*khanqahs*), however, would have stood in closer relation to Guru Nanak's community. The Sufis' vision of a theocentric universe, their ethic of social responsibility, and some of their institutions, in particular the community kitchen (*langarkhana*) and donations for support (*futuh*), all remind one of what Guru Nanak was trying to nourish at Kartarpur.

It appears, then, that early Sikhism possessed a closer affinity to Islam than has frequently been recognized. The oversight is understandable. Most people drawn into the early Sikh community were Hindus, and many of these continued to maintain close ties with caste fellows in the parent Hindu community. Furthermore, the eighteenth-century confrontation between Sikhs and Muslims translated itself into a tendency on the part of the Sikhs to demonize Muslims and reject everything Islamic. This historical tendency became even more marked when marginal groups such as the Udasis and Nirmalas became the official spokesmen of the tradition. For centuries these factors have discouraged an objective analysis of doctrinal and social parallels between Sikhs and Muslims.

Yet there is a difference between recognizing this and propounding a syncretic view of Sikhism—that is, seeing it as an attempt to offer a common ground between Hinduism and Islam, with the conception of the object of worship closer to the Semitic side and the means of worship closer to medieval Vaishnavism. I found it was not easy to get students to see this distinction. On the whole, it was easier to persuade them, on the basis of the *Adi Granth,* that Guru Nanak had a distinct and independent theological vision.

Having laid this foundation, we went on to trace the evolution of the community at both the doctrinal and the social levels. Although the very phrase "doctrinal evolution" is repugnant to many Sikh scholars, who see Sikh truths as eternal and unchanging, Sikhism in fact presents an important case study for students of comparative religion interested in the evolution of religious ideas. In analyzing this evolution, we emphasized its gradual movement, both with respect to ideas in existence before Guru Nanak and with respect to later developments. In particular we found ourselves questioning scholars who insist that the advent of Sikhism constituted a complete break from earlier thinking. Secondly, as I have hinted, we took a definite interest in parallels with Islam, which many recent scholars have missed.

A case in point is the early community's belief in the universality of Guru Nanak's message and his special relationship with God. Much more commonly recognized is the Hindu background for the concept of *guru*, which is used in Guru Nanak's poetry to mean either God or the voice of God as spoken in human heart. Both motifs underwent a definite evolution as subsequent Gurus were invested with Guru Nanak's spiritual authority. Much of this takes place in the *janam-sakhi* literature, which again has been more readily compared with Hindu hagiography than with the hagiographic anecdotes (*tazkiras*) of Sufi saints. The Sufi parallel is at least as close. Taking our cue from McLeod's readings on the *janam-sakhis*, we discussed these documents as a valuable source for understanding the evolving image of Guru Nanak in the community of his followers.

The belief that the living Guru was the representative of Guru Nanak, and that his words, like those of Guru Nanak, were the voice of God, resulted in the idea that the writings (*bani*) of the Sikh Gurus were the most precious treasure of the community. The process of collection began extraordinarily early and developed through several phases, from the writing of the Goindval *pothis* (1570) to the compilation of the *Adi Granth* itself (1603–4). Again, the distinct Sikh concern with the written word aligns it more directly with Islam than with most Hindu communities. It is not accidental that dated Sikh manuscripts go further back in time than manuscripts associated with other *panths* of the period.

By the end of the sixteenth century, under the social and religious authority of Guru Arjan, the Sikhs had successfully developed a spiritual kingdom—a reign of humility (*halimi raj*), as they called it—with an abode dedicated to God, the Golden Temple (*harimandar*), and the beginnings of Amritsar, the city established to house it. Again, the possible parallel presented by the spiritual kingdoms (*wilayas*) of medieval Sufi masters is instructive. But unlike Sufis, Sikhs could not avoid confrontation with temporal authority, which was exercised by Muslims. The first brush resulted in the martyrdom of Guru Arjan in Lahore, in 1606.

The doctrinal vitality of the tradition was powerful enough to stand this shock, and the successor Guru readily took over the role of being both spiritual and temporal mentor to the community. This gave rise to the formal doctrine of spiritual and temporal authority (*miri* and *piri*), which manifested itself in the construction of the Akal Takhat (throne of the Immortal One) in the vicinity of the

Golden Temple. The doctrine of spiritual and temporal authority seems to have been but a verbal articulation of what already existed in practice. The Guru during this period was addressed as the true lord (*sacha patishahu*), a key epithet for God in Guru Nanak's compositions. The true lord of the Sikhs thus stood in contrast to the Mughal emperor (*patishahu*), a false lord from the Sikh point of view. For the Sikh community, the Guru was the sole authority to be recognized, for he alone represented the ultimate authority, namely God.

The emerging situation demanded a revised posture arising out of the need to defend the community from external attack as well as protect the crucial Sikh doctrine that only the sovereignty of God deserves submission. The Sikh acceptance of the sword, symbolizing God's power and justice, as a valid means of self-defense seems to have emerged during this confrontation with the temporal power at Lahore, before the core Sikh community was forced to move to the Shivalik hills. For this reason we argued against the view that Sikhs derived their symbol of the potency of the sword from Hindu goddess (*devi*) cults prominent in the Shivalik area.

In sum, we traced the formulation of a coherent doctrinal position about the role of the Sikhs as bearers of their Sovereign's victory (*fateh*) on earth, right up to the concept of the *khalsa*. God's victory, in its purest form, was conceived as a Sikh kingdom (*khalsa raj*). The martyrdom of Tegh Bahadur (1675), the ninth Sikh Guru, provided the immediate context for the formulation of the concept of the *khalsa*, but the earlier doctrinal considerations of the sovereignty of God had laid the groundwork long before. Sikhs had formally rejected all temporal authority both within the community (*masands*) and without (the Mughal *patishahu*) and had prepared to wage a holy war (*dharamyudh*) against any infringement of God's sovereignty. Although Muslims were the enemy, insofar as they held the central power, the Sikh concepts of martyrdom (*shahadat*) and holy war (*dharamyudh*) are hardly understandable without taking into account parallel concepts in Islam.

Having covered the early doctrinal evolution of the community, we paused to comment on its social development during this period. For someone deeply influenced by Weber, as I am, it is obvious that doctrinal developments have their social contexts, and the Sikh tradition provides a rich store of information suggesting that the community paid close attention to its collective institutions. Early on there were pilgrimage centers and biennial gatherings in the presence of the Gurus, and a system that established a secondary level of authority among distant congregations through the Guru's designated representatives (*manjis,* and later on *masands*). The founding of the Golden Temple and the city of Amritsar away from the immediate royal scrutiny—unlike the earlier Goindwal, which lay on the highway connecting Delhi and Lahore—was an important administrative decision, and it reflected a definite theological bias in the direction of independent rule. Here the earlier concepts of charity (*dan*) and personal purity (*ishnan*) translated themselves into the practice of sending a tithe (*dasvand*) to the central treasury and coming to Amritsar to bathe in the pool at the Golden Temple, meet fellow brethren in the faith (*gurbhai*), and have an audience (*darshan*) with the Guru.

Importantly, the earlier social composition of the community also underwent change, with the Jats joining it in large numbers at this point in history. The Jats were nomadic tribes considered low-caste in the traditional Hindu hierarchy, but with strong traditions of egalitarianism among themselves, and pride in a militant past. Why they joined the Sikh movement and in what way their presence shaped its future are significant questions—not the least for anyone interested in the general phenomenon of religious conversion.

Often, the Jat conversion to Sikhism is explained as being initiated by a desire for upward mobility since merchant-class Khatris were the major constituents of the early Sikh community. Yet one wonders if this does not unfairly downplay an ideological element: a likely attraction on the part of Jats toward the Sikh doctrine of the sole sovereignty of God and of the Sikh Guru as his sole representative on earth. Jats can only have welcomed a mode of thought that questioned temporal authority since they had an illustrious traditions of open rebellion, as shown in documents as early as the *Chach Nama* (A.D. eighth century). It is not just that the Sikh community offered them a more positive self-image than they might have found elsewhere; the Sikh belief in sovereignty of God provided them with a framework that made overarching sense of their earlier tradition of resistance to temporal authority.

At this early stage of Sikh history, then, we see a powerful blending of the doctrinal and social resources for dealing with threats to the community—with the use of force, if necessary. The death of Guru Arjan in official custody at Lahore, in 1606, galvanized the community into taking such action. It was not just a challenge to its physical survival, as it is so often depicted, but a challenge to its doctrinal foundation: sole submission to the divine authority of God and Guru. The Jats, with their martial heritage, heroically led the confrontation. Their historical mastery of the sword suddenly achieved a new theological and ideological meaning: they were instruments of God's justice on earth.

Thus, the formal entry of militancy into the Sikh tradition after the death of Guru Arjan was not a sudden development but the result of a long and growing tradition. As for the institution of the *khalsa,* if one thinks in Hindu terms, it may look like a "sinister transformation" to grasp political power, as Toynbee said, but it makes perfect sense if one takes a more Semitic view of the role of religion, as in Islam and Christianity, where the sword was used for both the defense of faith and its propagation. We argued against the view that the *khalsa* was a reversal of early Sikh religious concerns. Such a view is rooted in a misunderstanding of Guru Nanak's own key concerns, which had a strong social dimension. The dream of a Sikh kingdom (*khalsa raj*) seemed a natural outgrowth of the concept of a city of God (Kartarpur), which Guru Nanak founded and nourished during the later part of his life.

The position we developed on these matters is midway between the Sikh understanding as expressed by Harbans Singh or Jagjit Singh, who in their own ways present the key developments of the period primarily as a result of the decisions of the Sikh Gurus, and W. H. McLeod and other scholars beginning with J. D. Cunningham in the mid-nineteenth century, who see the entry of Jats into the Sikh fold as being primarily responsible for later ideological developments. From our point of view, the weakness of the traditional view lies in its inability to give any weight to the changing social composition of the community. But McLeod's view also seems flawed since it emerges from his analysis of early Sikhism as essentially a religion of the interior. This misses the ideological underpinnings that would have brought Jats into the Sikh community in the first place and then provided them with a framework to continue their resistance to reigning authorities of the time.

There was a general receptivity among students to my view that the evolution of the Sikh community is to be read as blending of its distinctive ideology and social strengths. Although there was some initial resistance to my emphasis on Islamic parallels, by the time we reached this point in the course, there was general agreement that Islamic ideas are far more helpful than anything available in Hinduism for understanding the Sikh concept of the *khalsa,* the single most important development of the period.

The death of Guru Gobind Singh, in 1708, began a new chapter in the history of the Sikh community. With the limited sources at our disposal, it is hard to understand clearly how the community effectively filled the vacuum caused by the passing away of the Guru and the dissolution of this central Sikh institution. Why was the guruship discontinued? The tradition interprets the development as a result of the decision of Guru Gobind Singh at the time of his death in Nander. Banda Singh Bahadur and a few others seem to have emerged as potential successors to Guru Gobind Singh, but the twin doctrines of scripture (*guru granth*) and corporate community (*guru panth*) crystallized rapidly enough to prevent an individual from succeeding Guru Gobind Singh as the community's central religious authority. The collective will (*gurmata*) formulated in a corporate assembly (*sarbat khalsa*) in the presence of the scripture (*guru granth*) became the standard method of communal response to emerging situations of threat from the outside. In their own areas of influence, however, Sikh leaders were completely autonomous, and *gurmata* was not held to be applicable. Obviously, the whole period is of great interest from a comparative point of view: how does a religious tradition deal with the dissolution of a central authoritative institution? One of the more fascinating aspects, in the Sikh case, is that while the mainstream community emphatically rejected the possibility of a living guru after Guru Gobind Singh, several sects continued to shape themselves around individual charismatic figures.

Behind the Sikh struggle for power in the eighteenth century remained the doctrine of the sole sovereignty of God, and it continued to assert itself during the period when Sikh leaders carved out for themselves a major political role in the Punjab. From Banda Singh Bahadur to the Sikh kingdom under Maharaja Ranjit Singh, sovereignty was declared to be vested in God and in the Gurus, his representatives on earth. Coins were minted in their name and titles were avoided as a matter of principle. This religious belief did not conflict with the routine functioning of the Sikh state, nor did it obstruct the centralizing of power in the hands of the Sikh chiefs.

This period also saw the growth of Sikh literature pertaining to the conduct (*rahit*) of a *khalsa* Sikh, which is crucial for our understanding of how Sikh identity evolved then and subsequently. Again an Islamic institution, *sharia,* suggests parallels, but the heightened hostility of the Sikhs toward Muslims gave *rahit* documents an anti-Islamic flavor. In this period Muslims are no longer viewed by Sikhs as fellow monotheists, as they had been in the *Zafar Nama* of Guru Gobind Singh, but as instruments of evil (*dushat*). A problem for students, then, is understanding how Sikhs of the period could model themselves on Muslims in one respect and reject them so utterly in another.

The sway that the eighteenth century exerts on the contemporary Sikh psyche can be approached as a fine example of how symbol systems play an active role in the lives of religious communities. This period is often seen as providing the backdrop for the contemporary struggle of Sikhs against the central Indian government. Delhi has been the historic enemy, so it strikes Sikhs as of no surprise that battle lines should be drawn there again. Diverse Sikh groups struggling to create an independent Sikh state are deeply immersed in symbols of heroism, martyrdom, and the destiny of Sikhs to rule, all of which are associated with Sikh history of eighteenth century. These modern groups see their functioning as parallel to the activities of the small groups of Sikh warriors (*misals*) that were responsible in the collapse of Mughal and Afghan political dominance in eighteenth-century Punjab.

Yet victory is hardly the only major theme in eighteenth-century Sikh history. Banda Singh was cruelly executed in Delhi in 1716, and the refusal of Sikhs to bow to temporal authority wielded by Muslims led to severe persecution, resulting in the temporary disappearance of *khalsa* Sikhs from central Punjab. They once again moved to the Shivalik area and would limit themselves to twice-yearly visits to Amritsar. Over time, this had a deep impact on central Sikh institutions of worship, which slowly slipped into the hands of Udasis who remained in the plains.

The Udasis were an ascetic sect founded by Baba Srichand, the elder son of Guru Nanak; many *gurdwaras* fell under their control during this period. Most Sikh scholars rightly feel that the Udasis had but a marginal loyalty to Sikh doctrine. Under their influence Sikh doctrine adopted a strong Vedantic bias. The Nirmalas, a parallel sect which claimed to have been sent to Banaras for Sanskrit education by Guru Gobind Singh, added their share to this trend of vedanticization, portraying the *Adi Granth* as the fifth Veda, that is, the culminating aspect of the Hindu scriptural tradition.

The issue of who actually represented the majority community in this period is a difficult one. Was it the group that was fighting for the religious and political domination of Sikhs in the Punjab, or was it the group that could move easily between multiple identities, making no distinction between Hindus and Sikhs and, seemingly, changing as the winds might demand? The question is difficult to address because the latter—the Udasis, Sevapanthis, and Nirmalas—were the main forces in literary activity at the time. The only sources to come down to us are theirs. The use of these sources is problematic, and scholars who confidently declare on the basis of this literature that there were no boundaries between Sikhism and Hinduism throughout this period must be questioned.

Although by the end of the eighteenth century Sikhs were able to establish their political dominance in the form of the *khalsa raj,* no effort was made to liberate the doctrinal heritage from Udasis and Nirmalas. To the contrary, the benevolent monarchy of Maharaja Ranjit Singh bestowed rich land grants upon *gurdwaras* under Udasi control, thus winning the good will of Udasis and enlarging their influence over local population. An important question for scholars who see a tension between the militant *khalsa* and assimilationist Udasis, is how Sikh militarism—if it was the great force leading to the victory of Maharaja Ranjit Singh—could have taken such a neutral attitude toward what seems so clearly to be the doctrinal ambiguity that emanated from Udasi and Nirmala institutions. In class, it was hard to map out the circumstances that would make this position fully intelligible.

Another important issue that divides scholars with different leanings within the Sikh community is whether the period of Sikh ascendency under Maharaja Ranjit Singh is to be interpreted as a period of great Sikh glory (for the first time in South Asian history, the tide of invasion was reversed as the Maharaja's armies knocked at the gates of Kabul) or as one that saw a great erosion of Sikh moral values. While some Sikhs would lay down their lives for the prospect of reviving Maharaja Ranjit Singh's kingdom, others hold him responsible for a downward trend that sanctioned an increasing Hindu influence on the Sikh tradition, and for the weakening of such illustrious Sikh concepts as the corporate community (*guru panth*) and its collective will (*gurmata*).

My own inclination was to argue against the position that holds the maharaja responsible for a perceived decline of Sikh values. I believe he saw himself working within the broad framework of the ultimate sovereignty of God. In his understanding, this did not stop him from functioning like any monarch of his times. He did discourage Sikh institutions such as *sarbat khalsa* (corporate gatherings for a communal decision) since they could interfere with the routine functioning of the kingdom, but he did not deliberately dismantle them. Nor did he actively encourage a Hinduizing of the Sikh tradition.

In our study of this period of Sikh history, beginning with the death of Guru Gobind Singh, we often found traditional explanations for key events to be wanting in evidence and used reading from Grewal and McLeod to help provide a critical reevaluation of these issues. But our readings and lectures made it clear that answers for all questions are not readily available, and students understood this basic problem. As a counterpoise to such uncertainties, students enjoyed delving into the confident symbolic use of the period in contemporary Sikh struggles. This led to a lively discussion on the complexity of the process by which communal symbols are selected from history, depending upon each new situation and the challenges it presents to the community.

In the next phase of the course, we considered the arrival of the British, when Sikhs became a querulous group unable to understand the exact cause of their defeat and the collapse of their kingdom. As for the conquerors, they expected a quick decline in Sikh religion as a natural corollary to the Sikhs' crumbled political fortunes. As is well known, however, relations between Sikhs and the British changed markedly with the mutiny of 1857, when Sikhs supported the British against the rebelling soldiers (*purbias*). The motive was revenge: Sikhs thought the *purbias* had been responsible for the Sikh defeat some years before, and they saw this as an opportunity to settle scores with the soldiers of their old enemy, the Mughal emperor in Delhi. The episode of Sikhs killing the sons of Bahadur Shah at the same site where the ninth Guru, Tegh Bahadur, was martyred is indicative of their general motivation. Indian historians may paint the mutiny as "the first war of Indian independence," but for Sikhs it was a chance to take revenge. To an historian of religion, the potency of Sikh symbols of martyrdom and of Sikh convictions about divine justice is a matter of significant interest.

The Sikh support for the British at this crucial juncture resulted in a complete change of British attitude toward them and the Punjab. The Sikh aristocracy was offered official recognition and general respect; the custodians of the Sikh shrines were given full rights over their institutional properties; and the Sikh peasantry was helped by reduced land revenue and the offer of large-scale employment in the army. The Punjab was also earmarked for extensive development projects, which produced a stability the Punjab had not known since the death of Maharaja Ranjit Singh, and led to an enthusiastic acceptance of the British.

This relative stability of Sikh society in the latter half of the nineteenth century prepared the ground for considerable introspection about matters religious, and the circumstances causing this stability affected the way in which it proceeded. The opening of the

Punjab to Christian missionaries and Brahmo Samajis had much to do not only with the founding of the Singh Sabha, in 1873, but with the basic agenda it set for itself: bringing back the pristine purity of the Sikh tradition. The Arya Samajis, who had their own program of reform, later added to this momentum. A fact often forgotten is that at this early stage all sects, including the Udasis, showed enthusiastic support for the Singh Sabha's reformist agenda; but as time passed and *khalsa* Sikh identity was increasingly taken to have been the substance of pristine Sikhism, non-*khalsa* groups such as the Udasis were marginalized and became slowly alienated from the movement.

Sikh activists set about to revive the fundamentals of Sikhism, as known in the period of the Gurus, by removing what they saw to be later accretions. History was rewritten, Sikh ceremonies were revitalized or created anew, so as to be distinct from the Hindu ones, and much emphasis was placed on the use of Punjabi written in Gurmukhi as the language of the Sikhs. Singh Sabha scholars held up the *Adi Granth* as the final criterion for determining the characteristics of a distinct Sikh tradition, and attempted to dilute the overt anti-Muslim bias prevalent in the *rahit* literature of the eighteenth century.

Much interest has recently been lavished on this period, especially by Western scholars like Gerald Barrier who believe that the now commonly accepted concept of a Sikh identity is basically the construct of Singh Sabha activists. Building on our analysis of the earlier tradition, I argued that the boundaries drawn between Hinduism and Sikhism in this period were not actually new. They were old but had been obscured by the Udasi and Nirmala ascendency to positions of religious authority and by the large-scale conversion of Hindus to the faith during the reign of Maharaja Ranjit Singh. Such Hindu converts were at best ambivalent about their religious identity after the Sikh kingdom collapsed. Admittedly, the clarity with which Sikh identity was understood in the earlier period must have varied from group to group, but it is hard to accept that Sikhs saw themselves as Hindus. Clearly, the most important institutions of the Sikh kingdom—the court (*khalsa darbar*), the government (*khalsa sarkar*), and army (*khalsa fauj*)—were all conceived in terms of a *khalsa* Sikh identity, and in other respects too it is hard to accept Harjot S. Oberoi's view that in this period there was no marked distinction between the religious world views of Hindus and Sikhs.

The British, who simply continued older Sikh traditions having to do with the army, are often accused of deliberately encouraging this *khalsa* identity at the expense of other options that were available to Sikhs, with the intent of achieving a permanent split between Sikhs and Hindus. But such allegations do not seem to have much substance, and they tend to rely uncritically on the assumption that Hindus and Sikhs constituted one religious community before the arrival of the British. It seems more fruitful to understand the Singh Sabha as responding to a natural desire in the community for clear boundaries. Newly opened avenues of local power made that possible.

The Chief Khalsa Diwan, the central Sikh forum during the first two decades of the present century, functioned in the same broad framework. Its achievements included the passage of the Anand Marriage Act (which created a legal rubric for Sikh marriage, as distinct from those of other religious communities), the exclusion of the Sikh sword from the Indian Arms Act of 1904, and the acceptance of Punjabi in the postal service and on signboards at railway stations. The Chief Khalsa Diwan also made a substantial contribution to Sikh education, but its most innovative activity was the use of legislation for religious purposes.

British legal codes became a problem, however, in other areas. With the increasing doctrinal assertion of a distinct Sikh identity, a concerted effort was made to release the *gurdwaras* from the control of Udasis. Here Sikh activists, quite unexpectedly and to their great dismay, found themselves pitted against the British administration, which missed the religious dimension of the struggle and decided to handle it as a law-and-order problem having to do with property rights. In subsequent years others too have missed the religious dimension: nationalist historians often attempt to present the Gurdwara Reform Movement as a battle for Indian freedom. I argued against this, seeing the movement as motivated, if anything, by Sikh nationalism—a dream of retrieving the Sikh kingdom and the era of Maharaja Ranjit Singh. Mahatma Gandhi tried to mesh this regional struggle with the nationalist cause, but failed, as Sikh leaders jealously kept the agitation in their own hands. Even the Indian National Congress's offer of non-Sikh volunteers to join the movement was politely rejected, and there was more than a little wariness of the discomfort Gandhi felt at the idea of "dehinduizing" Sikhism by removing *gurdwaras* from Udasi control and ousting the Hindu icons from the precincts of the Golden Temple.

The Gurdwaras Act of 1925 confirmed the success of the Gurdwara Reform Movement in establishing Sikhism as an independent entity. Communal thinking in the previous fifty years had largely gone into framing answers to the fundamental doctrinal questions of who is a Sikh and what is a *gurdwara*. With the Act, the Singh Sabha's answers to these questions acquired legal sanction and served once and for all to define the core identity of Sikhs. Groups such as the Udasis were distinctly marginalized and have remained so ever since. *Khalsa* identity became identical with Sikh identity.

Parallel to this doctrinal development was an administrative one: the Shiromani Gurdwara Prabandhak Committee (SGPC) became the most important Sikh institution of its day and, indeed, of this century. As British administrators conceded the Sikh activists' demands, the major Sikh shrines came under the control of this committee of elected Sikh representatives, providing them both with financial resources and effective platforms to reach local Sikh audiences. The Shiromani Akali Dal, which led the struggle for the establishment of the SGPC, survives as the oldest regional party on the Indian scene today.

From this point onward, our course increasingly gravitated toward a discussion of the conflicts between region and nation—and, implicitly, between one religion and another—that are still being worked out in the Punjab today. It was as inevitable for students as for the instructor to fix their eyes on these developments, in an attempt to understand the forces leading to the struggles that dominate present-day life in the Punjab. Already in the earlier part of the course, but especially in this section, I took it as one of my central tasks to justify my conviction that what many see as a newly radical Sikh cause which grew up in the 1980s gains its sustenance from much deeper strands in twentieth-century Sikh history.

We had already come up against tensions between Sikhs and the Indian national movement. This was to continue as Sikhs concerned themselves with the political issue of garnering additional representation in the provincial government. Building on the work of K. L. Tuteja, we focused on the communal interests that actually shaped the policy of the Akali Dal and rejected the view that the Akali Dal was an enthusiastic participant in the struggle for freedom in the country as a whole. We observed that whenever Sikh interests came into conflict with larger national goals, as in the Nehru Report, the Communal Award, and the war effort in the Second World War, the Akalis parted ways with the Congress until such time as a new compromise could be formulated on mutually beneficial terms. It was the rising demand for Pakistan, which put Sikhs in a very difficult situation demographically, that finally forced them to link their fate with India's. The colossal human tragedy of the partition, with its displacing of twelve million people in the Punjab, reinforced this by causing a resurgence of the old eighteenth-century hatred between Sikhs and Muslims. The scale of the loss of human life and its attendant agony is perhaps beyond comparison with any other situation in human history.

One bright spot, as Sikh refugees from west Punjab laboriously settled themselves in the east, was that for the first time the Sikhs found themselves in the majority in central districts of the Punjab. This was to add new cogency to demands for a Sikh state. Of course, such regional aspirations ran counter to those of the central leadership. The government under Pundit Nehru, committed to national reconstruction, had no patience for the communal vision of the Akali Dal, and indications of growing tension began to appear soon after partition. Within months Master Tara Singh, the key Sikh leader, began to question the national leaders' promise of a "glow of freedom" for Sikhs. Hence the Akali members of the Constituent Assembly abstained from formally signing the Indian constitution. The conflict became sharper, and its tactics rougher, as the years passed.

As the linguistic reorganization of the country began in the early 1950s, Akali leaders demanded a Punjabi state, but this was denied them by Pundit Nehru, who feared—perhaps rightly—that the granting of a Punjabi-speaking state would soon lead to a demand for a Sikh state. The government's attitude encouraged local Hindus, who were the majority, to deny that Punjabi was their mother tongue—an act that earned them considerable Sikh enmity for years to come—and the Congress Party set a precedent of interfering in internal Akali politics by helping to dislodge Master Tara Singh, who supported the idea of a Sikh state. When a Punjabi-language state did finally come into being, in 1966, many issues remained unsolved, especially the state to which Chandigarh and other Punjabi-speaking regions should be allocated and the proper distribution of river waters. This situation persists today.

These unresolved tensions mitigated against the success of Sant Fateh Singh and later Parkash Singh Badal, Sikh leaders who in the years following 1967 showed a willingness to share regional power with the Jan Sangh, a Hindu Party. Had such cooperation succeeded, it would have trimmed many of the sharp edges from the Sikh vision of regional autonomy. The general degeneration of

Indian politics under Mrs. Gandhi made such initiatives extremely difficult to translate into an effective harmony between Sikhs and Hindus.

The emergence of Sant Jarnail Singh Bhindranwale brought forth an increasingly stark assertion that Sikh nationalism and Indian nationalism are mutually exclusive, and the Akali effort to build some kind of coexistence between the two was branded as being outside the spirit of Sikh religion. Sant Bhindranwale, who was thoroughly immersed in the great symbols of eighteenth-century Sikh history, especially the belief that it was the Sikh destiny to rule, touched a raw nerve by repeatedly explaining to his large audiences how Sikhs had been humiliated by Hindus in Delhi. Hindus may have been a new force in the imperial capital, but Delhi was still Delhi, and Sant Bhindranwale succeeded in convincing many Sikhs that the whole weight of history argued against negotiating with anyone there. Sikhs must take control of their own affairs, he said, and use their own time-tested methods to sort out their problems. Khalistan, the unsaid word, was the goal, and violent force was the right means to achieve it.

By ensconcing himself in the Golden Temple, Sant Bhindranwale aligned himself with another great Sikh symbol. "The foundation of Khalistan will be laid on the day government troops attack the Golden Temple, and we sacrifice our lives defending it," he said. With Mrs. Gandhi's decision to go on the offensive against Sant Bhindranwale's forces, these words came to be prophetic. The riots that followed Mrs. Gandhi's subsequent death—they were especially widespread and bloody in Delhi—proved to many Sikhs the real attitude of Hindu India toward Sikhs and matched, once again, with the great historical paradigm of the necessity for struggle against a central authority based in Delhi. We closed our study, then, on a pessimistic note as to the possibility of an arrangement that would allow Sikhs to live happily within India, and we attempted to look forward to a future that would more adequately bear the burden of the past.

The Class Experience

As threaded our way through such difficult issues, it was natural that the class should have strong and not always uniform reactions. I made it a policy, therefore, that questions should be raised at any time during the lecture, and this happened regularly. As I went about constructing my undoubtedly controversial reading of Sikh history and religion, there arose a number of healthy disagreements.

The tone of the class was established at the beginning of the course, when we addressed the question of the origin of the Sikh tradition. Several students resisted my attempts at drawing parallels between Semitic and Sikh theological visions of a powerful personal God to whom humans must submit in love and fear. It took some effort to provide a criticism of McLeod's persuasive analysis, which tends to give less than adequate weight to the social and ethical dimensions of Guru Nanak's thinking and thereby assimilates him relatively easily into a broad Hindu context. I believe that all students, consciously or unconsciously, began the course with the assumption that Sikhs belong to a Hindu context. As we sorted out this early disagreement and realized that differences were going to arise more frequently than one might have expected, we were able to strike a working relationship and move rapidly and comfortably through later segments of the course. The opening lectures caused the most strenuous debate.

If the relationship between Sikhism and Hinduism was the most difficult point for non-Sikh students, Sikh students were most concerned about protecting their conviction that Sikh revelation was unique and divine. Their initial discomfort with the analytical approach taken in the class surfaced quickly. Before long they were able to see that this approach did not challenge the Sikh belief that the revelation to Guru Nanak was divine, and they accepted that divine revelations have to be received in the context of specific cultures. I believe they came to agree with me, as well, that it is always enlightening to understand religions in a comparative way. Interestingly, they had far less difficulty in responding to our discussion of the nature of *janam-sakhi* literature as set out in terms of McLeod's perceptive analysis than they had in confronting the *Adi Granth* itself.

Discussions of the effects of the social composition of the early Sikh community, the provision of central authority after the death of the tenth Guru, the role of the Udasis in the vedanticization of the Sikh thought, the Singh Sabha effort, and the contemporary Punjab crisis, were all lively. My line of argument was not always acceptable to everyone, nor had I expected it to be. At several points things had to be left hanging, with satisfactory answers yet not available. If the Sikh tradition holds the *Adi Granth* so dear, for example, why was the original *granth* permitted to stay with a family with which the *khalsa panth,* according to the *rahit* literature, was not supposed to have any social dealings? If it is agreed that caste is fundamentally opposed by Sikh doctrine, then how has it persisted? How can the community address this issue today? Such questions, I found, were enlivening, not threatening, and my personal lesson was that the best way one can learn a subject is by actually attempting to teach it. One learns not only by one's own effort, but by the response one elicits in others.

Our weekend visits to local Sikh families were very well received. Students interested in participating in this venture were picked up on a Saturday afternoon by local Sikh families and returned on Sunday. On Saturday the students had the opportunity for a firsthand exposure to Sikh family life in the United States. On Sunday they visited the *gurdwara,* participating in Sikh worship and the community meal (*langar*). This visit was timed to take advantage of ten weeks of classroom experience; it provided students with a chance to test out their ideas on real-life Sikhs. It created a milieu in which many questions about the Sikh diaspora, which was then being discussed in class, could effectively be raised.

I was also fortunate in being able to arrange three visiting lectures, and a course on Sikhism taught in almost any part of North America would afford a similar opportunity. Our three visitors were Professors Darshan Singh Maini, Gurcharan Singh, and John C. B. Webster. Professor Maini, of the Department of English at New York University, spoke on the partition of the Punjab. Having lost family members and having translated specimens of the poetry of the period, he was an excellent person to present the intensity of the tragedy. Professor Gurcharan Singh, who teaches international affairs at Marymount Manhattan College and has been in the New York area for three decades, addressed the issue of Sikh life beyond South Asia. He spoke candidly of his reasons for leaving the Punjab and the problems he faced when he arrived in this country, and of those he now faces with two grown-up Sikh-American children. Dr. Webster, a Presbyterian missionary who for many years was the director of the Christian Institute of Sikh Studies in Batala, Punjab, spoke on the theme of diversity within the Sikh community. Having done a book on the Nirankaris and organized a seminar on the nature of guruship within the Sikh community, he was in a good position to present the concerns of both mainstream and sectarian Sikhs.

I hope to develop my collection of slides dealing with basic themes in Sikh life—ceremonies, religious rituals, art and architecture, even folk dances—to give students a more vivid sense of Sikh

life in the Punjab. These materials will be made available for others'
use at the Southern Asian Institute of Columbia University and can
be duplicated.

Such resources are of great help in varying and enlivening the
classroom experience, and they provide a healthy balance for the instructor's own views. For the latter, however, there is no need to
apologize. As long as students understand that the classroom is
theirs and that discussion is open, and as long as examinations and
papers are evaluated as to effort, care, and depth rather than for
their ideological correctness, it cannot but be good for teachers of
Sikhism to present the issues the way they see them. There is room
for disagreement at many points, but I hope I have made it clear
that for me, at least, much of the excitement of teaching a course on
Sikhism lies right there. The subject is challenging, and for many
intensely personal as well. That combination can make for a truly
stimulating course—for students and teachers alike.

8

A Brief History of Sikh Studies in English

*

J. S. Grewal

In the present essay I will be limiting myself to works on Sikh studies that have been published in English. Many other important contributions to the field have been made, especially in Punjabi, but it is possible to say that the bulk of serious work so far has been in English. For the community of scholars living in North America, this is a fortunate thing. I will observe a second limitation, as well. Rather than speaking at length about each and every work published, I will describe the broad development of Sikh studies over the past century and a half, a development that can be outlined with reference to the work of selected individual writers. Regrettably, in a survey chapter such as this, much has to be omitted.[1]

Of crucial significance in the context of the development of Sikh studies is the work of Joseph Davey Cunningham. He published *A History of the Sikhs* in 1849. It has been reprinted several times subsequently and even today is treated with respect by students of Sikh history. In a way, his work was the culmination of the British interest in the Sikhs. By the late eighteenth century several travelers, diplomats, administrators, and scholars had written about the Sikhs, their history and their religion. This interest was inspired by the belief that the Sikhs were politically important in the northwestern parts of the Indian subcontinent; it was therefore useful to have information about them. An understanding of their past was meant to elucidate their present, so that sound political action could be taken in the near or distant future. This practical interest was supported and supplemented by the intellectual curiosity of the few who pursued universal history or the history of religion, and for a writer such as John Malcolm, author of *A Sketch of the Sikhs* (1812), there was no incompatibility between these two kinds of interests. In his view, to know about the Sikhs was necessary for practical purposes, yet to know the Sikhs one had to know not just their history but their religion, manners, and customs.

Those who wrote after Malcolm and before Cunningham were more frankly interested in Sikh politics and, therefore, in the then recent political history of the Sikhs. After the death of Ranjit Singh in 1839, a political interest in his kingdom excluded every other, and a great variety of information was obtained and published. Similarly, after the first Anglo-Sikh War (1845–46), those who wrote on the Sikhs reveled in the war and its events. Almost invariably they gloated over the success of British arms, blamed the Sikhs for bringing about the war, and justified the official policy of the British rulers of India. This immediate background, as much as the larger background of nearly three-quarters of a century, enables us to understand the significance of Cunningham's work.

Cunningham had read all that his predecessors had written; he had consulted almost every source of Sikh history then published. He wrote his work on the eve of the extinction of the kingdom of Lahore, combining the practical and intellectual interests of his predecessors and his contemporaries. His *History* represented a high-water mark of early British scholarship on the Sikhs, for once the Punjab was annexed to the British Empire, the nature of the British interest in the Sikhs underwent a sudden change. No British writer on the Sikhs has ever seriously attempted to replace the work of J. D. Cunningham.

This is not to say, however, that Cunningham's work survived merely for negative reasons, or merely because he had successfully summarized existing knowledge. Cunningham had thought deeply about the subject of his study and was essentially in sympathy with it. He was the first British historian to postulate that Sikhism was a distinct faith, meant to transcend both Hinduism and Islam; he was the first to see a close connection between the essential teachings of Guru Nanak and Guru Gobind Singh; and he was the only British historian to look upon Sikh polity as closely linked with the Sikh faith. He thought of the Sikhs as being a distinct nation. Unlike most writers of his time, Cunningham opposed the idea of annexing the Sikh kingdom to the British Empire. In his view, the Sikhs as "a nation" had the right to be independent. These, and many other ideas of his, have found favor with Indian writers, and he has left a deep mark on subsequent studies.

In the present century, the bulk of the work published on Sikh history has been produced in India. The advance of Western education and the rise of nationalist movements in South Asia have made this possible. It was no accident, therefore, that two of the earliest contributors to Sikh Studies were Bengalis: N. K. Sinha and Indubhushan Banerjee. They complement each other and, together, they cover the whole of Cunningham's ground. In fact, one of Sinha's books is dedicated to Cunningham. Whereas Banerjee was interested in the socioreligious history of the Sikhs and covered the period of the Guru Nanak and his nine successors in the *Evolution of the Khalsa,* Sinha was interested in political history and wrote on Ranjit Singh and the rise of the Sikh power in the eighteenth century.

With better sources at their command, Sinha and Banerjee amplified and supported, with a few exceptions, the theses propounded by Cunningham. Banerjee's interpretation of Guru Nanak's mission is different from Cunningham's; he does not regard Guru Nanak as the founder of a distinct faith and he does not believe that Guru Nanak's message had far-reaching social implications. On most other points, however, he agrees with Cunningham. In *Evolution of the Khalsa,* the contribution of the first four successors of Guru Nanak to the development of the Sikh *panth* is discussed in detail to demonstrate that the Sikhs had come to form a distinct socioreligious group with distinctive ideals and institutions; they formed a state within the Mughal Empire.

Banerjee does not see any essential departure from the early evolutionary process in the so-called new deal of Guru Hargobind, who foreshadowed Guru Gobind Singh. Banerjee underlines the essentially religious interests of the latter and places his wars and the institution of the *khalsa* in that perspective. He emphasizes the importance of the Jat element in the composition of the Sikh *panth* and tries to relate some of the measures taken by the Sikh gurus to the Jat presence. Cunningham had been the first to recognize the relevance of the Jat peasantry to the history of the Sikh *panth* in the seventeenth and eighteenth centuries.

The broad similarity between Sinha's work and Cunningham's is equally marked. Sinha looks upon the measure introduced by Guru Gobind Singh as being relevant to the rise of the Sikhs to power; he sees a close connection also between the political institutions of the Sikhs and their faith; he accepts Cunningham's conception of Sikh polity as "theocratic confederate feudalism"; and he looks upon Ranjit Singh as by far the most important Sikh ruler, indeed, as one of the heroes of Indian history. Ranjit Singh, in Sinha's view, is important in his own right and not because of his relations with the British.

Cunningham's interpretation of Sikhism in relation to Indian tradition as the counterpart to Christianity within the greater Judaic tradition was not acceptable to many a British administrator, who tended to veer toward the position of Christian missionaries in the role they imagined for Christianity in India. In the course of the nineteenth century, as the Indian subcontinent came under British rule, a general wave of aggressive optimism prevailed among the protagonists of Christian evangelical work in India, which left little room for envisaging a constructive role to be played by any other religion. Sikhism was no exception, as the work of Ernest Trumpp clearly showed. Trumpp was encouraged to translate the *Adi Granth* out of the conviction that to know the religion of the Sikhs it was necessary to know their scriptures and that to persuade the Sikhs to accept Christianity it was necessary to know what they thought of their own religion. Trumpp gave an introduction to his translations from the *Adi Granth* in which his comments on the character of the Sikh scriptures and the nature of Sikh theology reveal his contempt for both. An English translation of the *Adi Granth* in the late nineteenth century was meant to be a major advance in Sikh studies, for nothing on this scale had been done before. But Trumpp's unconcealed hostility toward the Sikhs and their religion made his work unpopular with the Sikhs. It may not be too much to say that the most fruitful result of Trumpp's work was the reaction it evoked after its publication in the late 1870s.

Max Arthur Macauliffe's six volumes, entitled *The Sikh Religion,* published by Oxford University Press in 1909, were intended to replace the *Adi Granth* of Ernest Trumpp. They cover almost the same ground, but with a palpable difference. Whereas Trumpp had written with a total disregard for Sikh sensibilities, Macauliffe wrote on behalf of the Sikhs. His translations from the *Adi Granth* are closer to the Sikh's own interpretation of their scriptures and have therefore been received by Sikhs as more acceptable in general than Trumpp's. Also, Macauliffe's work has been very widely regarded as more authentic. However, in his anxiety not to offend the sentiments of his Sikh contemporaries, Macauliffe deliberately adhered to Sikh traditions regarding the lives both of the Sikh Gurus and of those saints (*bhagats*) whose compositions were included in the *Adi Granth*. More recent scholarship has suggested this may have been a dubious practice, but if faced with a choice between the hypercritical attitude of Trumpp and the uncritical attitude of Macauliffe, most scholars have certainly been happy to choose the latter. A student of Sikhism who does not have a working knowledge of *gurmukhi* has to lean on Macauliffe even today, though other English translations of the *Adi Granth* have appeared more recently.

Foreign scholars and missionaries after Macauliffe have continued to take interest in Sikh studies. J. C. Archer's *The Sikhs* (1946) is an example of this. Similarly, C. H. Loehlin has devoted a number of years to the study of the writings of Guru Gobind Singh. The recent work of W. H. McLeod, *Guru Nanak and the Sikh Religion,* demonstrates the usefulness of a reexamination and reinterpretation of sources and themes covered by earlier writers. It casts serious doubt on the value of the *janam-sakhi* traditions to the biographer of Guru Nanak. The only legitimate reply to McLeod is to demonstrate the value of those traditions to such a biographer, but McLeod's attempt at a scholarly analysis of the most important form of evidence for the life of Guru Nanak has too often been criticized without rational argument. The evidence of *janam-sakhi* traditions is extremely valuable insofar as it reflects the aspirations and attitudes of the people among whom they became current, but if a *sakhi* is believed to contain the kernel of biographical truth, that has to be demonstrated rather than merely assumed. McLeod's reinterpretation of Guru Nanak's religion, at any rate, has been generally applauded. His is probably the best interpretation of Guru Nanak's faith to appear so far in English.

Until India's independence, the scope of Sikh studies remained largely confined to the period up to the fall of the Sikh kingdom, in 1849. Teja Singh, for instance, wrote about the ideals and institutions of Sikhism almost entirely on the basis of its early history. In *A Short History of the Sikhs* (1950), written conjointly with Ganda Singh, much of the eighteenth century is also covered. Ganda Singh wrote on several phases and aspects of Sikhism and Sikh history. Even so, he showed a much greater interest in the period covered by Cunningham than in later Sikh history. In fact, he made a substantial contribution to the study of two very important figures of the eighteenth century: Banda Singh Bahadur and Ahmad Shah Durrani. Similarly H. R. Gupta produced three detailed volumes on the rise of Sikh power in the eighteenth century.

Ranjit Singh, the great Sikh ruler, has continued to be a popular subject with modern historians of the Sikhs. R. R. Sethi's *Lahore Darbar,* which aims at studying diplomatic relations between the Sikhs and the English, is a tribute to the political sagacity of Ranjit Singh. More recently, Khushwant Singh has produced a biography of the Maharaja, while Syed Waheeduddin has brought out the essential traits of Ranjit Singh's personality in *The Real Ranjit*

Singh. Fauja Singh Bajwa, in *The Military System of the Sikhs,* has concentrated upon the army of Ranjit Singh, just as G. L. Chopra, back in the 1920s, had studied the administration of Ranjit Singh in *The Punjab as a Sovereign State.*

The decade from Ranjit Singh's death to the British annexation of the Punjab, a decade that saw the decline and fall of Sikh power, has attracted the attention of several writers, notably Sita Ram Kohli, Khushwant Singh, B. J. Hasrat, and S. S. Bal, B. R. Chopra, and Fauja Singh. Since the publication of Cunningham's work, one major question has agitated the minds of writers who consider the demise of the Sikh kingdom. Did the British deliberately subvert the power of Ranjit Singh's successors, or were the intrinsic weaknesses of the Sikh state responsible for its fall? Almost every writer on this decade has tried, directly or indirectly, to answer this question. While Kohli, Khushwant Singh, and Chopra have written directly on the successors of Ranjit Singh, Hasrat and Bal have concentrated on the British side of the situation by studying Anglo-Sikh relations and British policy toward the Punjab.

Reinterpretations of historical events become more meaningful when historians have the advantage of some fresh evidence at their command. Such evidence has indeed been brought to light over the course of the present century. The publication of a large number of *hukamnamas* by Ganda Singh, for example, has opened up new possibilities of interpretation. Similarly, the publication of the official orders of the Sikh chiefs of the late eighteenth century (as contrasted with those of Ranjit Singh and his representatives) in *The Mughal and Sikh Rulers and the Vaishnavas of Pindori,* by B. N. Goswamy and myself, should oblige historians of the Sikhs to revise their conceptions of Sikh polity. Indu Banga and I had the same objective in mind when we wrote *Civil and Military Affairs of Ranjit Singh.* Unfortunately, it often takes general historians—and, naturally enough, lay historians—a certain amount of time to integrate new information about particular periods and places into their broader view. One merely hopes that the new information bearing on eighteenth-century Sikh history will soon enter the general stream.

It is understandable that there should have been a relative lessening of interest in the fortunes of the Sikhs after the loss of their political power in 1849. From the very beginning the British interest in the Sikhs was a tribute to their political power. As subjects, however, the Sikhs were of little special interest; only information relating to government and administration was avidly collected by the British. For many years this was true of Punjabi and, more broadly, Indian authors too. Many chose to debate with their British predecessors on the latter's own grounds. This situation changed in the wake of the socioreligious movements that flourished in India during the late nineteenth century and the political awakening that characterized the early decades of the twentieth. These inspired an interest in the socioreligious origins of the Sikhs and in their early political development. Yet this new interest in origins did little to alter the general apathy that prevailed in relation to more recent periods of Sikh history. Thus for nearly a century after the fall of the kingdom of Lahore in 1849, the Sikhs appeared to have a more or less distant past, but no immediate past or present.

Only after the end of British rule in India did some writers turn to the Sikhs of the British period. Considerable attention has been paid to the Namdharis, or Kukas, as the protagonists of a religious movement with political undertones, as in the *Freedom Fighters* of M. L. Ahluwalia and *The Kuka Movement* of Fauja Singh Bajwa. More recently, N. G. Barrier has brought out a comprehensive bibliography for the period between 1849 and 1919, entitled *The Sikhs and Their Literature*. It contains a brief but meaningful introduction to the Singh Sabha Movement.

Although the history of the Sikhs during the British period is just beginning to receive serious study, Khushwant Singh has attempted a general history of this period in the second volume of his *History of the Sikhs*. A first-rate journalist, they say, is better than a second-rate historian. But for some years Khushwant Singh was not in competition with second-rate historians; his was the only general history of this period. In his ambitious but premature attempt, he presented Sikhism as the spearhead of Punjabi nationalism.

In the course of the last twenty years, Khushwant Singh's work has ceased to be the only general history of the Sikhs. It has been joined by Hari Ram Gupta's *History of the Sikhs,* the first four volumes of which have already been published (in 1978–84) as a third revised edition. This may be taken as an index of their popularity. Besides Professor Gupta's *History* and my own *The Sikhs of the Punjab* (1990), which forms a part of *The New Cambridge History of India,* there is Gopal Singh's voluminous *History of the Sikh People, 1469–1978,* first published in 1979. Additionally, Harbans Singh's

Heritage of the Sikhs was revised and published in 1983, and Rajiv A. Kapur's *Sikh Separatism: The Politics of Faith* (1986) also covers the whole range of Sikh history, if from a particular viewpoint.

In the last two decades, there have also been major institutional advances in the study of the Sikhs. In 1962 Ganda Singh came to be associated with the Punjabi University at Patiala, and he was joined there by Fauja Singh to establish a center for historical studies related to the Punjab. Their achievement is reflected, among other things, in the continuous publication, since 1967, of the journal *Panjab Past and Present,* and, since 1965, *The Proceedings of the Punjab History Conference.* Both are indispensable for research in the field of Punjab history and in relation to Sikh studies. All the work of the Department of Guru Granth Studies at Punjabi University is directly relevant for Sikh studies, and much of the interest of the Department of Comparative Religion is concentrated on Sikh studies, too, especially the projected *Encyclopaedia of Sikhism* under the general editorship of Harbans Singh. Individually, as well, Ganda Singh, Fauja Singh, and Harbans Singh have published a number of important books. Whereas Fauja Singh has concentrated on the early nineteenth century, Harbans Singh and Ganda Singh have shown greater interest in the period of the Gurus, and in Sikh resurgence under colonial rule.

Another center for Sikh studies has more recently evolved at Amritsar, in Guru Nanak Dev University, with its Department of Guru Nanak Studies, Department of History, and School of Punjabi Studies. All three departments publish journals: respectively, the *Journal of Sikh Studies,* the *Journal of Regional History,* and *Khoj Darpan.* Between them, these departments and their journals intend to cover Sikh history, faith, and literature for purposes of research and publication. In historical studies, the most significant thrust has undoubtedly been in the area of socioeconomic history, as represented by Indu Banga's *Agrarian System of the Sikhs* (1978) and my own *Maharaja Ranjit Singh: Structure of Power, Economy and Society* (1981). One also finds some attention to the historical analysis of Sikh literature in the doctoral dissertation of S. S. Hans and my own *Guru Nanak in History* (1969), but there has been very little political history or interest in Sikh history as part of the regional history of the Punjab.

Returning to the work of individual scholars, we may notice that the ground covered earlier by Indubhushan Banerjee and N. K. Sinha has been covered by A. C. Banerjee in three books: *Guru Nanak and His Times* (1971), *Guru Nanak to Guru Gobind Singh*

(1978), and *The Khalsa Raj* (1985). It is difficult to say that Banerjee has made a substantial advance over his predecessors. It can be safely stated, however, that Niharranjan Ray's *Sikh Gurus and the Sikh Society* (1970) does contain many new insights. In a related field Avtar Singh's *Ethics of the Sikhs,* published in the same year, is the first systematic study of the subject. And an attempt is made by Ravinder G. B. Singh to study Guru Nanak's concepts in the broad context of Indian philosophy in the work entitled *Indian Philosophical Tradition and Guru Nanak,* published in 1983.

A major development of the last two decades is the emergence of an interest in Sikh history during the period of colonial rule, among both Indian and foreign scholars. Important titles are Mohinder Singh's *Akali Movement* (1978), Kailash Chander Gulati's *Akalis Past and Present* (1974), and Gobinder Singh's *Religion and Politics in the Punjab* (1986). If the latter two flow over into the post-independence era, Richard G. Fox's *Lions of the Punjab,* published in 1985 as a study of culture in the making, places the Akali Movement in the broad context of colonial rule. The same period receives study in Ethene K. Marenco's *Transformation of Sikh Society* (1974), a book meant to scrutinize social mobility and social change among the Sikhs during the period of British rule. Tom G. Kissinger's *Vilayatpur* (1974) is a study of socioeconomic change in a Sikh village under colonial rule, continuing into the post-independence phase, until the mid-1960s.

Interest in the post-independence phase of Sikh history has been inspired almost exclusively by politics. Baldev Raj Nayar's *Minority Politics in the Punjab,* which envisaged no change in the near future, was published, ironically, in the year that the erstwhile Punjab was divided to create a Punjabi-speaking state in 1966. Ajit Singh Sarhadi's *Punjabi Suba,* published in 1970, celebrated the struggle from the viewpoint opposite to Nayar's. Joyce Pettigrew's *Robber Noblemen* (1975) is meant to be a study of the political system of the Sikh Jats; she shows how traditional attitudes survived in a new political framework. Paul R. Brass's work, published a year earlier, brings in a new dimension altogether by studying politics in relation to two other important categories of experience, as its title suggests: *Language, Religion and Politics in North India.* The book, which covers the Punjab in addition to other areas of north India, could be subtitled "political articulation based on cultural reorientation." Satya M. Rai's *Punjab Since Partition* (1986) is a continuation of her earlier work on the partition of the Punjab; this time she analyzes the Punjab's quick recovery from the trauma. The events of past decade have, if anything, further increased interest in contemporary history, as is evident, for example, from Mark Tully and Satish Jacob's *Amritsar* (1985), which portrays Operation Bluestar as "the last battle" of Indira Gandhi, and from two edited volumes: *The Tragedy of Punjab: Bluestar and After* (1984), edited by Khushwant Singh and Kuldip Nayar, and *Punjab in Indian Politics* (1985), edited by Amrik Singh.

These authors are journalists, but journalists are not the only category of writers who have started taking an interest in Sikh history. There are retired administrators, judges, teachers, and creative writers as well. A sampler of some of their works would include Gobind Singh Mansukhani's *Life of Guru Nanak* (1974), *Guru Ram Das: His Life, Work and Philosophy* (1979), and *Aspects of Sikhism* (1982); K. S. Duggal's *The Sikh Gurus: Their Lives and Teachings* (1980); Daljeet Singh's *Sikhism: A Comparative Study of its Theology and Mysticism* (1979) and *The Sikh Ideology* (1984); Jagjit Singh's *The Sikh Revolution* (1981) and *Perspectives on Sikh Studies* (1985); Balwant Singh Anand's *Guru Nanak: His Life Was His Message* (1983); and Justice Gurdev Singh's edited volume, *Perspectives on Sikh Tradition* (1986), which contains a longish introduction of his own. What impels authors such as these to write on Sikh history of Sikh faith is not altogether clear. It seems unlikely to be merely a desire to see their names in print, especially since one can scarcely hope to make a fortune from such publications. Is it then an act of piety? Certainly each of these writers desires to project a particular image of the Sikh past and of Sikh tradition, so perhaps one concludes that they are writing for "self-understanding." In any case, this popular interest in Sikh studies is a significant and new phenomenon of recent decades.

The increasing interest in Sikh studies among foreign scholars, as shown in the entire thrust of the present book, is also a significantly recent phenomenon. One clue to this development lies in the publications such as A. W. Helweg's *Sikhs in England: The Development of a Migrant Community* (1979), Parminder Bhachu's *Twice Migrants: East African Sikh Settlers in Britain* (1985), and W. H. McLeod's *Punjabis in New Zealand* (1986). Such titles suggest that a substantial part of the new interest springs from the presence of Sikhs in countries other than their own. An attempt to understand Sikhs' background or tradition is only a small step from this initial interest. Such a movement of thought is clearly demonstrated in W. Owen Cole and Piara Singh Sambhi's *The Sikhs: Their Religious Beliefs and Practices,* published in 1978. Cole has followed up this volume with *The Guru in Sikhism* (1982) and *Sikhism and its Indian Context 1469–1708* (1984).

Of course, other motives also bring non-Indian, non-Punjabi, and non-Sikh authors to the study of Sikhism. A purely academic interest seems to have inspired Christopher Shackle, of the School of Oriental and African Studies in London, to publish his *An Introduction to the Sacred Language of the Sikhs* in 1983. A revised edition of his more general study, *The Sikhs,* appeared in 1986. Still another motive for a commitment to Sikh studies on the part of foreigners can be found in people like W. H. McLeod and John C. B. Webster, both of whom resided in the Punjab for a number of years. Webster's growing interest in the Nirankaris led to the publication of *The Nirankari Sikhs* in 1979.

N. G. Barrier, one of whose works was earlier cited, has continued to publish on Sikh and related themes, and he was joined by Mark Juergensmeyer, another American, in the 1970s. Their scholarly interest in Sikh studies was reflected in the work they edited in 1979: *Sikh Studies: Comparative Perspectives on a Changing Tradition.* Sheer quantity cannot always be a sound argument, but the much thicker volume published from Toronto in 1988 under the editorship of Joseph T. O'Connell and four other scholars is surely evidence of an intensified interest in Sikh studies in recent years. Like the earlier volume, this book, entitled *Sikh History and Religion in the Twentieth Century,* was based on an international seminar held in 1987 that was intended to survey the various portions of the field of Sikh studies. Efforts on the part of affluent or enlightened Sikh immigrants to establish new centers for Sikh studies in North America are detailed elsewhere in the present book. Thus there are clear signs that academic as well as popular interest in Sikh studies has increased in recent years, both in India and abroad.

Over the past quarter century, one scholar has shown an interest in Sikh studies more consistently than perhaps any other: W. H. McLeod. His *Guru Nanak and the Sikh Religion* was followed by *The Evolution of the Sikh Community* in 1975, which was followed by the *Early Sikh Tradition: A Study of the Janam-sakhis* in 1980. He published an English translation of a *janam-sakhi* in 1981 as *The B40 Janamsakhi,* and then in *Textual Sources for the Study of Sikhism* (1984), he published extracts, in English translation, from a large number of works from the time of Guru Nanak to the present day. McLeod published another important text with English translation as *The Chaupa Singh Rahit-Nama* in 1987, and more recently he has come out with *The Sikhs: History, Religion and Society,* published by Columbia University Press, and *Who Is A Sikh?*, which deals with the issue of Sikh identity and is published by his old publishers, Oxford University Press. As is plain from the length of this list and the influence of the works included in it, few scholars have dedicated their lives to the critical study of the Sikh tradition as McLeod has.

Because of an understandable tension between critical scholarship and faith in what is perceived to be the Sikh tradition, a measure of controversy has accompanied the recent interest in Sikh studies. Many chapters in this book attempt to respond to its existence. Controversy as such is not new in Sikh studies, but its present character certainly is. This has much to do with the crisis through which the Sikh community at home appears to be passing, and it affects members of the broader Sikh community wherever they happen to be. There is a strong reaction in certain quarters against the work published by Professor McLeod and by a few other scholars. The issues raised by this controversy are not new ones, but they are very important: the character of the Sikh faith and the question of its "origins," the nature and character of sources relating to the life of Guru Nanak (and the other Sikh Gurus), the societal composition of the early Sikhs *panth* and its bearing on the supposed transformation of the early *panth* into something rather different, the problem of authority within the *panth* after the death of Guru Gobind Singh, and the question of equality and caste in the Sikh *panth*.

This controversy can be quite fruitful if it causes critical scholars to become more aware of the implications of their apparently innocuous findings for believers and if it helps their critics from within the faith to become more clearly aware of the real implications of the "methodological atheism" that characterizes all rational-empirical research in the world today. At the present moment, such developments are only beginning to take place, and with much pain on both sides. One only hopes that the decades to come will tell a happier tale as Sikh studies achieve a rapidly approaching maturity both within the academic community and within the community of faith.

Notes

1. An earlier version of the first portion of this chapter was delivered as an inaugural address at the Christian Institute of Sikh Studies, Baring

Union Christian College, Batala, in 1972. It was published by the institute under the title "The Present State of Sikh Studies" and subsequently reprinted in my *Miscellaneous Articles* (Amritsar: Guru Nanak Dev University, 1974). Full citations for all works mentioned in the course of the chapter will be found in the general bibliography that follows, and readers interested in a more detailed consideration of the topic are referred to the bibliographic essay contained in my *The Sikhs of the Punjab,* recently published as a volume in *The New Cambridge History of India.*

Glossary of Punjabi Terms

Note: We are grateful to the editors of *Sikh History and Religion in the Twentieth Century* (Toronto: Centre for South Asian Studies, University of Toronto, 1988) for permission to use their glossary as a point of departure in creating the one that appears here.

Adi Granth (*ādi granth*) "primal book": the Sikh scripture as compiled by Guru Arjan in 1604, including the compositions of the Sikh Gurus, and selected writings of fifteen poet-saints of medieval India, in addition to some bards from within the Sikh community. The writings of Guru Tegh Bahadur were added to the text in the 1670s. The honorific title used for the sacred book is *Guru Granth Sahib*.

Akal Purakh (akāl purakh) "Timeless Being": an epithet for God in Sikh sacred writing.

Akal Takhat (*akāl takhat/ akāl takht*) "Throne of the Timeless": historically came into being as seat of the temporal authority of the Guru located on the premises of the Golden Temple and developed into the central place where communal decisions are taken.

Akali (*akālī*) "devotee of the Timeless One": During the eighteenth and early nineteenth century, this title designated Sikh warriors noted for their bravery. Today it signifies member of the Akali Dal.

Akali Dal (*akālī dal*) "army of the Akalis": the prominent political party of the Sikhs. It came into being early in the twentieth century when Sikhs were agitating for freedom of the *gurdwaras* from private hereditary control.

akhand path (*akhand pāth*) "unbroken reading": an uninterrupted recitation of the entire *Guru Granth Sahib* by a group of readers.

amritdhari (*amritdhārī*) "one who has taken the nectar": a person who has undergone the initiation ceremony and is a *khalsa* Sikh.

ardas (*ardās*) "petition": the daily Sikh congregational prayer.

Baba (*bābā*) "father/grandfather": a term of affection and respect often used for religious figures, including the *Guru Granth
Sahib*.

Babbar Akali (*babar akālī*) "lion among the Akalis": a radical early
twentieth-century group of Sikh militants.

bani (*bānī*) "utterances/compositions": the compositions recorded in
the *Guru Granth Sahib*. The writings of the Gurus are called
gurbani: those of the saints are *bhagatbani.*

Bhai (*bhāī*) "brother": a title applied to Sikhs of acknowledged
learning and piety, or any Sikh congregational leader.

bhagati (*bhagatī*) "devotion": a tradition of ardent worship based on
an attitude of loving devotion (cf. Sanskrit, *bhakti*).

bhog (*bhog*) "completion": the completion of a reading of the *Guru
Granth Sahib*.

bir (*bīr*) "volume," "book."

charan pahul (*charan pahul*) "nectar of the feet": the pre-*khalsa*
form of the ritual for initiation, performed by administering
water sanctified with the touch of the toe of the right foot of
a holy figure, whether the Guru himself or his designated official (*masand*).

Dal Khalsa (*dal khālsā*) "the *khalsa* horde": the combined forces of
the several *khalsa* groups that existed during the eighteenth
century.

Dasam Granth (*dasam granth*) "book of the tenth Master": the text
includes the sacred writings attributed to Guru Gobind
Singh, the tenth Guru of the Sikhs.

dharam (*dharam*) "duty": appropriate moral and religious obligation (cf. Sanskrit, *dharma*).

dharamsala (*dharamsālā*) "place for temporary residence": in early
Sikh usage, a building in which Sikhs met for devotional
singing and prayer, that is, a *gurdwara.*

dharamyudh (*dharamyudh*) "war in defense of *dharam*": The term
may be used to apply to a political struggle with religious
overtones.

giani (*giānī*) "a learned man": a scholar well versed in Sikh scriptures (cf. Sanskrit, *jñānī*).

granth (*granth*) "book": religious scripture.

granthi (*granthī*) "keeper of the *Guru Granth Sahib*": the official
who is in charge of the *gurdwara,* leads the daily worship,
and performs ceremonies such as weddings and the naming
of newborn children. These ceremonies may or may not be
held in the *gurdwara.*

gurdwara (gurdvārā/gurduārā) "Guru's place": the Sikh place of worship. This term is often translated as literally meaning "door of the Guru" or "door to the Guru," and the word door *(dvar/ duar)* is indeed the basis for the term *(dvara/duara)* that describes the interior space to which a door leads, especially in the context of a temple. The key area of a Sikh *gurdwara* is a spacious room housing the *Guru Granth Sahib,* where people sit and listen to scriptural recitation. The *gurdwara* is also used as a center for social activity and has a community kitchen attached to it, in which meals are prepared and served.

gurmat (gurmat) "the advice of the Gurus": the sum total of the Gurus' teachings; the doctrines referred to as "Sikhism."

gurmata (gurmatā) "the intention of the Guru": the will of the eternal Guru, as expressed in a formal decision made by a representative assembly of Sikhs; a resolution of the *sarbat khalsa.*

gurmukhi (gurmukhī) "from the mouth of the Guru": the script in which the compositions of the Gurus were first written. It has become the script in which Punjabi is written by all Sikhs.

gurpurb (gurpurb/gurpurab) "the festival of the Guru": celebration of the birth or death anniversary of the Gurus.

Guru *(gurū)* "preceptor": the mode of God as teacher and guide which in the past was revealed to Sikhs in the form of ten human Gurus and persists in the form of the *Guru Granth Sahib* and the *guru panth.*

Guru Granth Sahib *(gurū granth sāhib)* "the honorable Guru in book form": honorific title of the *Adi Granth.*

guru panth (gurū panth) "community as the Guru": the doctrine of the authoritative presence of the eternal Guru in a Sikh assembly.

haumai (haumai, haume) "self-centeredness": the powerful impulse to disregard submission to God, which is the essential human obligation, and succumb to personal gratification.

hukam (hukam/hukm) "order": the divine command of the personal God, which governs the entire universe.

hukamnama (hukamnāmā) "decree": a decree issued from the Akal Takhat, considered to be binding on the entire Sikh community.

izzat (izzat) "prestige": honor, especially associated with the social status of one's family.

Janam-sakhi (janam-sākhī) "birth story": traditional hagiographic narratives of Guru Nanak.

Japji (*japjī/japujī*): a composition of Guru Nanak that is recited by
  Sikhs every morning. This is the most commonly known Sikh
  liturgical prayer.
Jat (*jat*): the landholding caste group that is dominant in the Punjab and comprises the majority of Sikhs; a member of that
  cluster of castes.
jatha (*jathā*) "military detachment": organized group of Sikhs with
  a particular mission of preaching and reform, or political
  agenda.
jathedar (*jathedār*) "commander": the title of a leader of Sikh band.
  The title is applied to custodians of the five historic *gur-*
  dwaras, singled out from the others and known as *takhats*
  (thrones).
kachha (*kachhā*) "pair of shorts": *Kachha, kangha,* and *kara* are
  three of the five items a *khalsa* Sikh is required to wear. The
  other two are *kes* (uncut hair) and *kirpan* (sword).
kangha (*kanghā*) "comb." See *kachha.*
kara (*karā*) "steel bracelet." See *kachha.*
karah parshad (*karāh parshād*) "sacramental food": Made of flour,
  sugar, and clarified butter, *karah parshad* is distributed after
  each *gurdwara* service.
Kaur (*kaur*) "princess": used as a name by female members of the
  khalsa, as a parallel to *singh* for men.
kes (*kes*) "hair": *Khalsa* Sikhs are required to keep their hair uncut.
kesdhari (*kesdhārī*) "hair-bearing": a term used for Sikhs who do
  not cut their hair.
Khalistan (*khālistān*) "the land of the *khalsa*": the proposed name
  for a Sikh state independent of India.
khalsa (*khālsā*) "God's own": Sikhs who have undergone the initiation ceremony of taking nectar prepared with the double-
  edged sword and have thus responded to the call of
  dedicating themselves to God and working for his victory on
  the earth. The word *khalsa,* derived from Arabic *khalis,*
  meaning pure, connotes not simply "pure" (as it is often
  translated) but one who is purified by God. The word *khalsa*
  was also a common revenue term in Mughal administration,
  used to denote territories under direct royal control. Consequently, *khalsa* Sikhs are those who owe allegiance to God
  alone, and should reject all sources of temporal authority.
khande di pahul (*khande dī pahul*) "the nectar made with the
  double-edged sword": This name was given to the *khalsa* initiation ceremony instituted by Guru Gobind Singh, symbol-

izing militancy and a self-perception within the *khalsa* that it constitutes an elect group chosen by the Guru for its role.

Khatri (*khatrī*) "merchant-caste." Although the name derives from Sanskrit *kshatriya*, which designates the warrior or ruling castes, *khatri* in Punjabi usage refers to a cluster of merchant castes including Bedis, Bhallas, and Sodhis.

kirpan (*kirpān*) "sword": required to be worn by a member of the *khalsa* as part of the five possessions appropriate to it.

kirtan (*kīrtan*) "devotional singing": a significant part of Sikh piety.

langar (*langar*) "community kitchen": attached to every *gurdwara*, from which food is served to all, regardless of caste or creed.

mahant (*mahant*) "abbot": title traditionally used for Udasi custodians of the Sikh *gurdwaras*. The position tended to be hereditary before the Gurdwaras Act of 1925.

Majha (*mājhā*) "middle": the area of central Punjab between the Beas and the Ravi rivers.

masand (*masand*) "[Guru's] deputy": authorized leader of a local congregation of Sikhs.

miri-piri (*mīrī-pīrī*) "temporal-spiritual": the assumption of temporal and spiritual authority on the part of the Gurus. This doctrine goes back to Guru Hargobind, who symbolically donned two swords, one for each type of authority.

misal (*misal/misl*) "equal": a Sikh military band of the eighteenth century; also a Sikh principality in that century.

mulmantar (*mūlmantar*) "the root formula": the Sikh creedal statement placed at the head of the text of the *Guru Granth Sahib*. It reads: "There is one Supreme Being, the Eternal Reality. He is the Creator, without fear, and devoid of enmity. He is the immortal, never incarnated, self-existent, reached through the grace of the Guru."

Namdharis (*nāmdhārīs*) "the bearers of the Name": a nineteenth-century millenarian revivalist movement started by Baba Balak Singh (1799–1861). He advocated the simplification of Sikh ceremonies, and his followers were known for their loud shrieks at the time of devotional chanting. Namdharis have a base in Ludhiana, from which a number of them have moved to Southeast Asia.

nam-simran (*nām-simran*): "remembering the Name": repetition of a name of God and the devout singing of hymns from the *Guru Granth Sahib*.

Nanak-panth (*nānak panth*) "the way of Nanak": term often used for the early Sikh community, as a way of refering to the fact that they were followers of Guru Nanak.

Nirankari (*nirankārī*) "a follower of Nirankar": a revivalist Sikh movement started by Baba Dayal in the middle of the nineteenth century. At present the movement has bases in Chandigarh and Delhi.

Nirmala (*nirmalā*) "a pure one": a line of Sikh scholars said to have originated during the time of Guru Gobind Singh (1666–1708). Because of their emphasis on Sanskrit learning, their interpretation of Sikh scriptures has a strong Vedantic coloring. Like several other *sant* groups, their places of learning are known as *akharas* (arenas, wrestling rings), a reference to the association between physical and intellectual discipline.

Nath Yogi (*nāth yogī*): a member of a Shaivite sect of ascetics that was very influential in medieval Punjab. The writings of the Sikh Gurus indicate their engagement with these ascetics, whose seats were known as *tillas* ("mounds").

panj kakke (*panj kakke*) "five k's": the five items, each of whose name begins with letter "k," that a *khalsa* Sikh should wear. (See *kachha*.)

panj piare (*panj piāre*) "the beloved five": leaders who constitute the chief authority in the Sikh *panth*. This designation recalls the five men who offered their lives to Guru Gobind Singh.

patit (*patit*) "fallen": one who, once having undergone the baptism of the *khalsa,* no longer follows its code of conduct.

pothi (*pothī*) "volume," "book": title used for early Sikh manuscripts including the first canonical version of the *Guru Granth Sahib.*

qaum (*kaum*) "a people who stand together": The Sikh usage of this term has connotations of both community and nation.

rahit (*rahit/rehat/reht*): the *khalsa* code of conduct, which attained written form in the eighteenth century.

rahit maryada (*rahit maryādā/rehat maryādā*): the code of discipline of the *khalsa;* also a specific text on this subject.

rahit-nama (*rehat-nāmā*): one of several manuals of Sikh conduct.

raj karega khalsa (*rāj karegā khālsā*) "the *khalsa* shall rule": This phrase, which appears in the concluding couplet in daily Sikh prayer, became current in the eighteenth century as part of Sikh aspirations for sovereign rule.

Ramgaria (*rāmgaṛīā*) the carpenter caste. After the Jats, this is the second largest caste within the Sikh community.

Sacha Patishahu (*sachā pātshāh*) "True Lord": a key epithet for God in the writings of Guru Nanak. The term came to be used to address the Sikh Gurus, who were seen as the representatives of God on earth.

sahajdhari (*sahajdhārī*) "simple adherent": someone who has not received initiation into the *khalsa* but affirms full allegiance to the *Guru Granth Sahib*. In its Sikh context, the term is used in contrast to *amritdhari* and *kesdhari*.

sangat (*sangat*) "congregation": With its considerable emphasis on community, Sikhism gives great importance to congregational worship (cf. Sanskrit, *sangha*).

sant (*sant*) "saint": a title for a Sikh holy person; is also used to describe a devotional tradition of North India in which God is worshipped as formless, and transcendental reality.

sant-sipahi (*sant-sipāhī*) "saint soldier": one who combines the spirituality of the devout believer with the bravery and obedience of a true soldier.

sarbat khalsa (*sarbat khālsā*) "the entire *khalsa*": an assembly of representatives of the whole Sikh community, historically gathered at the Akal Takhat, Amritsar, to resolve some crisis facing the Sikh community.

Sati Sri Akal (*sati srī akāl*) "God is truth": the common Sikh greeting. The generally accepted translation of this phrase, "Truth is eternal" or "Truth is timeless," is not accurate. This translation ignores the word "*sri*," an honorific preceeding "*akal*," meaning God, which often appears in the *Dasam Granth*.

seva (*sevā*) "service": Holding the remembrance of God in one's heart and serving the community are the two pillars of Sikh faith.

shabad (*shabad*) "word": The term is used to refer both to the divine Word received from God and to a hymn contained within the *Guru Granth Sahib* which expresses that Word (cf. Sanskrit *śabda*).

Sikh (*sikh*) "disciple," "learner": any person who believes in God, in the ten Gurus, in the *Guru Granth Sahib* and other teachings of the Gurus, in the *khalsa* initiation ceremony, and in the doctrinal system of no other religion. This definition, coined in the middle of the twentieth century, is considered authoritative in the mainstream Sikh community.

Singh (*singh*) "lion": name used by male Sikhs.

Singh Sabha (*singh sabhā*) "the Singh Society": a late nineteenth- or early twentieth-century movement based on several local societies dedicated to religious and educational reform among Sikhs.

Sufi (*sufī*) "Muslim mystic": As a group, Sufis had a major religious impact in medieval Punjab. From centers known as *khanqahs,* these saints taught their disciples, fed travelers, and gave medicine to the sick.

takhat (*takhat/takht*) "throne": one of the five major seats of authority among Sikhs. The *takhats* are located at Amritsar, Anandpur, Damdama (all in the Punjab), Patna (in Bihar), and Nander (in Maharashtra).

taksal (*taksāl*) "mint": Sikh seminaries where religious education is offered.

Tat Khalsa (*tat khālsā*) "the true *khalsa*": the more rigorous, reformed mode of being Sikh advocated within the Singh Sabha movement.

Udasi (*udāsī*) "disinterested; stoic": an order of ascetics begun by Baba Srichand, the eldest son of Guru Nanak. During the eighteenth century, the Udasis became the custodians of Sikh *gurdwaras* and the key interpreters of Sikh religious thought. In line with the reformed Sikh self-definition created by the Singh Sabha, the close Sikh-Udasi link was largely severed, and Udasis increasingly regarded themselves as Hindus rather than Sikhs.

updeshak (*updeshak*) "preacher": a Sikh functionary who instructs, advises, and motivates the faithful.

Vahiguru (*vāhigurū*) "Wonderful Guru": presently the most commonly used epithet for God in the Sikh tradition.

Select Bibliography of Works in English

Textual Sources

Ashta, Dharam Pal. *The Poetry of the Dasam Granth.* New Delhi: Arun, 1959.

Bedi, Gursharan Singh. *The Epistle of Victory: An English Translation of Zafrarnama in Verse.* Amritsar: the author, 1960.

Doabia, Harbans Singh. *Life Story of Satguru Gobind Singh Ji Mahraj and Some of His Hymns.* Chandigarh: Harbans Singh Doabia Charitable Trust, 1974.

———. *Sacred Nitnem.* Amritsar: Singh Brothers, 1974.

———. *Sacred Sukhmani.* Amritsar: the author, 1979.

Duggal, K. S. *Fatehnama and Zafarnama.* Jalandhar: Institute of Sikh Studies, 1980.

Fauja Singh. *Hukamnamas Shri Guru Tegh Bahadur Sahib.* Patiala: Punjabi University Press, 1976.

Gopal Singh. *Sri Guru Granth Sahib,* 4 vols. Delhi: Gurdas Kapur & Sons, 1960–62.

———. *Thus Spake the Tenth Master.* Patiala: Punjabi University Press, 1978.

Greenless, Duncan. *Selections from the Adi Granth.* Adyar: Theosophical Publishing House, 1975.

Gursaran Singh. *Guru Nanak's Japji.* Delhi: Atma Ram, 1972.

Hawley, J. S., and Mark Juergensmeyer, *Songs of the Saints of India.* New York: Oxford University Press, 1988.

Jodh Singh. *Thirty-Three Swaiyas.* Ludhiana: Lahore Book Shop, 1953.

Khushwant Singh. *Hymns of Guru Nanak.* New Delhi: Orient Longmans, 1969.

Kanwaljit Kaur and Inderjit Singh. *Rehat Maryada: A Guide to the Sikh Way of Life.* London: Sikh Cultural Society, 1969.

Loehlin, Clinton H. *The Sikhs and their Scriptures.* Lucknow Publishing House, 1964.

――――. *The Granth of Guru Gobind Singh and the Khalsa Brotherhood.* Lucknow: Lucknow Publishing House, 1971.

Macauliffe, Max Arthur. *The Sikh Religion, Its Gurus, Sacred Writings and Authors,* 6 vols. 1909. Reprint. Delhi: S. Chand & Co., 1985.

Maighowalia, B. S. *Bachittar Naatak.* Hoshiarpur: the author, 1978.

Manmohan Singh. *Sri Guru Granth Sahib,* 8 vols. Amritsar: Shiromani Gurdwara Prabandhak Committee, 1962–69.

Mansukhani, G. S. *Hymns from the Holy Granth.* New Delhi: Hemkunt Press, 1975.

McLeod, W. H. *The B 40 Janam-sakhi.* Amritsar: Guru Nanak Dev University Press, 1980.

――――. *Early Sikh Tradition: A Study of the Janam-sakhis.* Oxford: Clarendon Press, 1980.

――――. *Textual Sources for the Study of Sikhism.* 1984. Reprint. Chicago: University of Chicago Press, 1990.

――――. *The Chaupa Singh Rahit-nama.* Dunedin: University of Otago Press, 1987.

Nirbhai Singh. *Bhagat Namdev in Guru Granth.* Patiala: Punjabi University Press, 1981.

Pashaura Singh. "The Text and Meaning of the Adi Granth." Ph.D. diss., University of Toronto, 1991.

Peace, M. L. *Asa di Var.* Amritsar: Chief Khalsa Diwan, 1971.

Randhawa, G. S. *Guru Nanak's Japuji.* Amritsar: Guru Nanak Dev University Press, 1990.

Sawan Singh. *Tales of the Mystic East.* Beas: Radha Soami Satsang, 1964.

Sekhon, Sant Singh. *Unique Drama: Translation of Benati Chaupai, Bachitra Natak and Akal Ustati.* Chandigarh: Guru Gobind Singh Foundation, 1978.

Sohan Singh. *Asa di Var: The Ballad of God and Man.* Amritsar: Guru Nanak Dev University Press, 1982.

Swami Rama. *Japji: Meditation in Sikhism.* Honsdale, Pa.: Himalayan International Institute, 1987.

――――. *Sukhmani Sahib: Fountain of Eternal Joy.* Honsdale, Pa.: Himalayan International Institute, 1988.

Talib, Gurbachan Singh, et al. *Guru Tegh Bahadur: Martyr and Teacher.* Patiala: Punjabi University Press, 1975.

——. *Japuji: The Immortal Prayer Chant.* Delhi: Munshiram Manoharlal, 1977.

——. *Bani of Sri Guru Amardas.* New Delhi: Sterling, 1979.

——. *Selections from the Holy Granth.* New Delhi: Guru Nanak Foundation, 1982.

——. *Sri Guru Granth Sahib,* 4 vols. Patiala: Punjabi University Press, 1985–1990.

Teja Singh. *Asa di Var or Guru Nanak's Ode in the Asa Measure.* Amritsar, Shiromani Gurdwara Prabandhak Committee, 1957.

Trilochan Singh. *Hymns of Guru Tegh Bahadur: Songs of Nirvana.* Delhi: Delhi Sikh Gurdwara Management Committee, 1975.

Trilochan Singh et al. *Selections from the Sacred Writings of the Sikhs.* London: Allen and Unwin, 1960.

Trumpp, Ernest. *The Adi Granth or the Holy Scripture of the Sikhs.* 1877. Reprint. Delhi: Munshiram Manoharlal, 1978.

Beliefs and Practices

Aggarwal, S. C. *Sketch of the Sikhs: Their Customs and Manners.* Chandigarh: Vinay, 1981.

Avtar Singh. *Ethics of the Sikhs.* Patiala: Punjabi University Press, 1983.

Bajwa, Fauja Singh. *Guide to Sikh Shrines and Historical Places in Delhi.* New Delhi: Delhi Gurdwara Prabandhak Committee, 1953.

Cole, W. Owen. *The Guru in Sikhism.* London: Darton, Longman and Todd, 1982.

Cole, W. Owen, and Piara Singh Sambhi. *The Sikhs, Their Religious Beliefs and Practices.* Boston: Routledge and Kegan Paul, 1978.

Daljeet Singh. *The Sikh Ideology.* New Delhi: Guru Nanak Foundation, 1984.

Daljit Singh. *Sikh Sacred Music.* Ludhiana: Sikh Sacred Music Society, 1967.

Ganda Singh. *The Sikhs and their Religion.* Redwood City, Calif.: The Sikh Foundation, 1974.

Gopal Singh. *The Religion of the Sikhs.* Bombay: Asia Publishing House, 1971.

Gurnam Kaur. *Reason and Revelation in Sikhism*. New Delhi: Cosmo, 1990.

Jogendra Singh. *Sikh Ceremonies*. 1941. Reprint. Chandigarh: Religious Book Society, 1968.

Johar, Surinder Singh. *The Sikh Gurus and their Shrines*. Delhi: Vivek, 1976.

Kapoor, Sukhbir Singh. *Sikh Festivals*. England: Wayland, 1985.

Khan, Mohammad Walliullah. *Sikh Shrines in West Pakistan*. Karachi: Department of Archaeology, 1962.

Khushwant Singh. *Religion of the Sikhs*. Madras: University of Madras Press, 1968.

Kohli, Surinder Singh. *Sikh Ethics*. New Delhi: Munshiram Manoharlal, 1975.

Madanjit Kaur. *Golden Temple: Past and Present*. Amritsar: Guru Nanak Dev University Press, 1983.

Mansukhani, Gobind Singh. *Indian Classical Music and Sikh Kirtan*. New Delhi: Oxford & IBH, 1982.

McLeod, W. H. *The Sikhs: History, Religion, and Society*. New York: Columbia University Press, 1989.

McMullan, Clarence O., ed. *The Nature of Guruship*. Batala: Christian Institute of Sikh Studies, 1976.

——— . *Religious Beliefs and Practices of the Sikhs in Rural Punjab*. New Delhi: Manohar, 1989.

Mehar Singh. *Sikh Shrines in India*. Delhi: Publication Division, Government of India, 1975.

Nripinder Singh. *Sikh Moral Tradition*. New Delhi: Manohar, 1990.

Paintal, Ajit Singh. "The Nature and Place of Music in Sikh Religion and its Affinity with Hindustani Classical Music." Ph. D. diss., Delhi University, 1972.

Parkash Singh. *The Sikh Gurus and the Temple of Bread*. Amritsar: Shiromani Gurdwara Prabandhak Committee, 1971.

Sabi, Joginder Singh. *Sikh Shrines in India and Abroad*. Faridabad: Common World Publication, 1978.

Sher Singh. *Thoughts on Forms and Symbols in Sikhism*. Lahore: Mercantile Press, 1927.

Shergill, N. S. *International Directory of Gurdwaras and Sikh Organizations*. London: the author, 1985.

Sikhism and Indian Society: Transactions of the Indian Institute of Advanced Studies. Simla: Indian Institute of Advanced Studies, 1967.

Teja Singh. *Sikhism: Its Ideals and Institutions.* Calcutta: Orient Longmans, 1951.

Thursby, Gene R. *The Sikhs.* New York: E. J. Brill, 1992.

Trilochan Singh. *Historical Sikh Shrines in Delhi.* Delhi: Delhi Gurdwara Prabandhak Committe, 1967.

Webster, John C. B., ed. *Popular Religion in the Punjab Today.* Delhi: Christian Institute of Sikh Studies, Batala, 1974.

Origins of the Sikh Faith [*the Guru Period*]

Ahluwalia, Jasbir Singh. *The Sovereignty of the Sikh Doctrine.* New Delhi: Bahri Publications, 1983.

Ahuja, A. M. *Significance of Guru Tegh Bahadur's Martyrdom: A True Perspective.* Chandigarh: Kirti Publishing House, 1975.

Ahuja, N. D. *The Great Guru Nanak and the Muslims.* Chandigarh: Kirti Publishing House, 1971.

Anand, Balwant Singh. *Guru Nanak Religion and Ethics.* Patiala: Punjabi University Press, 1968.

―――. *Guru Tegh Bahadur: A Biography.* New Delhi: Sterling, 1979.

―――. *Guru Nanak: His Life was His Message.* New Delhi: Guru Nanak Foundation, 1983.

Archer, John Clark. *The Sikhs, in Relation to Hindus, Moslems, Christians and Ahmadiyas: A Study in Comparative Religion.* Princeton: Princeton University Press, 1946.

Bal, Sarjit Singh. *Life of Guru Nanak.* Chandigarh: Panjab University Press, 1969.

Banerjee, Anil Chandra. *Guru Nanak and His Times.* Patiala: Punjabi University Press, 1971.

―――. *Guru Nanak to Guru Gobind Singh.* New Delhi: Rajesh, 1978.

―――. *The Sikh Gurus and the Sikh Religion.* New Delhi: Munshiram Manoharlal, 1983.

Banerjee, Indubhushan. *Evolution of the Khalsa,* 2 vols. 1936. Reprint Calcutta: A. Mukherjee, 1979–80.

Cole, W. Owen. *Sikhism and its Indian Context 1469–1708*. New Delhi: D.K. Agencies, 1984.

Daljeet Singh. *Sikhism: A Comparative Study of Its Theology and Mysticism*. New Delhi: Sterling, 1979.

———. *Essay on the Authenticity of Kartarpuri Bir and the Integrated Logic and Unity of Sikhism*. Patiala: Punjabi University Press, 1987.

Darshan Singh. *Indian Bhakti Tradition and the Sikh Gurus*. Chandigarh: Punjab Publishers, 1968.

Dass, J. R. *Economic Thought of the Sikh Gurus*. New Delhi: National Book Organisation, 1988.

Dhillon, Dalbir Singh. *Sikhism: Origin and Development*. New Delhi: Atlantic, 1988.

Duggal, K. S. *Sikh Gurus: Their Lives and Teachings*. New Delhi: Vikas, 1980.

Fauja Singh. *Guru Amardas: Life and Teachings*. New Delhi: Sterling, 1979.

Fauja Singh et al. *Sikhism*. Patiala: Punjabi University Press, 1969.

Fauja Singh and A. C. Arora, eds. *Papers on Guru Nanak: Proceedings of Punjab History Conference*, 4th session. Patiala: Punjabi University Press, 1970.

Fauja Singh and Gurbachan Singh Talib. *Guru Tegh Bahadur: Martyr and Teacher*. Patiala: Punjabi University Press, 1975.

Fauja Singh and Rattan Singh Jaggi, eds. *Perspectives on Guru Amardas*. Patiala: Punjabi University Press, 1982.

Fields, Dorothy. *The Religion of the Sikhs*. New York: Dutton, 1914.

Ganda Singh, ed. *Sources on the Life and Teachings of Guru Nanak*. Patiala: Punjabi University Press, 1969.

———. *Guru Gobind Singh's Death at Nanded: An Examination of Succession Theories*. Faridkot: Guru Nanak Foundation, 1972.

Gandhi, Surjit Singh. *History of the Sikh Gurus: A Comprehensive Study*. Delhi: Gur Das Kapur & Sons, 1978.

Gopal Singh. *The Sikhs*. Bombay: Popular, 1970.

———. *A History of the Sikh People, 1469–1978*. New Delhi: World Sikh University Press, 1979.

Grewal, J. S. *Guru Nanak in History*. Chandigarh: Panjab University Press, 1969.

———. *From Guru Nanak to Maharaja Ranjit Singh: Essays in Sikh History. 1972.* Rev. ed. Amritsar: Guru Nanak Dev University Press, 1982.

———. *Guru Tegh Bahadur and the Persian Chroniclers.* Amritsar: Guru Nanak Dev University Press, 1976.

———. *The Sikhs of the Punjab.* Cambridge: Cambridge University Press, 1991.

Grewal, J. S., and S. S. Bal. *Guru Gobind Singh: A Biographical Study.* 1967. Reprint. Chandigarh: Panjab University Press, 1987.

Gupta, Hari Ram. *History of the Sikhs,* 4 vols. New Delhi: Munshiram Manoharlal, 1978–84.

Gurdev Singh, ed. *Perspectives on Sikh Tradition.* Chandigarh: Siddharth, 1986.

Gurmukh Nihal Singh, ed. *Guru Nanak, His Life, Times and Teachings.* New Delhi: Guru Nanak Foundation, 1969.

Ishar Singh. *The Philosophy of Guru Nanak.* Delhi: Atlantic, 1985.

Jodh Singh. *Guru Nanak Lectures.* Madras: University of Madras Press, 1969.

Johar, Surinder Singh. *Guru Tegh Bahadur: A Biography.* Delhi: Abhinav, 1975.

Hans, Surjit. *Reconstruction of Sikh History from Sikh Literature.* Jalandhar: ABC, 1988.

Harbans Singh. *Guru Gobind Singh.* Chandigarh: Guru Gobind Singh Foundation, 1966.

———. *Guru Nanak and the Origin of the Sikh Faith.* Bombay: Asia Publishing House, 1969.

———, ed. *Perspectives on Guru Nanak.* Patiala: Punjabi University Press, 1975.

———. *Guru Tegh Bahadur.* New Delhi: Sterling, 1982.

———. *The Heritage of the Sikhs.* New Delhi: Manohar, 1983.

Jagjit Singh. *Sikh Revolution: A Perspective View.* New Delhi: Kendri Singh Sabha, 1981.

———. *Perspectives on Sikh Studies.* New Delhi: Guru Nanak Foundation, 1985.

———. *In the Caravan of Revolutions.* Chandigarh: the author, 1987.

Jain, Nirmal Kumar. *Sikh Religion and Philosophy.* New Delhi: Sterling, 1979.

Juergensmeyer, Mark, and N. Gerald Barrier, eds. *Sikh Studies: Comparative Perspectives on a Changing Tradition*. Berkeley: Berkeley Religious Studies Series, 1979.

Kapur Singh. *Parasarprasna*. 1959. Rev. ed. Amritsar: Guru Nanak Dev University Press, 1988.

Kavishar, Sardul Singh. *Sikh Studies*. Lahore: The National Publication, 1937.

Kharak Singh, G. S. Mansukhani, and Jasbir Singh Mann. *Fundamental Issues in Sikh Studies*. Chandigarh: Institute of Sikh Studies, 1992.

Khushwant Singh. *The Sikhs*. London: George Allen & Unwin, 1953.

————. *The Sikhs Today*. Bombay: Orient Longmans, 1964.

————. *A History of the Sikhs*. 2 vols. 1963. Rev. ed. Delhi: Oxford University Press, 1991.

Kohli, Surinder Singh. *A Critical Study of the Adi Granth*. 1961. Reprint. Delhi: Motilal Banarsidas, 1976.

————. *Philosophy of Guru Nanak*. Chandigarh: Panjab University Press, 1969.

————. *Outline of Sikh Thought*. New Delhi: Munshiram Manoharlal, 1978.

————. *Life and Ideals of Guru Gobind Singh*. New Delhi: Munshiram Manoharlal, 1986.

Lahori, Lajwanti. *The Concept of Man in Sikhism*. New Delhi: Munshiram Manoharlal, 1985.

Macauliffe, Max Arthur. *The Sikh Religion, Its Gurus, Sacred Writings and Authors*, 6 vols. 1909. Reprint. New Delhi: S. Chand & Co., 1985.

Macauliffe, Max Arthur et al. *The Sikh Religion: A Symposium*. Calcutta: S. Gupta, 1958.

Mann, Jasbir Singh, and Harbans Singh Saraon, eds. *Advanced Studies in Sikhism*. Irvine, Calif.: Sikh Community of North America, 1989.

Mansukhani, Gobind Singh. *The Quintessence of Sikhism*. Amritsar: Shiromani Gurdwara Prabandhak Committee, 1965.

————. *Introduction to Sikhism*. Delhi: India Book House, 1968.

————. *Life of Guru Nanak*. New Delhi: Guru Nanak Foundation, 1974.

————. *Guru Ramdas: His Life Work and Philosophy*. New Delhi: Oxford & IBH, 1979.

————. *Life of Guru Ramdas: His Life Work and Philosophy*. New Delhi: Oxford & IBH, 1979.

McLeod, W. H. *Guru Nanak and the Sikh Religion*. Oxford: Clarendon Press, 1968.

———. *The Evolution of the Sikh Community*. Oxford: Clarendon Press, 1976.

———. *Who is a Sikh? The Problem of Sikh Identity*. Oxford: Clarendon Press, 1989.

Narang, Gokal Chand. *Transformation of Sikhism*. New Delhi: New Book Society, 1956.

———. *Glorious History of Sikhism*. Delhi: New Book Society, 1972.

Nirbhai Singh. *Philosophy of Sikhism: Reality and its Manifestations*. New Delhi: Atlantic Publishers, 1990.

Pritam Singh, ed. *Sikh Concept of the Divine*. Amritsar: Guru Nanak Dev University Press, 1985.

Raj, Hormise Nirmal. *Evolution of the Sikh Faith: The Historical Formation and Development of Sikhism under the Gurus*. New Delhi: Unity Book Service, 1987.

Ravinder, G. B. Singh. *Indian Philosophical Tradition and Guru Nanak: A Study Based on the Conceptual Terminology Used in Guru Nanak's Bani*. Patiala: Punjab Publishing House, 1983.

Ray, Niharranjan. *The Sikh Gurus and the Sikh Society: A Study in Social Analysis*. Patiala: Punjabi University Press, 1970.

Sahib Singh, *Guru Gobind Singh: His Mission*. Jalandhar: Raj, 1967.

———. *Guru Nanak Dev and His Teachings*. Jalandhar: Raj, 1969.

Schomer, Karine, and W. H. McLeod, eds. *The Sants: Studies in a Devotional Tradition of India*. Berkeley: Berkeley Religious Studies Series; Delhi: Motilal Banarsidass, 1987.

Sethi, Amarjit Singh. *Universal Sikhism*. Delhi: Vikas, 1972.

Sher Singh. *Philosophy of Sikhism*. 1944. Reprint. Amritsar: Shiromani Gurdwara Prabandhak Committee, 1986.

Talib, Gurbachan Singh. *The Impact of Guru Gobind Singh on Indian Society*. Chandigarh: Guru Gobind Singh Foundation, 1966.

———. *Guru Nanak: His Personality and Vision*. New Delhi: Gur Das Kapur & Sons, 1969.

———, ed. *Guru Tegh Bahadur: Background and the Supreme Sacrifice: A Collection of Research Articles*. Patiala: Punjabi University Press, 1976.

Taran Singh, ed. *Guru Nanak and the Indian Religious Thought*. Patiala: Punjabi University Press, 1970.

――― . *Teachings of Guru Nanak Dev*. Patiala: Punjabi University Press, 1977.

――― , ed. *Sikh Gurus and the Indian Spiritual Tradition*. Patiala: Punjabi University Press, 1981.

Teja Singh and Ganda Singh. *A Short History of the Sikhs*. 1950. Reprint. Patiala: Punjabi University Press, 1989.

Trilochan Singh. *Guru Tegh Bahadur: Prophet and Martyr*. Delhi: Gurdwara Prabandhak Committee, 1967.

――― . *Guru Nanak, Founder of Sikhism*. Delhi: Gurdwara Prabandhak Committee, 1969.

――― . *Life of Guru Harikrishan: A Biography and History*. Delhi: Delhi Sikh Gurdwara Management Committee, 1981.

Uberoi, Mohan Singh. *Sikh Mysticism: The Sevenfold Yoga of Sikhism*. Amritsar: the author, 1964.

Wazir Singh. *Aspects of Guru Nanak's Philosophy*. Ludhiana: Lahore Book Shop, 1969.

――― . *Humanism of Guru Nanak: A Philosophic Inquiry*. Delhi: Ess Ess, 1977.

Period of Sikh Ascendence

Alam, Muzaffar. *The Crisis of Empire in Mughal North India, Awadh and the Punjab, 1707–48*. Delhi: Oxford University Press, 1986.

Ali, Shahamat. *The Sikhs and the Afghans*. 1847. Reprint. Patiala: Punjab Language Department, 1970.

Banerjee, Anil Chandra. *The Khalsa Raj*. New Delhi: Abhinav, 1985.

Banga, Indu. *Agrarian System of the Sikhs*. New Delhi: Manohar, 1978.

Bhagat Singh. *Sikh Polity in the Eighteenth and the Nineteenth Century*. New Delhi: Oriental, 1978.

Chopra, Barkat Rai. *Kingdom of the Punjab, 1839–45*. Hoshairpur: Vishveshvaranand Institute, 1969.

Chopra, Gulshan Lal. *The Punjab as a Sovereign State*. 1929. Reprint. Lahore: Al-Biruni, 1977.

Cunningham, Joseph Davy. *A History of the Sikhs, From the Origin of the Nation to the Battle of the Sutlej.* 1849. Reprint. New Delhi: S. Chand & Co., 1985.

Farooqi, Bashir Ahmad. *British Relations With Cis-Sutlej States, 1809–1823.* 1942. Reprint. Patiala: Punjab Language Department, 1971.

Fauja Singh. *Military System of the Sikhs.* Delhi: Motilal Banarsidass, 1964.

———, ed. *Historians and Historiography of the Sikhs.* Delhi: Oriental, 1978.

———. *After Ranjit Singh.* New Delhi: Master, 1982.

———. *State and Society under Ranjit Singh.* New Delhi: Master, 1982.

Fauja Singh and A. C. Arora, eds. *Maharaja Ranjit Singh: Politics, Society and Economy.* Patiala: Punjabi University Press, 1984.

Forster, George A. *A Journey From Bengal to England, through the Northern Part of India, Kashmere, Afghanistan and Persia and into Russia by the Caspean Sea.* Vol. 1. London: R. Faulder, 1798.

Ganda Singh, ed. *Early European Accounts of the Sikhs.* Calcutta: Indian Studies, 1962.

———. *Baba Banda Singh Bahadur: His Life and Achievements and the Place of his Execution.* Sirhind: Historical Research Society, 1976.

Gandhi, Surjit Singh. *Struggle of the Sikhs for Sovereignty.* Delhi: Gur Das Kapur & Sons, 1980.

Goswami, B. N., and J. S. Grewal. *The Mughal and Sikh Rulers and the Vaishnavas of Pindori.* Simla: Indian Institute of Advanced Studies, 1969.

Grewal, J. S. *Historian's Punjab: Miscellaneous Articles.* Amritsar: Guru Nanak Dev University Press, 1974.

———. *The Reign of Maharaja Ranjit Singh: Structure of Power, Economy and Society.* Patiala: Punjabi University Press, 1981.

———. *Maharaja Ranjit Singh.* Amritsar: Guru Nanak Dev University Press, 1982.

Grewal, J. S., and Indu Banga. *The Civil and Military Affairs of Maharaja Ranjit Singh.* Amritsar: Guru Nanak Dev University Press, 1987.

Gupta, Hari Ram. *Punjab on the Eve of the First Sikh War.* Chandigarh: Panjab University Press, 1975.

Hasrat, Bikrama Jit. *Anglo-Sikh Relations 1799–1849.* Hoshairpur: V. V. Research Institute, 1968.

————. *Life and Times of Ranjit Singh: A Saga of Benevolent Despotism.* Hoshiarpur: V. V. Research Institute, 1977.

Khushwant Singh, *Ranjit Singh: Maharaja of the Punjab.* London: George Allen & Unwin, 1962.

————. *The Fall of the Kingdom of the Punjab.* Bombay: Orient Longmans, 1962.

Kirpal Singh. *Life of Maharaja Ala Singh of Patiala.* Amritsar: Shiromani Gurdwara Prabandhak Committee, 1954.

Kohli, Sita Ram. *Sunset of the Sikh Empire.* New Delhi: Orient Longmans, 1967

Lafont, Jean Marrie. *French Administrators of Maharaja Ranjit Singh.* Delhi: National Book Shop, 1986.

Latif, Syad Mohammad. *History of the Punjab from the Remotest Antiquity to the Present Time.* 1891. Reprint. Delhi: Eurasia Publishing House, 1964.

Mahajan, Jagmohan. *Circumstances leading to the Annexation of the Punjab.* Allahabad: Kitabistan, 1949.

Majumdar, B. N. *Military System of the Sikhs.* Delhi: Delhi Army Educational Stores, 1965.

Malcolm, Sir John. *Sketches of the Sikhs.* London: John Murray, 1812.

Malik, Arjan Dass. *An Indian Guerilla War: The Sikh People's War 1699–1768.* New Delhi: Wiley Eastern, 1975.

M'Gregor, W. L. *The History of the Sikhs,* 2 vols. London: James Maden, 1846.

Parmu, R. K. *A History of Sikh Rule in Kashmir, 1819–1846.* Srinagar: Department of Education, Government of Kashmir, 1977.

Princep, Henry T. *Origin of the Sikh Power and Political Life of Maharaja Ranjit Singh with an Account of Religion, Laws and Customs of the Sikhs.* 1834. Reprint. Patiala: Punjab Language Department, 1970.

Sethi, R. R. *Lahore Darbar: In the Light of Correspondence of Sir C. M. Wade, 1823–1840.* Delhi: Gulab Chand Kapur, 1950.

————. *The Mighty and Shrewd Maharaja Ranjit Singh's Relation with Other Powers.* Delhi: S. Chand & Co., 1960

Sinha, Narendra Krishna. *Ranjit Singh.* Calcutta: A. Mukherjee & Co., 1968.

————. *Rise of the Sikh Power.* 1936. Reprint. Calcutta: A. Mukherjee & Co., 1973.

Suri, V. S. *Umdat-ut-Tawarikh. Chronicles of the Reign of Maharaja Kharak Singh.* Chandigarh: Punjab Itihas Prakashan, 1972.

Waheeduddin, Fakir Syed. *The Real Ranjit Singh.* Karachi: Lion Art Press, 1965.

Sikhs Under the British

Adhikari, G. *Sikh Homeland through Hindu-Muslim Unity.* Bombay: People's Publishing House, 1944.

Ahluwalia, M. L., ed. *Select Documents, Gurdwara Reform Movement 1919–1925.* New Delhi: Ashoka International, 1985.

Ahluwalia, M. M. *Kukas, the Freedom Fighters of the Punjab.* Bombay: Allied, 1965.

Bal, S. S. *A Brief History of the Modern Punjab.* Ludhiana: Lyall, 1974.

————. *British Policy Towards Punjab 1844–49.* Calcutta: New Age, 1971.

————. *Political Parties and the Growth of Communalism in Punjab (1920–47).* Chandigarh: CRRID Publication, 1989.

Bal, Sukhmani. *Politics of the Central Sikh League.* Delhi: Books N' Books, 1990.

Barque, Ali Mohammand. *Eminent Sikhs of Today.* Lahore: Barque & Company, 1942.

Barrier, N. Gerald. *The Sikhs and their Literature.* Delhi: Manohar, 1970.

————. *Banned Controversial Literature and Political Control in British India 1907–1947.* New Delhi: Manohar, 1976.

Bhatia, Shyamala. *Social Change and Politics in Punjab 1898–1910.* New Delhi: Enkay, 1987.

Chander, Bushan. *The Punjab Belongs to the Sikhs.* Lahore: Modern Publications, 1947.

Darling, Malcolm Lyall. *The Punjab Peasant in Prosperity and Debt.* London: Oxford University Press, 1928.

Darbara Singh. *The Punjab Tragedy, 1947.* Amritsar: Steno House Agency, 1949.

Datta, V. N. *Jallianwala Bagh.* Ludhiana: Lyall, 1969.

Domin, Dolores. *India in 1857–59: A Study of the Role of the Sikhs in the People's Uprising.* Berlin: Akademie-Verlag, 1977.

Dungen, P. H. N. Van den. *The Punjab Tradition: Influence and Authority in Nineteenth Century India.* London: George Allen and Unwin, 1972.

Durlab Singh. *The Valiant Fighter: A Biographical Study of Master Tara Singh.* Lahore: Hero, 1942.

——. *Sikh Leadership.* Delhi: Sikh Literature Distributors, 1950.

Effenberg, Christine. *The Political Status of the Sikhs.* Stuttgart: South Asia Institute, Heidelberg, 1984.

Fauja Singh. *Kuka Movement: An Important Phase in Punjab's Role in India's Struggle for Freedom.* Delhi: Motilal Banarsidass, 1965.

——. *Eminent Freedom Fighters of Punjab.* Patiala: Punjabi University Press, 1972.

Fox, Richard G. *Lions of the Punjab: Culture in the Making.* Berkeley: University of California, 1985.

Ganda Singh. *History of Gurdwara Shahidganj, Lahore.* Amritsar: Khalsa College, 1935.

——, ed. *Some Confidential Papers of the Akali Movement.* Amritsar: Shiromani Gurdwara Prabandhak Committee, 1965.

——, ed. *The Singh Sabha and Other Socio-Religious Movements in the Punjab 1850–1925.* 1973. *Panjab Past and Present* 7, no. 1. Reprint. Patiala: Punjabi University Press, 1984.

Griffen, Sir Lepel Henry. *Chiefs and Families of Note in the Punjab.* 1890. Reprint. Lahore: Government Printing Press, 1940.

Grewal, J. S., and H. K. Puri, eds. *Letters of Udham Singh.* Amritsar: Guru Nanak Dev University Press, 1974.

Gulati, Kailash Chander. *The Akalis: Past and Present.* New Delhi: Ashajanak, 1974.

Ibbetson, Sir Denzil. *Punjab Castes.* Lahore: Government Printing Press, 1916.

Jones, Kenneth W. *Arya Dharm: Hindu Consciousness in 19th-Century Punjab.* Berkeley: University of California Press, 1976.

Juergensmeyer, Mark. *Religion as a Social Vision: The Movement Against Untouchability in 20th-Century Punjab.* Berkeley: University of California Press, 1982.

Josh, Sohan Singh. *Hindustan Gadar Party: A Short History.* New Delhi: People's Publishing House, 1977.

Khanna, K. *Sikh Leadership and Some Aspects of Anglo-Sikh Relations.* Patiala: Punjabi University Press, 1969.

Khilnani, N. M. *The Punjab Under the Lawrences.* Simla: Punjab Government Record Office, 1951

Khushdeva Singh. *Love is Stronger than Hate: A Rememberance of 1947.* Patiala: Guru Nanak Mission, 1973.

Kirpal Singh. *The Partition of the Punjab.* Patiala: Punjabi University Press, 1972.

Kissinger, Tom G. *Vilayatpur.* Berkeley: University of California Press, 1974.

Lakshman Singh, Bhagat. *Sikh Martyrs.* Ludhiana: Lahore Book Shop, 1923.

Leitner, G. W. *Indigenous Education in the Punjab Since Annexation.* 1882. Reprint. Patiala: Punjab Language Department, 1970.

Malhotra, S. L. *Gandhi: An Experiment with Communal Politics: A Study of Gandhi's Role in Punjab Politics (1921–1931).* Chandigarh: Panjab University Press, 1975.

———. *Gandhi, Punjab and the Partition.* Chandigarh: Panjab University Press, 1983.

Marenco, Ethene K. *The Transformation of Sikh Society.* Portland, Oregon: HaPi Press, 1974.

Mehta, H. R. *A History of the Growth and Development of Western Education in the Punjab 1846–1884.* 1929. Reprint. Patiala: Punjab Language Department, 1971.

Mittal, S. C. *Freedom Movement in Punjab (1905–29).* Delhi: Concept, 1977.

Mohan, Kamlesh. *Militant Nationalism in the Punjab, 1919–1935.* New Delhi: Manohar, 1988.

Mohinder Singh. *The Akali Movement.* New Delhi: Macmillan, 1978.

———. *The Akali Struggle: A Retrospect.* New Delhi: Atlantic, 1988.

Nahar Singh. *Guru Ram Singh and the Kuka Sikhs.* New Delhi: Amrit, 1965.

Oberoi, Harjot Singh. "A World Reconstructed: Religion, Ritual and Community among the Sikhs, 1850–1909." Ph.D. diss., Australian National University, Canberra, 1987.

Oxen, Stephen. *The Sikhs and the Punjab Politics 1921–1947.* Vancouver, University of British Columbia Press, 1964.

Petrie, D. *Developments in Sikh Politics (1900–1911).* Amritsar: Chief Khalsa Diwan, n.d.

Puri, Harish K. *Ghadar Movement: Ideology, Organization and Strategy.* Amritsar: Guru Nanak Dev University Press, 1983.

Puri, Nina. *Political Elite and Society in the Punjab.* New Delhi: Vikas, 1985.

Rai, Satya M. *Legislative Politics and Freedom Struggle in the Punjab 1897–1947.* New Delhi: Indian Council of Historical Research, 1984.

Rose, H. A. *A Glossary of the Tribes and Castes of the Punjab and North-West Frontier Province.* 3 vols. 1911. Reprint. Patiala: Punjab Language Department, 1970.

Sahni, Ruchi Ram. *Struggle for Freedom in Sikh Shrines.* Amritsar: Shiromani Gurdwara Prabandhak Committee, n.d.

Sethi, G. R. *Sikh Struggle for Gurdwara Reform.* Amritsar: Union Press, 1927.

Sadhu Swarup Singh. *The Sikhs Demand Their Home Land.* Lahore: Sikh University Press, 1946.

Sarsfield, Landen. *Betrayal of the Sikhs.* Lahore: Lahore Book Shop, 1946.

Talbot, Ian. *Punjab and the Raj 1849–1947.* New Delhi: Manohar, 1988.

Teja Singh. *Gurdwara Reform Movement and the Sikh Awakening.* 1922. Reprint. Amritsar: Shiromani Gurdwara Prabandhak Committee, 1984.

Tuteja K. L. *Sikh Politics 1920–1940.* Kurukshetra: Vishal, 1984.

Uprety, Prem. Raman. *Religion and Politics in the Punjab in the 1920s.* New Delhi: Sterling, 1980.

Walia, Ramesh. *Praja Mandal Movement in East Punjab States.* Patiala: Punjabi University Press, 1972.

Webster, John C. B. *The Nirankari Sikhs.* Delhi: Macmillan, 1979.

Sikhs in Independent India

Alakhdhari. *Case for United Punjab.* Ambala: Azad Hind, 1956.

Amarjit Kaur et al. *The Punjab Story.* New Delhi: Roli, 1984.

Amrik Singh, ed. *Punjab in Indian Politics: Issues and Trends.* Delhi: Ajanta, 1985.

Anand, Jagjit Singh et al. *Punjabi Suba: A Symposium.* Delhi: National Book Club, 1967.

Attar Singh. *Secularism and Sikh Faith*. Amritsar: Guru Nanak Dev University Press, 1973.

Bajwa, Harcharan Singh. *Fifty Years in Punjab Politics, 1920–1970*. Chandigarh: Modern, 1979.

Brass, Paul R. *Language, Religion and Politics in North India*. London: Cambridge University Press, 1974.

Chopra, V. D. et al. *Agony of the Punjab*. New Delhi: Patriot, 1984.

Dhillon, G. S. *Researches in Sikh Religion and History*. Chandigarh: Sumeet, 1989.

———. *India Commits Suicide*. Chandigarh: Singh and Singh Publishers, 1992.

G. B. Singh. *Transformation of Agriculture: A Case Study of Punjab*. Kurukshetra: Vishal, 1979.

Gobinder Singh. *Religion and Politics in the Punjab*. New Delhi: Deep and Deep, 1986.

Gopal Singh, ed. *Punjab Today*. New Delhi: Intellectual, 1987.

Gurmit Singh. *History of Sikh Struggles,* vol. 1. (1946–66). New Delhi: Atlantic, 1989.

Gurnam Singh. *A Unilingual Punjabi State and the Sikh Unrest*. New Delhi: Super Press, 1960.

Harjinder Singh. *Authority and Influence in Two Sikh Villages*. Delhi: Sterling, 1976.

Hershman, Paul. *Punjabi Kinship and Marriage*. Delhi: Hindustan Publishing Corporation, 1981.

Iqbal Singh. *Punjab under Siege: A Critical Analysis*. New York: Allen, McMillan and Enderson, 1986.

Izmirlian, Harry. *Structure and Strategy in Sikh Society: The Politics of Passion*. New Delhi: Manohar, 1979.

Jatinder Kaur. *The Politics of the Sikhs*. New Delhi: National Book Organization, 1986.

———. *Punjab Crisis: The Political Perceptions of Rural Voters*. New Delhi: Ajanta, 1989.

Jeffrey, Robin. *What is Happening in India?* London: Macmillan, 1986.

Joshi, Chand. *Bhindranwale: Myth and Reality*. New Delhi: Vikas, 1984.

Kapur, Anup Chand. *The Punjab Crisis: An Analytical Study*. New Delhi: S. Chand & Co., 1988.

Kumar, Parmod et al., eds. *Punjab Crisis: Context and Trends*. Chandigarh: CRRID, 1984.

Kapur, Rajiv A. *Sikh Separatism: The Politics of Faith.* London: Allen & Unwin, 1986.

Kapur Singh. *Some Documents on the Demand for the Sikh Homeland.* Chandigarh: All India Sikh Students Federation, 1956.

Leaf, Murray J. *Information and Behavior in a Sikh Village: Social Organization Reconsidered.* Berkeley: University of California Press, 1972.

Maini, D. S. *Cry the Beloved Punjab.* New Delhi: Siddharth, 1986.

Misra, Madhu Sudan. *Politics of Regionalism in India with Special Reference to Punjab.* New Delhi: Deep and Deep, 1988.

Narang, A. S. *Storm over the Sutlej: The Akali Politics.* New Delhi: Gitanjali, 1983.

————. *Punjab Politics in National Perspective.* New Delhi: Gitanjali, 1986.

Nayar, Baldev Raj. *Minority Politics in the Punjab.* Princeton: Princeton University Press, 1966.

Nayar, Kuldip and Khushwant Singh. *Tragedy of Punjab: Operation Bluestar & After.* New Delhi: Vision, 1984.

O'Connell, Joseph T. et al., eds. *Sikh History and Religion in the Twentieth Century.* Toronto: University of Toronto, Centre for South Asian Studies, 1988.

Patwant Singh and Harji Malik, eds. *Punjab the Fatal Miscalculation: Perspectives on Unprincipled Politics.* New Delhi: the editors, 1985.

Pavate, D. *My Days as Governor.* Delhi: Vikas, 1974.

Pettigrew, Joyce. *Robber Nobleman: A Study of the Political System of the Sikh Jats.* Boston: Routledge and Kegan Paul, 1975.

Rai, Satya M. *Partition of the Punjab: A Study of its Effect on Politics and Administration 1947–56.* New York: Asia Publishing House, 1965.

————. *Punjab Since Partition.* Delhi: Durga, 1986.

Saberwal, Satish. *Mobil Men: Limits to Social Change in Urban Punjab.* New Delhi: Vikas, 1976.

Sahota, Sohan Singh. *The Destiny of the Sikhs.* Delhi: Sterling, 1971.

Sarhadi, Ajit Singh. *Punjabi Suba: The Story of the Struggle.* Delhi: K. C. Kapur & Sons, 1970.

Tully, Mark, and Satish Jacob. *Amritsar: Mrs. Gandhi's Last Battle.* 1985. Reprint. New Delhi: Rupa & Co., 1988.

Wallace, Paul, and Surendra Chopra, eds. *Political Dynamics of Punjab.* 1981. Rev. ed. Amritsar: Guru Nanak Dev University Press, 1988.

The Sikh Diaspora

Agnihotri, R. K. "The Process of Assimilation: a Socio-linguistic Study of the Sikh Children in Leeds." D.Phil. diss., University of York, 1979.

Anwar, M. *Between Two Cultures: A Study of Relationships Between Generations in the Asian Community.* London: Community Relations Commission, 1976.

Ampalavanar, Rajeswary. "Politics of the Indian Community in West Malaysia and Singapore 1945–57." Ph.D. diss., University of London, 1979.

Arasaratnam, Sinnappah. *Indians in Malaysia and Singapore.* 1970. Reprint. Bombay: Oxford University Press, 1979.

Ashworth, Mary. *Immigrant Children and Canadian Schools.* Toronto: McCelland & Stewart, 1975.

Aurora, Gurdip Singh. *The New Frontiersmen: A Sociological Study of Indian Immigrants in the United Kingdom.* Bombay: Popular, 1967.

Barrier, N. Gerald, and Verne A. Dusenbery, eds. *The Sikh Diaspora: Migration and Experience Beyond Punjab.* Columbia, Mo.: South Asia Books, 1989.

Bath, K. S. "The Distribution and Spatial Patterns of Punjabi Population in Wolverhampton." M.A. diss., University of Wales, 1972.

Beetham, D. *Transport and Turbans: A Comparative Study in Local Politics.* London: Oxford University Press, 1970.

Bentley, S. "The Structure of Leadership Among Indians, Pakistanis and West Indians in Britain." M.Sc. diss., University of Bradford, 1971.

Bhachu, P. K. *Twice Migrants: East African Sikh Settlers in Britain.* New York: Tavistock Publications, 1985.

Bhatty, F. M. "East Indian Immigration into Canada 1905–1973." Ph.D. diss., University of Surrey, 1975.

Bradfield, Helen H. "The East Indians of Yuba City: A Study of Acculturation." M.A. diss., Sacramento State College, 1971.

Brooks, D. *Race and Labor in London Transport.* London: Oxford University Press, 1975.

Buchignani, Norman. "Immigration and Adaptation and the Management of Ethnic Identity: an Examination of Fijian East Indians in British Columbia." Ph.D. diss., Simon Fraser University, 1977.

Buchignani, Norman, and Doreen M. Indra. *Continuous Journey: A Social History of South Asians in Canada.* Toronto: McClelland and Stewart, 1985.

Calman, D. A. "History of Indians in Fiji, 1906–1949." M.A. dissertation, University of Sydney, 1952.

——. "Indian Labour Migration to Malaya 1867–1910." B.Litt diss., Oxford University, 1955.

Chadney, James G. *The Sikhs of Vancouver.* New York: AMS Press, 1984.

Chakarvarti, N. R. "The Political and Economic Conditions of Indians in Burma, 1900–1941." Ph.D. diss., University of London, 1969.

Chakarvarti, R. C. "The Sikhs of El Centro: a Study in Social Integration." Ph.D. diss., University of Minnesota, 1968.

Chandra, K. V. *Racial Discrimination in Canada.* San Francisco: R & E Research Associates, 1973.

Colaco, Lucy. "Labour Emigration from India to the British Colonies of Ceylon, Malaya, and Fiji 1850–1921." M.Sc. diss., University of London, 1957.

Cumpston, I. M. "The Problem of the Indian Immigrant in the British Colonial policy after 1834." D. Phil. diss., Oxford University, 1951.

Desai, Rashmi. *Indian Immigrants in Britain.* London: Oxford University Press, 1963.

DeWitt, J. *Indian Workers Association in Britain.* London: Oxford University Press, 1969.

Dusenbery, Verne. "Sikh Persons and Practices: A Comparative Ethnosociology." Ph.D. diss., University of Chicago, 1989.

Dosanjh, J. S. "A Study of the Problems in Educational and Social Adjustment of Immigrant Children from the Punjab in Nottingham and Derby." M.Ed. diss., University of Nottingham, 1968.

Gajraj Singh. *The Sikhs of Fiji.* Suva, Fiji: South Pacific Social Sciences Association, n.d. [1976–77].

Ghika, P. D. "Punjabi Immigrant Pupils in a Scottish Primary School." M.Ed. diss., University of Dundee, 1977.

Ghuman, P. A. S. *Cultural Context of Thinking: A Comparative Study of Punjabi and English Boys.* Windsor: N F E R, 1975.

Gibson, Margaret A. *Accommodation without Assimilation: Sikh Immigrants in an American High School.* Ithaca: Cornell University Press, 1988.

Gillion, K. L. *Fiji's Indian Migrants: A History to the End of Indenture in 1920.* Melbourne: Oxford University Press, 1962.

————. *The Fiji Indians: Challenge to European Dominance, 1920–1946.* Canberra: Australian National University Press, 1977.

Grimes, Eric. "Indians in New Zealand. The Socio-cultural Situation of Migrants from India in the Auckland Province." M.A. diss., University of Victoria, Wellington, 1957.

Gupta, Santosh. "The Accumulation of Asian Indians in Central Pennyslvania." Ph.D. diss., Pennsylvania State University, 1969.

Hardwick, Francis C., ed. *From Beyond the Western Horizon: Canadians from the Sub-continent of India.* Vancouver: Tantalus Research, 1974.

Helweg, A. W. *The Sikhs in England: The Development of a Migrant Community.* 1979. Rev. ed. Delhi: Oxford University Press, 1986.

Hind Balraj Singh. "Batra Sikhs in Bristol: Development of an Ethnic Community." M.Sc. diss., University of Bristol, 1977.

Hirabayashi, Gordon, and K. Victor Ujimoto. *Visible Minorities and Multiculturism: Asians in Canada.* Toronto: Butterworth, 1980.

Indra, Doreen M. "The Portrayal of Ethnicity in the Vancouver Press, 1906–1976." Ph.D. diss., Simon Fraser University, 1977.

Jain, Sushil K. *East Indians in Canada.* Windsor: Canadian Bibliographic Center, 1970.

James, Alan G. *Sikh Children in Britain.* London: Oxford University Press, 1974.

Jane Singh et al., eds. *South Asians in North America.* Berkeley: Center for South and Southeast Asian Studies, University of California, 1988.

Jassat, E. M. "A Sociological Analysis of the Interrelation of the Economic and the Political Activities of the Indian Traders in East and South Africa from 1850–1950." Ph.D. diss., University of Keele, 1977.

Jensen, Joan M. *Passage from India: Asian Indian Immigrants in North America.* New Haven: Yale University Press, 1988.

Johnston, Hugh. *The Voyage of the Kamagata Maru: The Sikh Challenge to Canada's Colour Bar.* Delhi: Oxford University Press, 1979.

Joy, Annama. "The Sikhs and Portuguese of the Okanagan Valley of British Columbia." Ph.D. diss., Concordia University, 1980.

Juergensmeyer, Mark, and N. Gerald Barrier, eds. *Sikh Studies: Comparative Perspectives on a Changing Tradition*. Berkeley: Berkeley Religious Studies Series, 1979.

Kalra, S. S. *Daughters of Tradition: Adolescent Girls and Their Accommodation to Life in British Society*. Birmingham: Diane Balbir Publication, 1980.

Kaul, Mohan Lal. "The Adaptive Style of Immigrants in the American Communities of Akron, Canton, Cleveland and Kent." Ph.D. diss., Case Western Reserve University, 1977.

LaBrack, B. W. *The Sikhs of Northern California: 1904–1986*. New York: American Migration Series, 1988.

Lal, B. "East Indians in British Columbia, 1904–1914: A Historical Study in Growth and Integration." M.A. diss., University of British Columbia, 1976.

Lepervanche, Marie M. de. *Indians in White Australia*. London: George Allen and Unwin, 1984.

Madan, Raj. *Colored Minorities in Great Britain*. Westport, Conn.: Greenwood Press, 1979.

Mahmud, M. "The Measurement of Social Support Among Immigrant Asian Women." M.Phil. diss., University of Edinburgh, 1978.

Mangat, J. S. *A History of the Asians in East Africa*. Oxford: Clarendon Press, 1970.

Marsh, Peter. *Anatomy of a Strike*. London: Institute of Race Relations, 1967.

Mayer, Adrian C. *Peasants in the Pacific: A Study of Fiji Indian Rural Society*. Berkeley: University of California Press, 1961.

McLeod, W. H. *Punjabis in New Zealand*. Amritsar: Guru Nanak Dev University Press, 1986.

Melendy, Brett H. *Asians in America*. New York: Hippocrene Books, 1981.

Morris, H. S. "Immigrant Indian Communities in Uganda" Ph.D. diss., University of London, 1963.

Nath, J. "Some Aspects of the Life of Indians and Pakistanis in New Castle with Special Reference to Women." M.A. diss., University of Durham, 1971.

Nesbitt, E. J. "Aspects of Sikh Tradition in Nottingham." M.Phil. diss., University of Nottingham, 1980.

Paige, J. P. "The Relation Between Punjabi Immigrants and Selected Schools in Coventry." M.Phil. diss., London University, 1977.

Pannu, R. S. "A Sociological Survey of Teachers from India Teaching in Alberta, 1958–65." M.Ed. diss., University of Alberta, 1966.

Pereira, Cecil Patrick. "East Indians in Winnipeg: A Study of the Consequence of Immigration for an Ethnic Group in Canada." M.A. diss., University of Manitoba, 1971.

Pocock, D. F. "Indians in East Africa with Special Reference to Their Social and Economic Relationships." D.Phil. diss., Oxford University, 1955.

Rashid, A. K. "The Comprehensibility of Punjabi Teachers in British Schools: A Phonological Enquiry into their Spoken Performance." M.Phil. diss., University of London, 1976.

Robinson, Vaughn. *Transients, Settlers, and Refugees.* Oxford: Clarendon Press, 1986.

Rosenstock, Janet, and Dennis Addair. *Multiracialism in the Class-room: A Survey of the Inter-racial Attitudes in Canadian Schools.* Don Mills, Ont.: Fulcrum Press, 1973.

Saint, C. K. "The Scholastic and Sociological Adjustment Problems of Punjabi Speaking Children in Smethwick." M.Ed. diss., University of Birmingham, 1964.

Sambhi, P. S. *Understanding Your Sikh Neighbor.* London: Lutterworth, 1980.

Sandhu, K. S. *Indians in Malaya.* Cambridge: Cambridge University Press, 1969.

Shah, S. "Aspects of Geographical Analysis of Asian Immigrants in London." D.Phil. diss., Oxford University, 1980.

Srivastava, S. R. "Asian Community in Glasgow." Ph.D. diss., University of Glasgow, 1975.

Stanworth, S.R. "The Assimilation of Immigrant Children in a Midland Town: A Sample Survey." M.Phil. diss., University of Leicester, 1975.

Tangri, R. K. "A Political History of the Asians in Kenya." M.Sc. diss., University of Edinburgh, 1967.

Tatla, Darshan Singh, and Eleanor M. Nesbitt. *Sikhs in Britain: An Annotated Bibliography.* Coventry: Centre for Research in Ethnic Relations, University of Warwick, 1987.

Thompson, M. A. "A Study of Generation Difference in Immigrant Groups with Particular Reference to the Sikhs." M.Phil. diss., University of London, 1970.

Tinker, Hugh. *A New System of Slavery: the Export of Indian Labour Overseas, 1830–1920*. London: Oxford University Press, 1974.

———. *Separate and Unequal: India and the Indians in the British Commonwealth*. Vancouver: University of British Columbia Press, 1976.

———. *The Banyan Tree: Overseas Emigrants from India, Pakistan and Bangladesh*. London: Oxford University Press, 1977.

Vaid, K. N. *The Overseas Indian Community in Hong Kong*. Hong Kong: Center of Asian Studies, University of Hong Kong, 1972.

Walker, S. K. "Home and School Expectation for Second Generation Asian Youth in Manchester." M.Ed. diss., University of Manchester, 1977.

Watson, J. L., ed. *Between Two Cultures*. Oxford: Basil Blackwell, 1977.

Wenzel, L. A. "The Identification and Analysis of Certain Value Orientations of Two Generations of East Indians in California." Ph.D. diss., University of the South Pacific, 1966.

Wood, Ann. "East Asians in California." M.A. diss., University of Wisconsin, 1966.

Yarwood, A. T. *Asian Migration to Australia: the Background to Exclusion, 1896–1923*. London: Melbourne University Press, 1964.

Punjabi Language and Literature

Ahluwalia, Jasbir Singh. *Punjabi Literature in Perspective. A Marxist Approach*. Ludhiana: Kalyani, 1973.

Arun, Vidya Bhaskar. *A Comparative Phonology of Hindi & Panjabi*. Ludhiana: Panjabi Sahitya Akademy, 1961.

Attar Singh. *Secularization of Modern Punjabi Poetry*. Chandigarh: Punjab Prakashan, 1988.

Bahri, Ujjal Singh. *An Introductory Course in Spoken Punjabi*. Chandigarh: Bahri, 1972.

Bahri, Vjjal Singh, and Paramjit Singh Walia. *Introductory Punjabi*. Patiala: Punjabi University Press, 1968.

Bhatia, Motia. *An Intensive Course in Punjabi*. Mysore: Central Institute of Indian Languages, 1985.

Gill, Harjeet Singh, and H. A. Gleason. *A Reference Grammar of Punjabi*. Patiala: Punjabi University Press, 1969.

———. *A Start in Punjabi*. Patiala: Punjabi University Press, 1972.

Gill, Harjeet Singh, ed. *Linguistic Atlas of the Punjab*. Patiala: Punjabi University Press, 1973.

Harbans Singh. *Bhai Vir Singh*. New Delhi: Sahitya Akademi, 1972.

Kohli, Mohinder Pal. *The Influence of the West on Punjabi Literature*. Ambala: Lyall, 1969.

Lajwanti, Rama Krishna. *Panjabi Sufi Poets, 1460–1900*. London: Oxford University Press, 1938.

Maini, Darshan Singh. *Studies in Punjabi Poetry*. New Delhi: Vikas, 1979.

Maya Singh. *The Punjabi Dictionary*. Patiala: Language Department, 1961.

Najm, Husain Sayyid. *Recurrent Patterns in Punjabi Poetry*. Lahore: Majlis Shah Hussain, 1968.

Pritam Singh, ed. *The Voices of Dissent*. Jalandhar: Seema, 1972.

Sandhu, Balbir Singh. "The Tonal System of the Punjabi Language." *Parakh* 2 (1968) [Chandigarh: Panjab University Press].

———. *The Articulatory & Acoustics Structure of the Punjabi Vowels*. Chandigarh: Panjab University Press, 1974.

Sethi, Jitendra. *Intonation of Statements and Questions in Punjabi*. Hyderabad: Central Institute of English and Foreign Languages, 1971.

Shackle, Christopher. *An Introduction to the Sacred Language of the Sikhs*. London: SOAS, University of London, 1983.

———. *A Guru Nanak Glossary*. New Delhi: Heritage, 1983.

Sharma Devi Datt. *Syllabic Structure of Hindi & Panjabi*. Chandigarh: Panjab University Press, 1971.

Talib, Gurbachan Singh, ed. *Rose-Garden of the Punjab: English Renderings from Punjabi Folk Poetry*. Patiala: Punjabi University Press, 1973.

Talib, Gurbachan Singh, and Attar Singh, eds. *Bhai Vir Singh: Life, Times and Works*. Chandigarh: Panjab University Press, 1973.

Vatuk, Ved Prakash. *Panjabi Reader*. Fort Collins: Colorado State University Research Foundation, 1964.

Academic Journals

Journal of Regional History
    Annual. Amritsar: Department of History,
    Guru Nanak Dev University. 1980–

Journal of Sikh Studies.
Semiannual. Amritsar: Department of Guru Nanak Studies,
Guru Nanak Dev University. February 1974–

Panjab Past and Present
Biennial. Patiala: Department of Punjab Historical Studies,
Punjabi University. 1967–

Punjab History Conference Proceedings
Annual. Patiala: Department of Punjab Historical Studies,
Punjabi University. 1965–

Punjab Journal of Politics
Biennial. Amritsar, Punjab: Department of Political Science,
Guru Nanak Dev University. 1977–

Sikh Religious Studies Information
Irregular. Stony Brook, N.Y.: Institute for Advanced Studies of
World Religion 1979–

Studies in Sikhism and Comparative Religion
Biennial. New Delhi: Guru Nanak Foundation. 1982–

The Journal of Religious Studies
Biennial. Patiala: Department of Religious Studies,
Punjabi University. 1969–

Contributors

N. Gerald Barrier is professor of history at the University of Missouri, Columbia. A specialist in Punjab and Sikh history, he has written or edited several volumes in that area, including *The Sikhs and Their Literature* (Manohar, 1970), *Banned* (University of Missouri Press, 1974), and *The Sikh Diaspora* (with Verne Dusenbery, South Asia Publications, 1989). He is currently working on a book-length study of religion and politics among Sikhs from about 1900 to 1920.

J. S. Grewal is director of the Indian Institute for Advanced Study, Simla. For many years he was professor of history at Guru Nanak Dev University, Amritsar, and is among the foremost figures in the study of Sikhism. His publications include *Guru Nanak in History* (Panjab University Press, 1969); *Medieval India: History and Historians* (Guru Nanak Dev University Press, 1975); and most recently *The Sikhs of the Punjab* (Cambridge University Press, 1991), which forms a part of the new Cambridge History of India.

John Stratton Hawley is professor and chair in the Department of Religion at Barnard College and director of the Southern Asian Institute at Columbia University. He has written on poetry and performance relating to Krishna (*At Play with Krishna*, Princeton University Press, 1981; *Krishna, the Butter Thief*, Princeton University Press, 1983), and on medieval Hindi literature and hagiography (*Sur Das*, University of Washington Press, 1984; *Songs of the Saints of India*, with Mark Juergensmeyer, Oxford University Press, 1988). His most recent edited volumes are a book on *sati* and one that investigates the ideology of gender among fundamentalist groups.

Arthur W. Helweg is professor of anthropology at Western Michigan University. He is the author of *Sikhs in England* (2d ed., Oxford University Press, 1986), *Perspectives on Punjab* (Asian Studies Center, Michigan State University, 1990), and various articles on Sikhs, Gujaratis, Pakistanis, overseas Indians, and the effects of emigration on various regions and communities in India. His current research concerns emigration from Kerala.

Mark Juergensmeyer is dean of the School of Hawaiian, Asian, and Pacific Studies at the University of Hawaii. In earlier years, as a professor at the Graduate Theological Union and the University of California, Berkeley, he drew together two major international conferences surveying Sikh studies. He is editor of *Sikh Studies: Comparative Perspectives on a Changing Tradition* (with N. G. Barrier, Berkeley Religious Studies Series, 1979) and author of *Religion as Social Vision* (University of California Press, 1982). Juergensmeyer's most recent works include *Radhasoami Reality* (Princeton University Press, 1991) and a series of edited volumes on the teaching of religious studies in a comparative context.

Gurinder Singh Mann, assistant professor of Sikh studies and South Asian religion at Columbia University, is the primary architect of the curriculum in Sikhism at Columbia. He teaches courses on Sikhism, Punjabi, and the Sikh scriptures, along with others that have a comparative thrust. He has recently completed his Ph.D. at Columbia with a dissertation on "The Making of Sikh Scripture," thus bringing to a conclusion a graduate career that has included an M.A. in English literature from the University of Kent, Canterbury, and an M.T.S. in comparative religion from Harvard. Mann is contributor of the entries on Sikhism that appear in the forthcoming *Harper's Dictionary of Religion.*

W. H. McLeod is professor of history at the University of Otago, Dunedin, New Zealand, and visiting professor of Sikh studies at the University of Toronto. He is the best known and widest ranging Western scholar of Sikhism. McLeod's recent works include *The Chaupa Singh Rahit-nama* (University of Otago Press, 1987), *The Sikhs: History, Religion, and Society* (Columbia University Press, 1989), *Who is a Sikh?* (Clarendon Press, 1989), and *Popular Sikh Art* (Oxford University Press, New Delhi, 1991).

Joseph T. O'Connell, professor of religious studies, St. Michael's College, University of Toronto, teaches and writes on the history of religion in South Asia, with special interest in its sixteenth- to twentieth-century devotional traditions: Hindu, Sikh, and Muslim. He is co-editor of *Sikh History and Religion in the Twentieth Century* (Centre for South Asian Studies, University of Toronto, 1988) and was program chairman for the major international conference from which the book emerged. O'Connell has also edited *Bengal Vaisnavism, Orientalism, Society, and the Arts* (Asian Studies Center, Michigan State University, 1985) and has published on Sikhs and Sikh studies in Canada.

Index